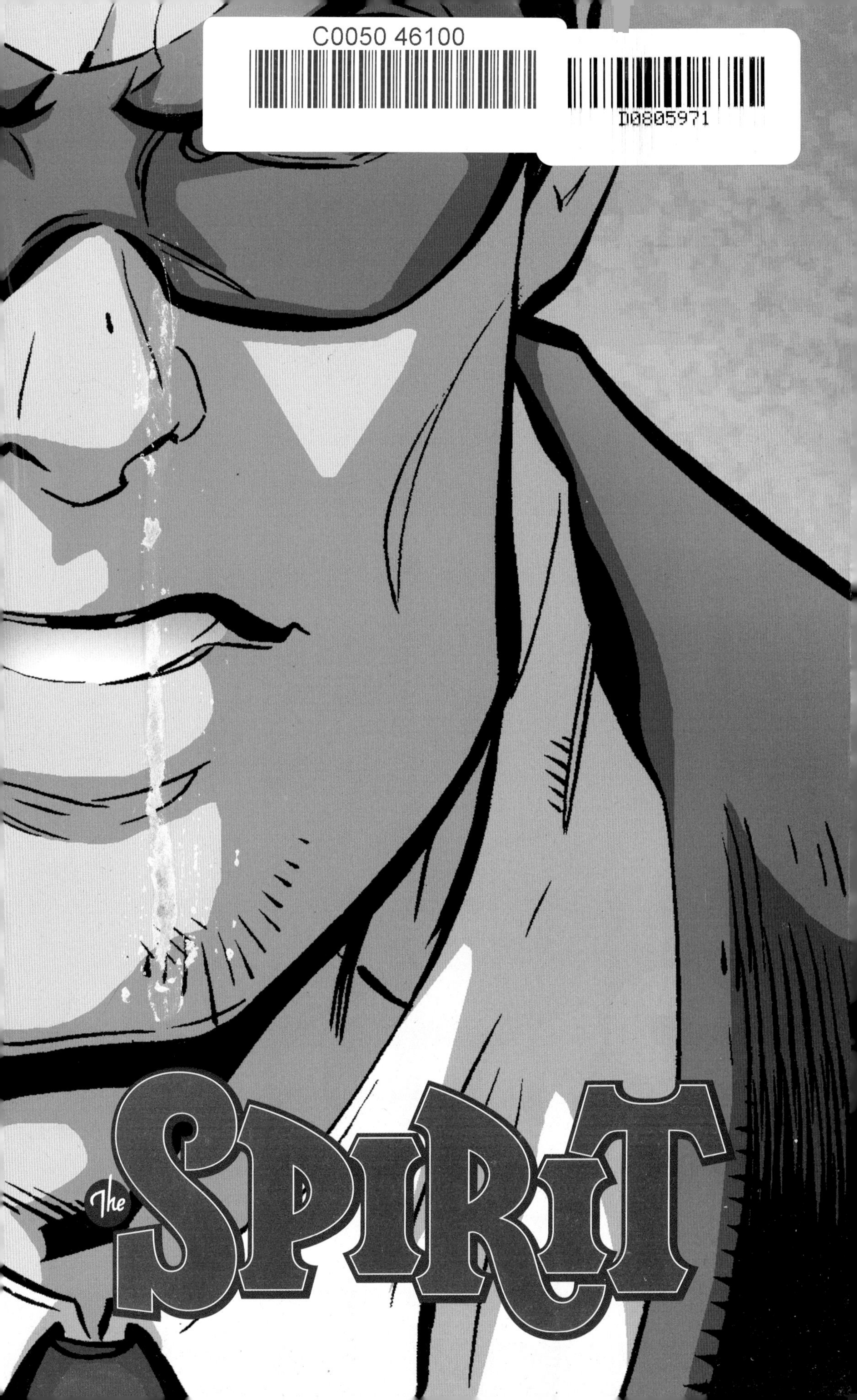
The SPIRIT

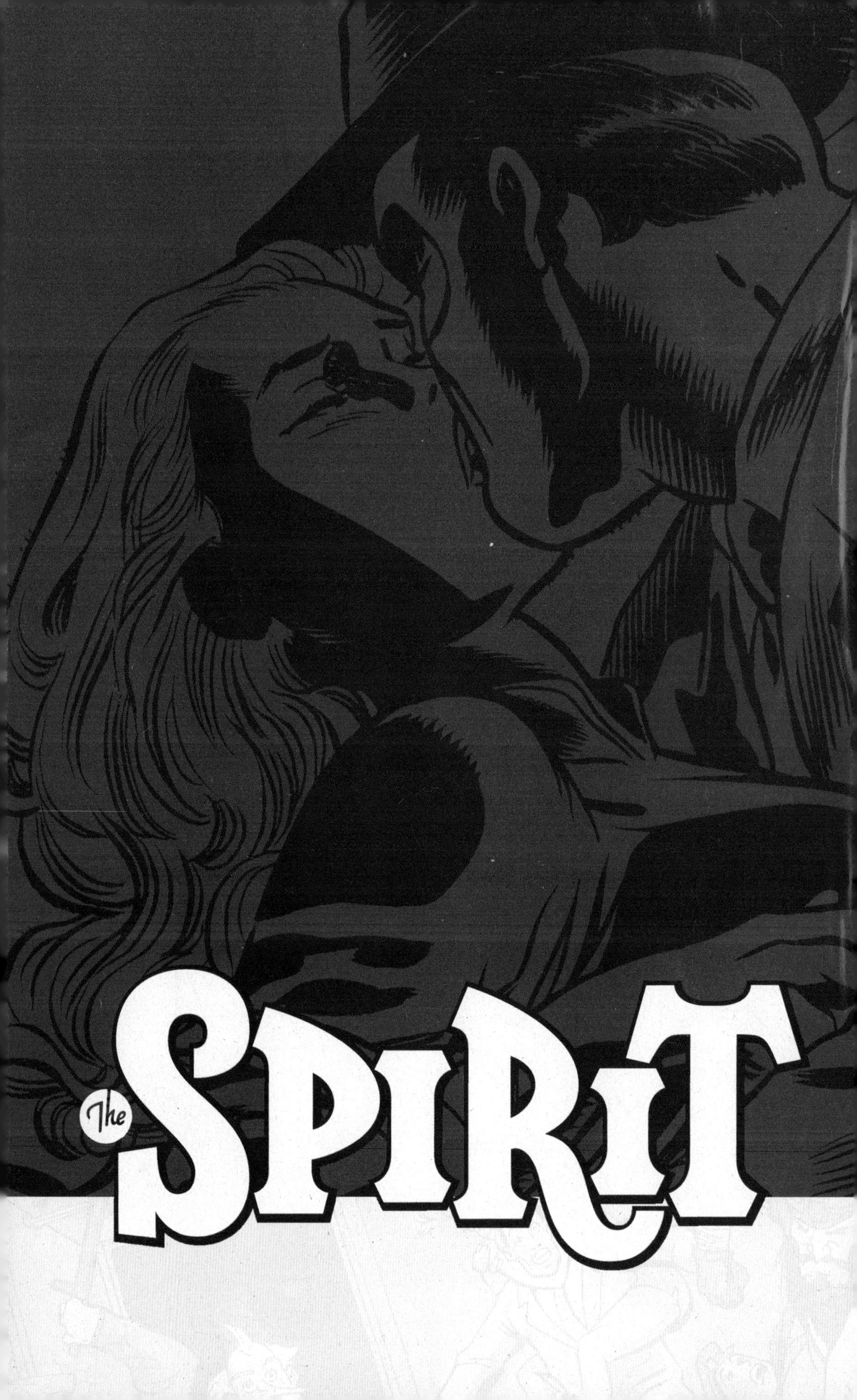
The
SPIRIT

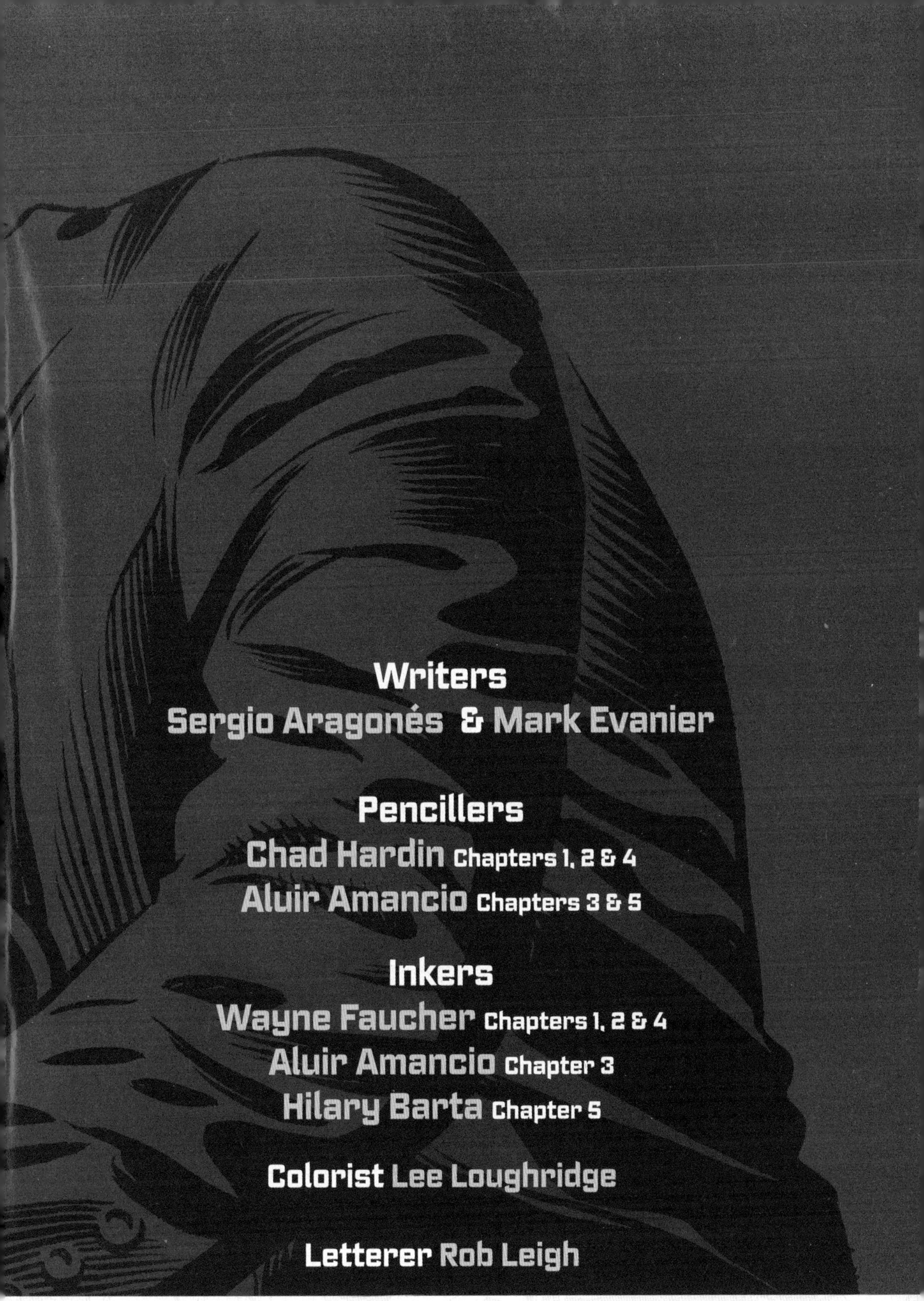

Writers
Sergio Aragonés & Mark Evanier

Pencillers
Chad Hardin Chapters 1, 2 & 4
Aluir Amancio Chapters 3 & 5

Inkers
Wayne Faucher Chapters 1, 2 & 4
Aluir Amancio Chapter 3
Hilary Barta Chapter 5

Colorist Lee Loughridge

Letterer Rob Leigh

Cover by Joe Kubert with Pete Carlsson
The Spirit created by Will Eisner

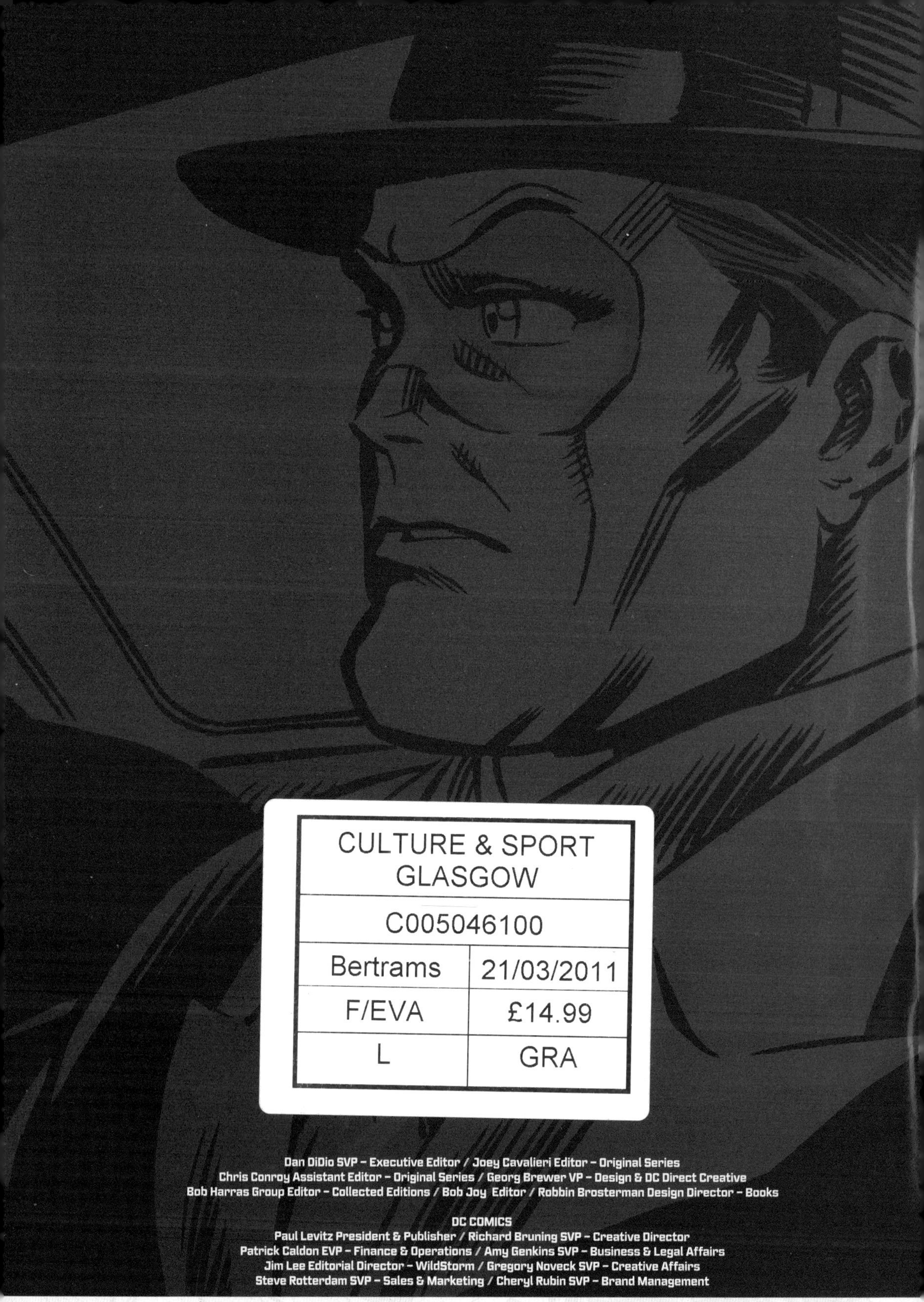

Dan DiDio SVP – Executive Editor / Joey Cavalieri Editor – Original Series
Chris Conroy Assistant Editor – Original Series / Georg Brewer VP – Design & DC Direct Creative
Bob Harras Group Editor – Collected Editions / Bob Joy Editor / Robbin Brosterman Design Director – Books

DC COMICS
Paul Levitz President & Publisher / Richard Bruning SVP – Creative Director
Patrick Caldon EVP – Finance & Operations / Amy Genkins SVP – Business & Legal Affairs
Jim Lee Editorial Director – WildStorm / Gregory Noveck SVP – Creative Affairs
Steve Rotterdam SVP – Sales & Marketing / Cheryl Rubin SVP – Brand Management

Printed by World Color Press, Inc., St-Romuald, QC, Canada. 10/21/2009. First Printing. ISBN: 978-1-4012-2505-6

1

ACTION • Mystery • ADVENTURE

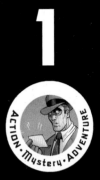

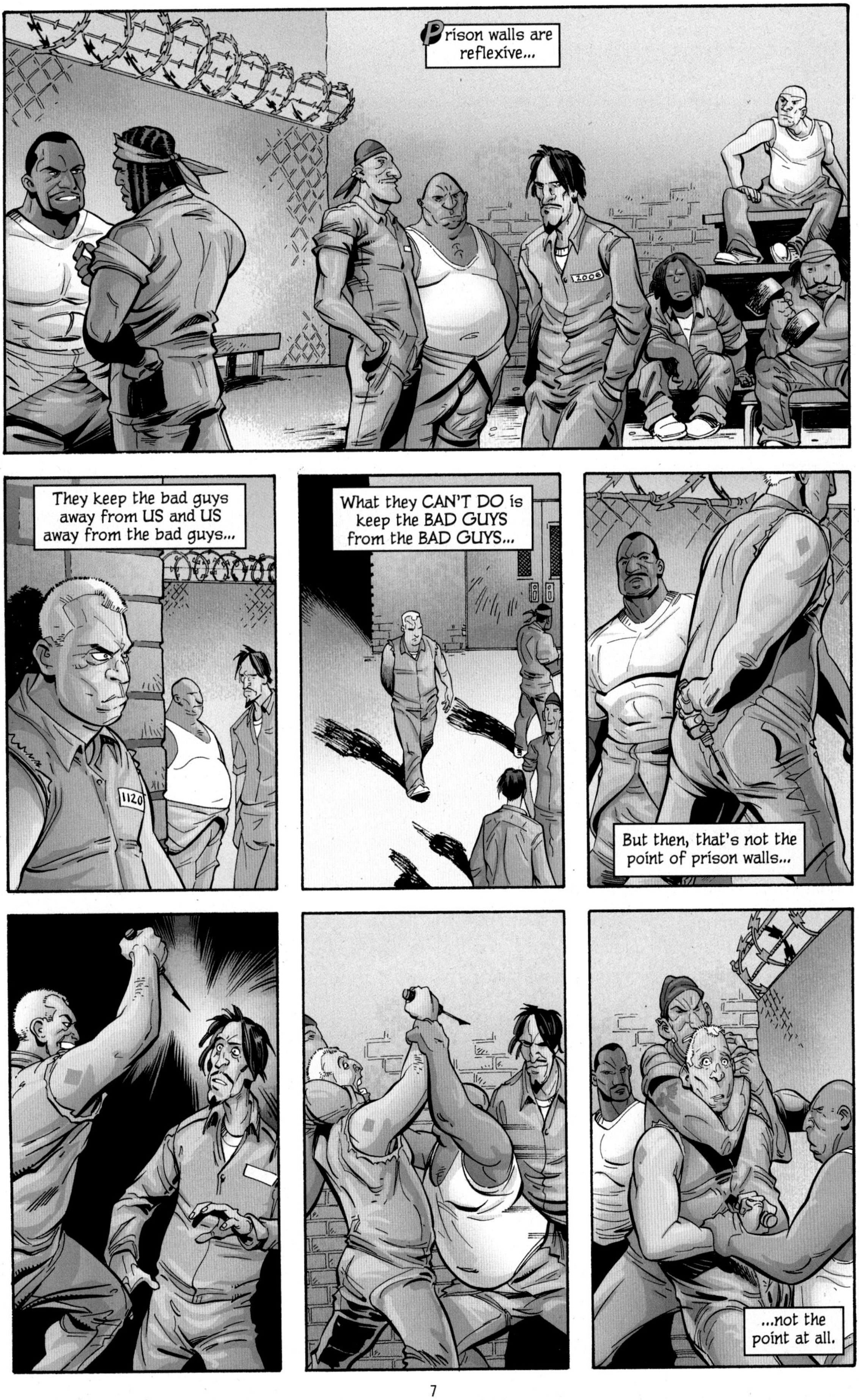
Prison walls are reflexive...
2006
They keep the bad guys away from US and US away from the bad guys...
1120
What they CAN'T DO is keep the BAD GUYS from the BAD GUYS...
But then, that's not the point of prison walls...
...not the point at all.

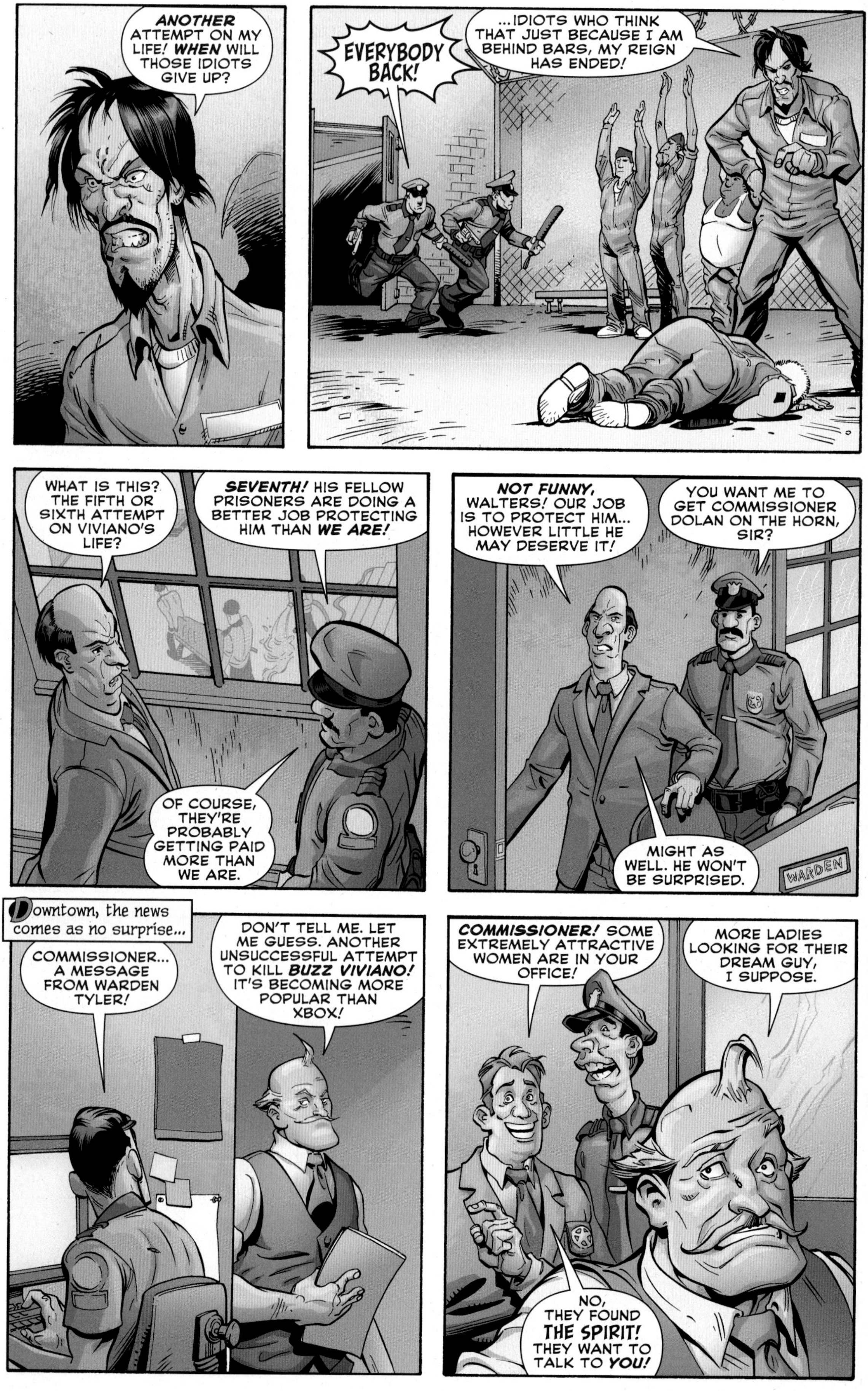

ANOTHER ATTEMPT ON MY LIFE! WHEN WILL THOSE IDIOTS GIVE UP?
EVERYBODY BACK!
...IDIOTS WHO THINK THAT JUST BECAUSE I AM BEHIND BARS, MY REIGN HAS ENDED!
WHAT IS THIS? THE FIFTH OR SIXTH ATTEMPT ON VIVIANO'S LIFE?
SEVENTH! HIS FELLOW PRISONERS ARE DOING A BETTER JOB PROTECTING HIM THAN WE ARE!
OF COURSE, THEY'RE PROBABLY GETTING PAID MORE THAN WE ARE.
NOT FUNNY, WALTERS! OUR JOB IS TO PROTECT HIM... HOWEVER LITTLE HE MAY DESERVE IT!
YOU WANT ME TO GET COMMISSIONER DOLAN ON THE HORN, SIR?
MIGHT AS WELL. HE WON'T BE SURPRISED.
WARDEN
Downtown, the news comes as no surprise...
COMMISSIONER... A MESSAGE FROM WARDEN TYLER!
DON'T TELL ME. LET ME GUESS. ANOTHER UNSUCCESSFUL ATTEMPT TO KILL BUZZ VIVIANO! IT'S BECOMING MORE POPULAR THAN XBOX!
COMMISSIONER! SOME EXTREMELY ATTRACTIVE WOMEN ARE IN YOUR OFFICE!
MORE LADIES LOOKING FOR THEIR DREAM GUY, I SUPPOSE.
NO, THEY FOUND THE SPIRIT! THEY WANT TO TALK TO YOU!

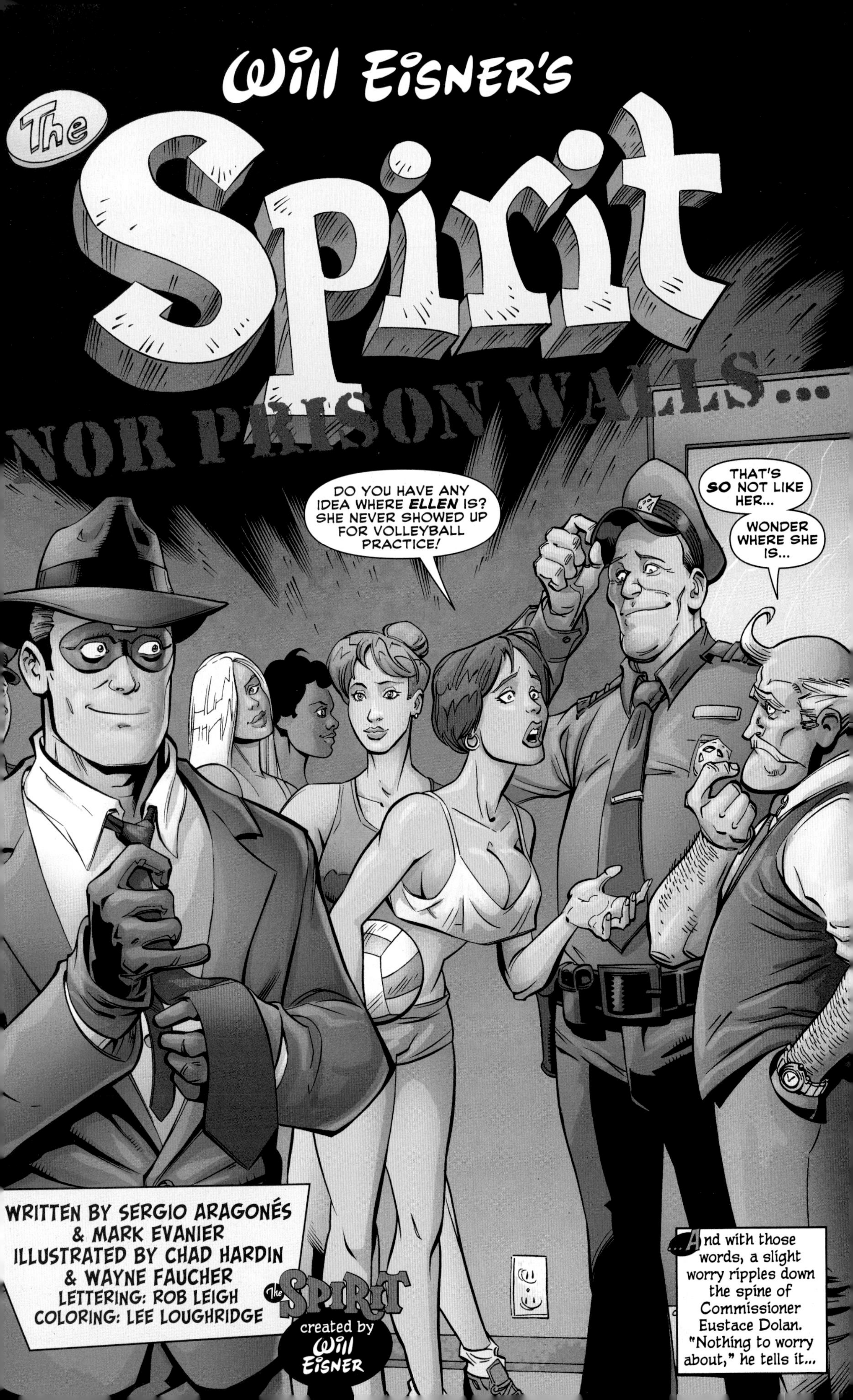
WILL EISNER'S
The Spirit
NOR PRISON WALLS...
DO YOU HAVE ANY IDEA WHERE ELLEN IS? SHE NEVER SHOWED UP FOR VOLLEYBALL PRACTICE!
THAT'S SO NOT LIKE HER...
WONDER WHERE SHE IS...
WRITTEN BY SERGIO ARAGONÉS & MARK EVANIER
ILLUSTRATED BY CHAD HARDIN & WAYNE FAUCHER
LETTERING: ROB LEIGH
COLORING: LEE LOUGHRIDGE
The SPIRIT created by Will Eisner
...And with those words, a slight worry ripples down the spine of Commissioner Eustace Dolan. "Nothing to worry about," he tells it...

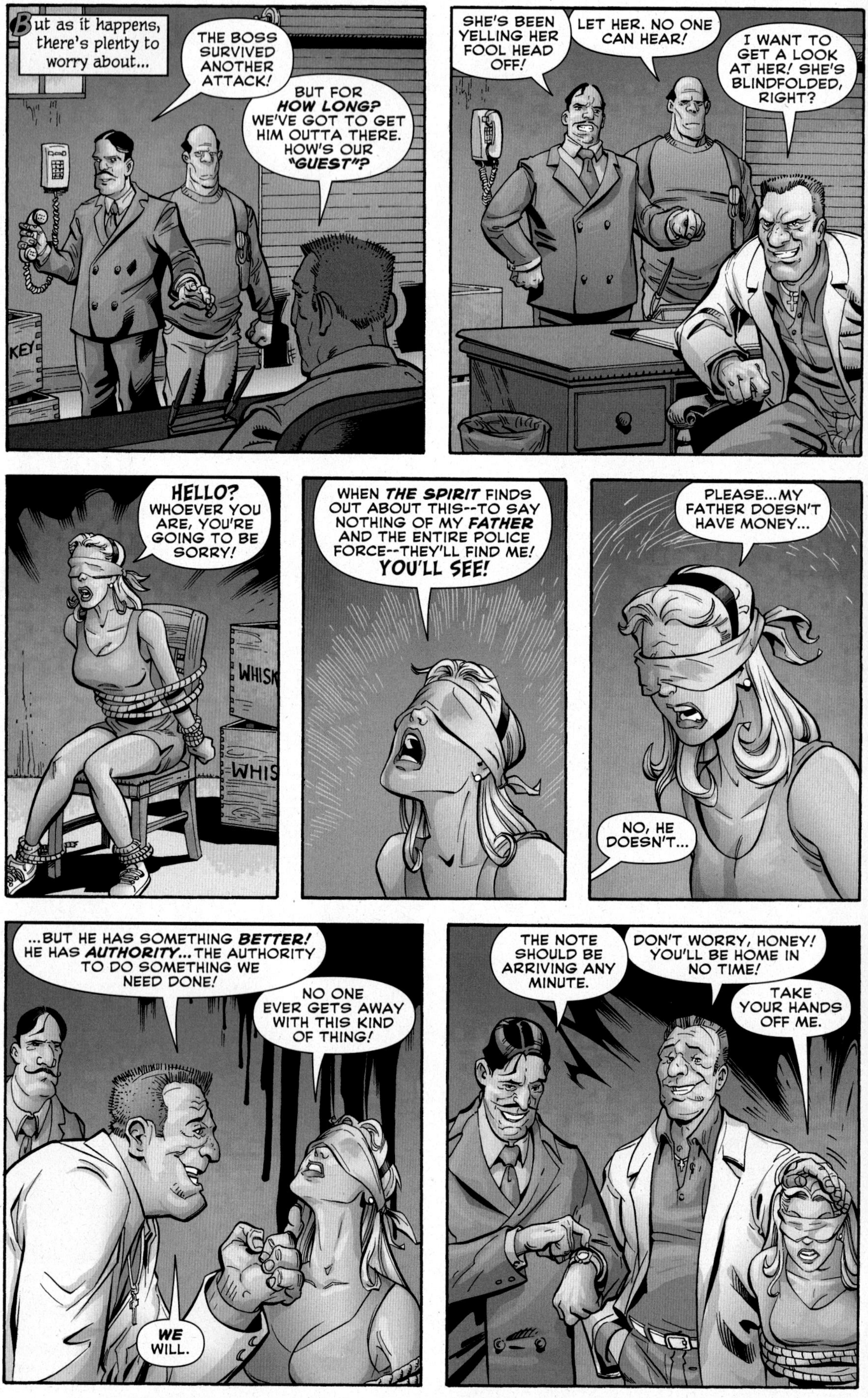
But as it happens, there's plenty to worry about...
THE BOSS SURVIVED ANOTHER ATTACK!
BUT FOR HOW LONG? WE'VE GOT TO GET HIM OUTTA THERE. HOW'S OUR "GUEST"?
KEY
SHE'S BEEN YELLING HER FOOL HEAD OFF!
LET HER. NO ONE CAN HEAR!
I WANT TO GET A LOOK AT HER! SHE'S BLINDFOLDED, RIGHT?
HELLO? WHOEVER YOU ARE, YOU'RE GOING TO BE SORRY!
WHISK
WHIS
WHEN THE SPIRIT FINDS OUT ABOUT THIS--TO SAY NOTHING OF MY FATHER AND THE ENTIRE POLICE FORCE--THEY'LL FIND ME! YOU'LL SEE!
PLEASE...MY FATHER DOESN'T HAVE MONEY...
NO, HE DOESN'T...
...BUT HE HAS SOMETHING BETTER! HE HAS AUTHORITY...THE AUTHORITY TO DO SOMETHING WE NEED DONE!
NO ONE EVER GETS AWAY WITH THIS KIND OF THING!
WE WILL.
THE NOTE SHOULD BE ARRIVING ANY MINUTE.
DON'T WORRY, HONEY! YOU'LL BE HOME IN NO TIME!
TAKE YOUR HANDS OFF ME.

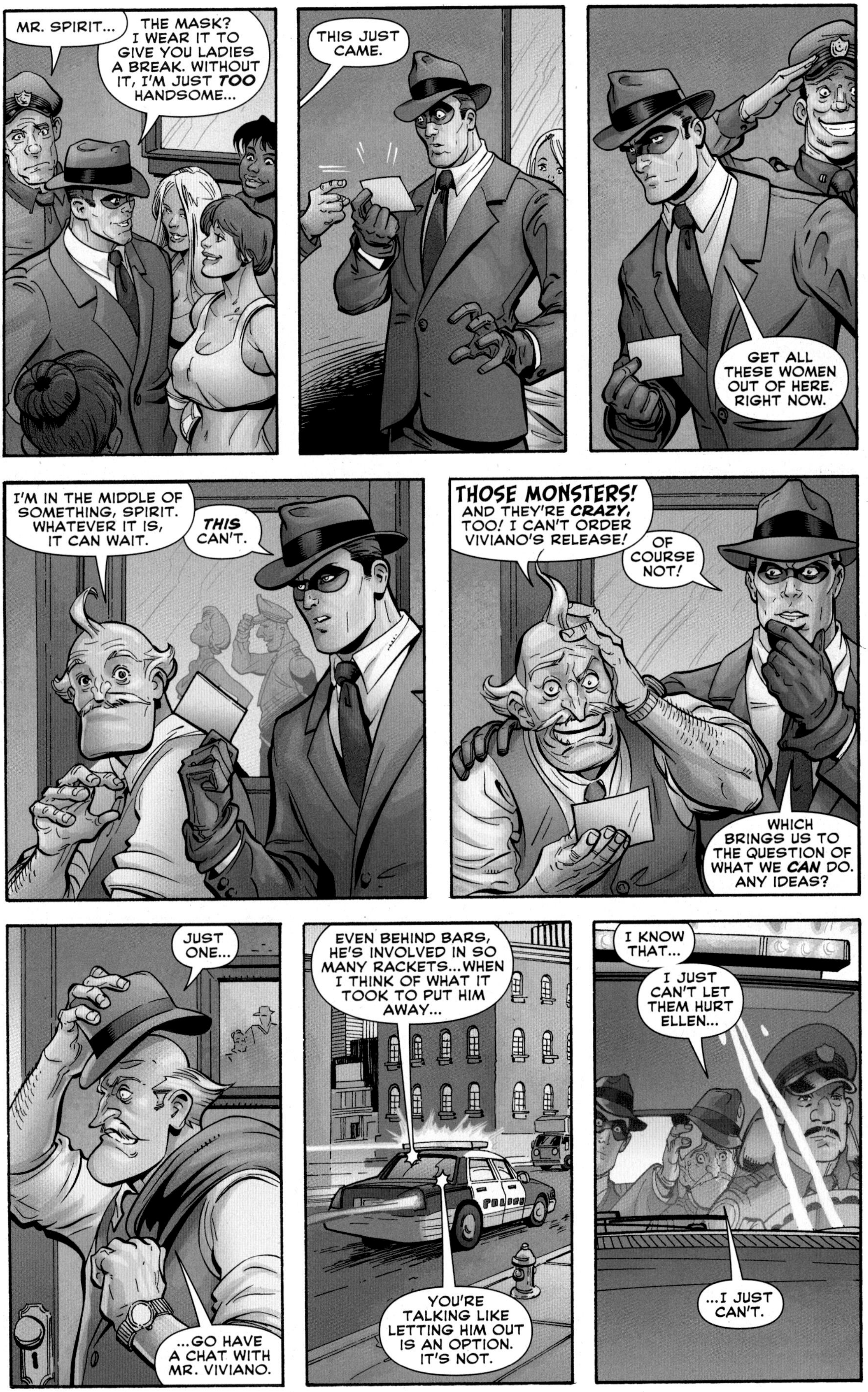
MR. SPIRIT...
THE MASK? I WEAR IT TO GIVE YOU LADIES A BREAK. WITHOUT IT, I'M JUST TOO HANDSOME...
THIS JUST CAME.
GET ALL THESE WOMEN OUT OF HERE. RIGHT NOW.
I'M IN THE MIDDLE OF SOMETHING, SPIRIT. WHATEVER IT IS, IT CAN WAIT.
THIS CAN'T.
THOSE MONSTERS! AND THEY'RE CRAZY, TOO! I CAN'T ORDER VIVIANO'S RELEASE!
OF COURSE NOT!
WHICH BRINGS US TO THE QUESTION OF WHAT WE CAN DO. ANY IDEAS?
JUST ONE...
...GO HAVE A CHAT WITH MR. VIVIANO.
EVEN BEHIND BARS, HE'S INVOLVED IN SO MANY RACKETS...WHEN I THINK OF WHAT IT TOOK TO PUT HIM AWAY...
YOU'RE TALKING LIKE LETTING HIM OUT IS AN OPTION. IT'S NOT.
I KNOW THAT...
I JUST CAN'T LET THEM HURT ELLEN...
...I JUST CAN'T.

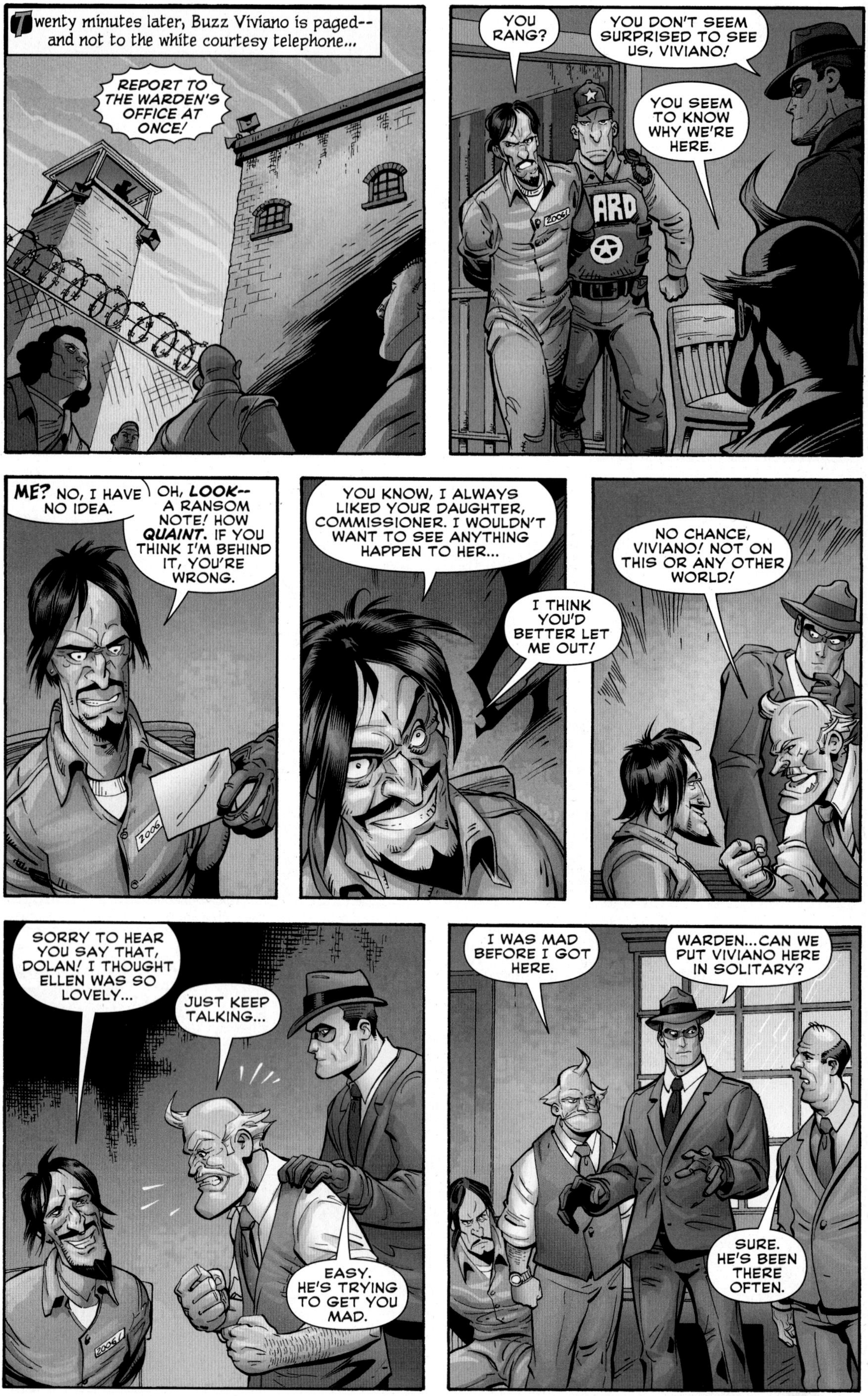
Twenty minutes later, Buzz Viviano is paged--and not to the white courtesy telephone...
REPORT TO THE WARDEN'S OFFICE AT ONCE!
YOU RANG?
YOU DON'T SEEM SURPRISED TO SEE US, VIVIANO!
YOU SEEM TO KNOW WHY WE'RE HERE.
ME? NO, I HAVE NO IDEA.
OH, LOOK-- A RANSOM NOTE! HOW QUAINT. IF YOU THINK I'M BEHIND IT, YOU'RE WRONG.
YOU KNOW, I ALWAYS LIKED YOUR DAUGHTER, COMMISSIONER. I WOULDN'T WANT TO SEE ANYTHING HAPPEN TO HER...
I THINK YOU'D BETTER LET ME OUT!
NO CHANCE, VIVIANO! NOT ON THIS OR ANY OTHER WORLD!
SORRY TO HEAR YOU SAY THAT, DOLAN! I THOUGHT ELLEN WAS SO LOVELY...
JUST KEEP TALKING...
EASY. HE'S TRYING TO GET YOU MAD.
I WAS MAD BEFORE I GOT HERE.
WARDEN...CAN WE PUT VIVIANO HERE IN SOLITARY?
SURE. HE'S BEEN THERE OFTEN.

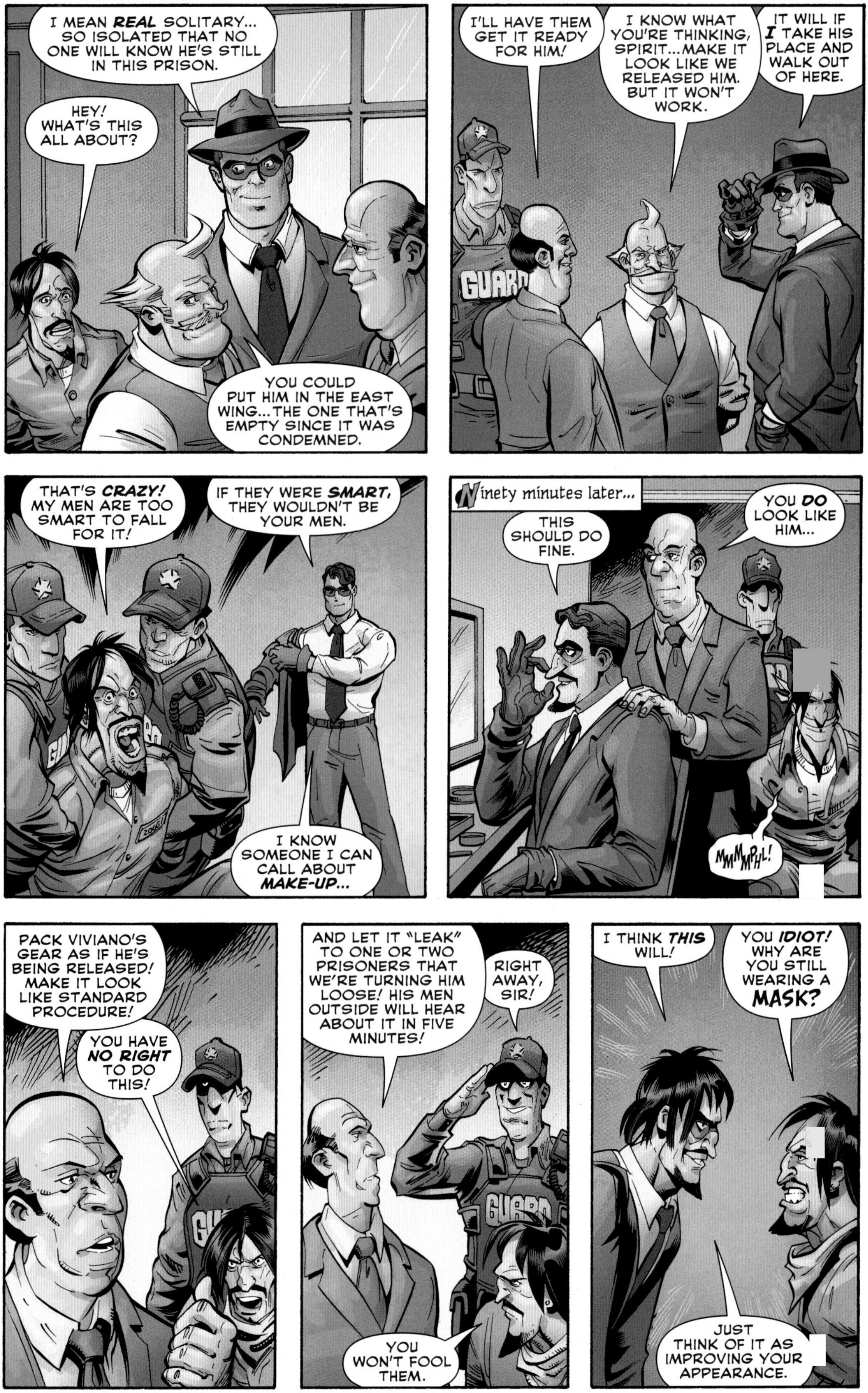
I MEAN REAL SOLITARY... SO ISOLATED THAT NO ONE WILL KNOW HE'S STILL IN THIS PRISON.
HEY! WHAT'S THIS ALL ABOUT?
YOU COULD PUT HIM IN THE EAST WING...THE ONE THAT'S EMPTY SINCE IT WAS CONDEMNED.
I'LL HAVE THEM GET IT READY FOR HIM!
I KNOW WHAT YOU'RE THINKING, SPIRIT...MAKE IT LOOK LIKE WE RELEASED HIM. BUT IT WON'T WORK.
IT WILL IF I TAKE HIS PLACE AND WALK OUT OF HERE.
GUARD
THAT'S CRAZY! MY MEN ARE TOO SMART TO FALL FOR IT!
IF THEY WERE SMART, THEY WOULDN'T BE YOUR MEN.
I KNOW SOMEONE I CAN CALL ABOUT MAKE-UP...
Ninety minutes later...
THIS SHOULD DO FINE.
YOU DO LOOK LIKE HIM...
MMMMPHL!
PACK VIVIANO'S GEAR AS IF HE'S BEING RELEASED! MAKE IT LOOK LIKE STANDARD PROCEDURE!
YOU HAVE NO RIGHT TO DO THIS!
AND LET IT "LEAK" TO ONE OR TWO PRISONERS THAT WE'RE TURNING HIM LOOSE! HIS MEN OUTSIDE WILL HEAR ABOUT IT IN FIVE MINUTES!
RIGHT AWAY, SIR!
YOU WON'T FOOL THEM.
I THINK THIS WILL!
YOU IDIOT! WHY ARE YOU STILL WEARING A MASK?
JUST THINK OF IT AS IMPROVING YOUR APPEARANCE.

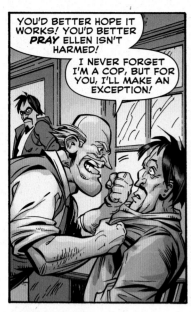

YOU'D BETTER HOPE IT WORKS! YOU'D BETTER **PRAY** ELLEN ISN'T HARMED!

I NEVER FORGET I'M A COP, BUT FOR YOU, I'LL MAKE AN EXCEPTION!

CHEER UP, VIVIANO! YOU'RE MAKING A DAPPER EXIT IN A NEW SUIT!

IF YOU DON'T GET BLOOD ON IT, I'LL BE ABLE TO WEAR IT WHEN I DO WALK OUT OF HERE!

YOU WORRIED, DOLAN?

AS A COP, NO. AS A FATHER... WELL, THAT'S WHAT FATHERS DO. WE WORRY.

HIS GANG GOT WORD OF THE RELEASE SOONER THAN I FIGURED. THERE'S A LIMO WAITING.

LOOK WHO'S GETTING SPRUNG!

I KNEW IT! I **KNEW** THEY COULDN'T KEEP BUZZ VIVIANO BEHIND BARS!

TIME OFF FOR **SOMEONE ELSE'S** BAD BEHAVIOR!

THANKS FOR COMING TO GET ME!

HI, BOSS! HEY, YOU LOOK LIKE YOU PUT ON A COUPLE OF POUNDS! MUST BE ALL THAT GREAT PRISON CHOW!

MY FATHER WILL **NEVER** GIVE IN TO YOUR RANSOM DEMANDS!

LATE-BREAKING BULLETIN, LADY...HE **JUST DID!** VIVIANO'S ON HIS WAY HERE NOW! WE NEED TO PREPARE A NICE **"WELCOME!"**

WHISKEY

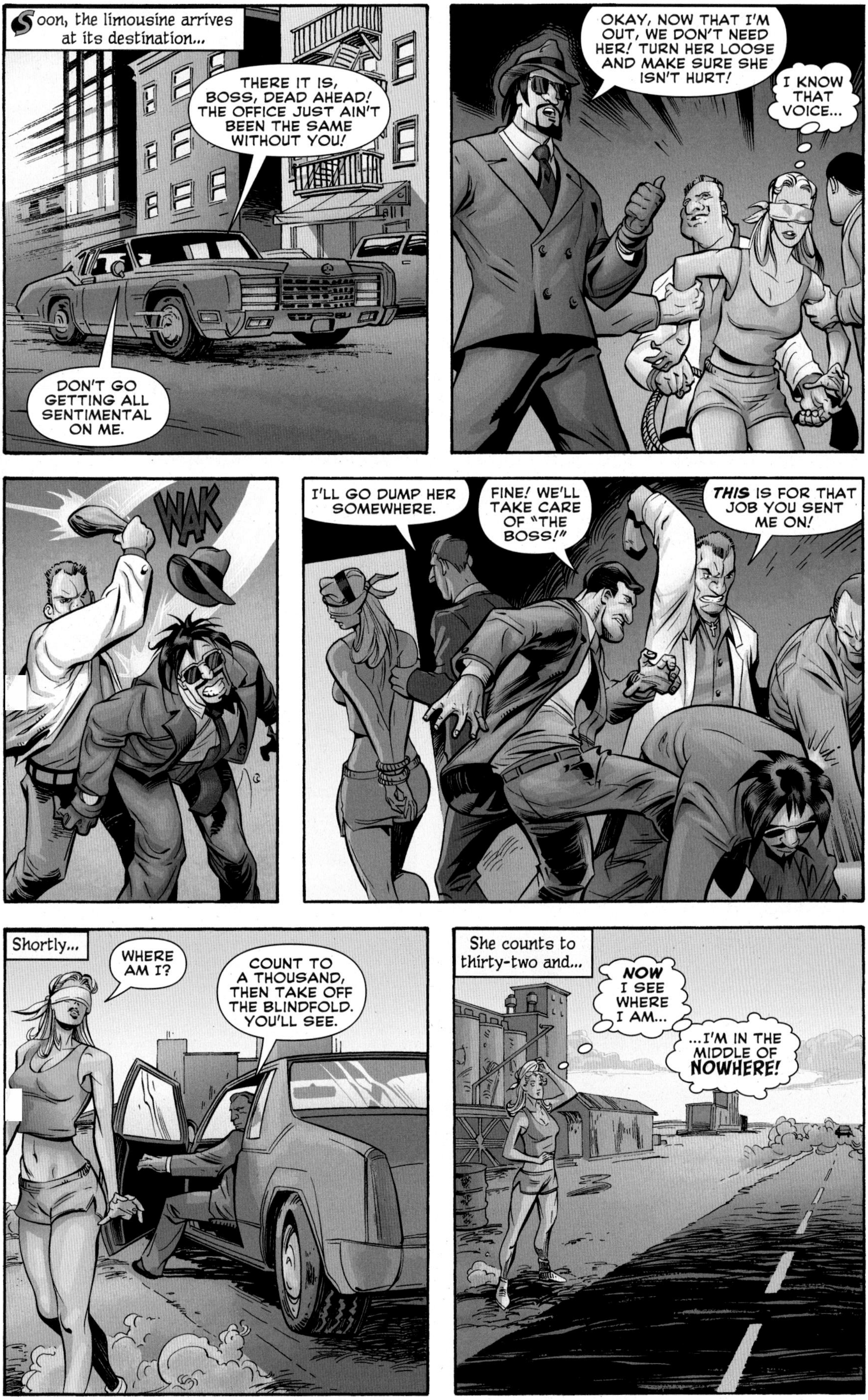
Soon, the limousine arrives at its destination...
THERE IT IS, BOSS, DEAD AHEAD! THE OFFICE JUST AIN'T BEEN THE SAME WITHOUT YOU!
DON'T GO GETTING ALL SENTIMENTAL ON ME.
OKAY, NOW THAT I'M OUT, WE DON'T NEED HER! TURN HER LOOSE AND MAKE SURE SHE ISN'T HURT!
I KNOW THAT VOICE...
WAK
I'LL GO DUMP HER SOMEWHERE.
FINE! WE'LL TAKE CARE OF "THE BOSS!"
THIS IS FOR THAT JOB YOU SENT ME ON!
Shortly...
WHERE AM I?
COUNT TO A THOUSAND, THEN TAKE OFF THE BLINDFOLD. YOU'LL SEE.
She counts to thirty-two and...
NOW I SEE WHERE I AM...
...I'M IN THE MIDDLE OF NOWHERE!

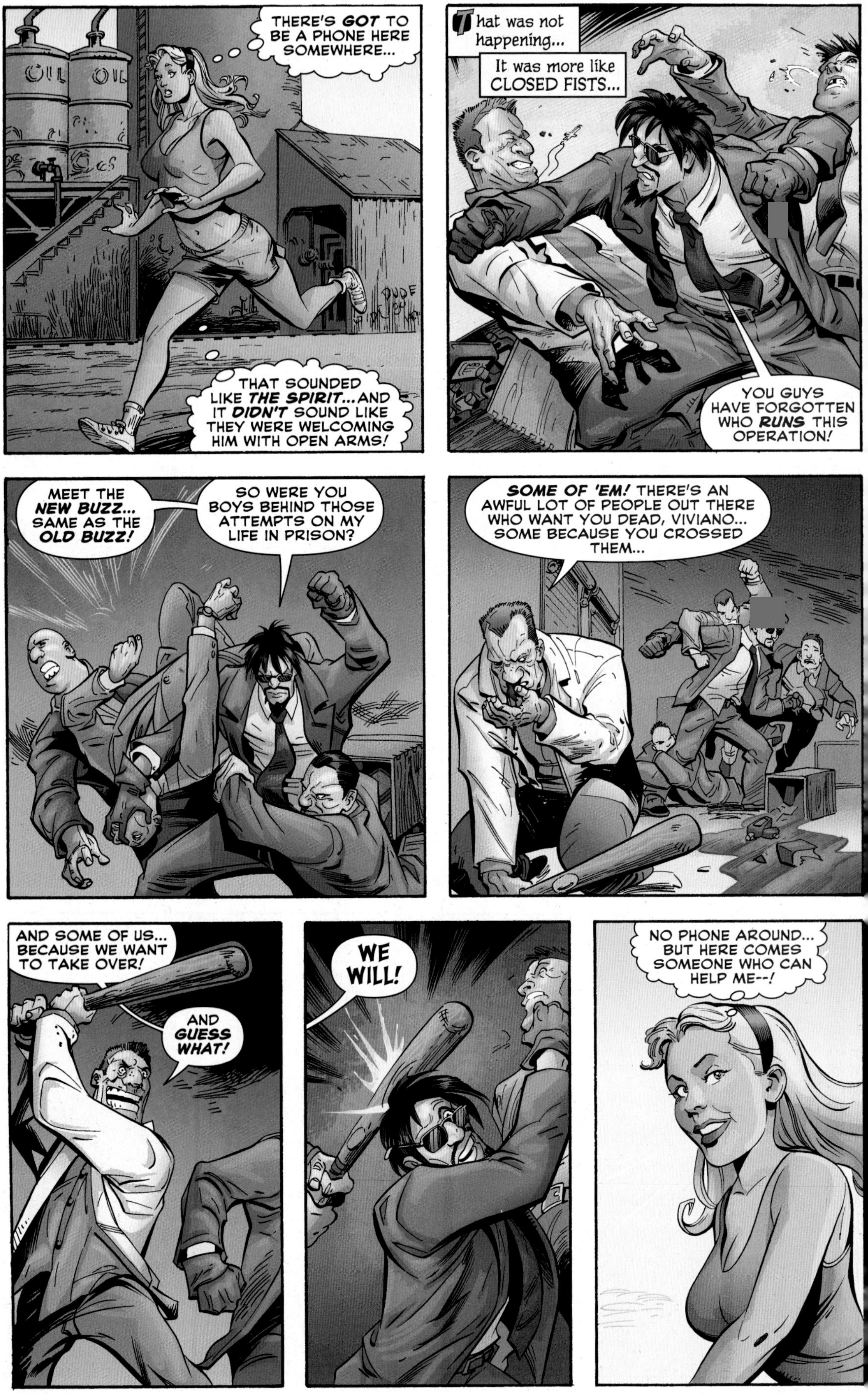
THERE'S GOT TO BE A PHONE HERE SOMEWHERE...
THAT SOUNDED LIKE THE SPIRIT...AND IT DIDN'T SOUND LIKE THEY WERE WELCOMING HIM WITH OPEN ARMS!
That was not happening...
It was more like CLOSED FISTS...
YOU GUYS HAVE FORGOTTEN WHO RUNS THIS OPERATION!
MEET THE NEW BUZZ... SAME AS THE OLD BUZZ!
SO WERE YOU BOYS BEHIND THOSE ATTEMPTS ON MY LIFE IN PRISON?
SOME OF 'EM! THERE'S AN AWFUL LOT OF PEOPLE OUT THERE WHO WANT YOU DEAD, VIVIANO... SOME BECAUSE YOU CROSSED THEM...
AND SOME OF US... BECAUSE WE WANT TO TAKE OVER!
AND GUESS WHAT!
WE WILL!
NO PHONE AROUND... BUT HERE COMES SOMEONE WHO CAN HELP ME--!

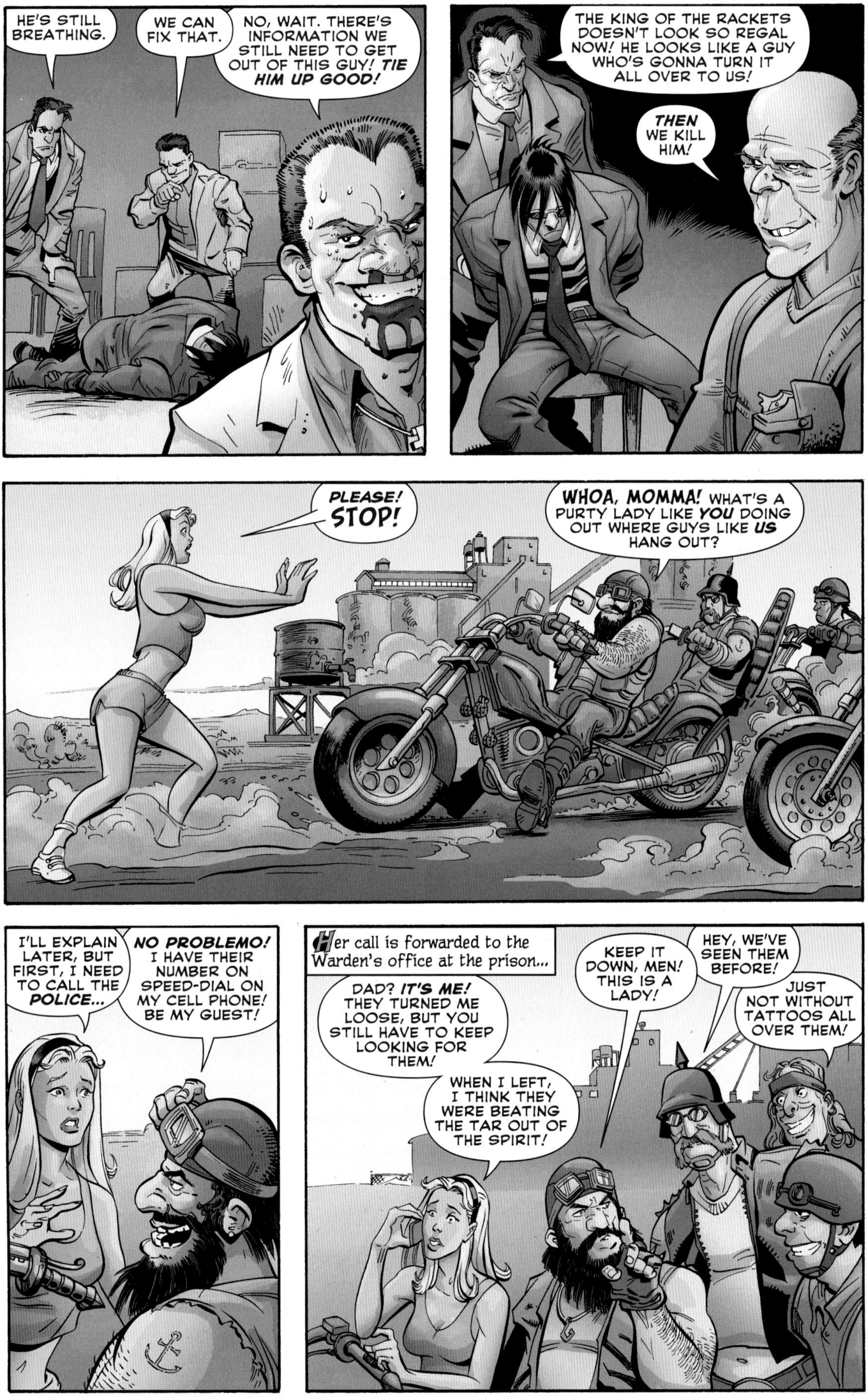
HE'S STILL BREATHING.
WE CAN FIX THAT.
NO, WAIT. THERE'S INFORMATION WE STILL NEED TO GET OUT OF THIS GUY! TIE HIM UP GOOD!
THE KING OF THE RACKETS DOESN'T LOOK SO REGAL NOW! HE LOOKS LIKE A GUY WHO'S GONNA TURN IT ALL OVER TO US!
THEN WE KILL HIM!
PLEASE! STOP!
WHOA, MOMMA! WHAT'S A PURTY LADY LIKE YOU DOING OUT WHERE GUYS LIKE US HANG OUT?
I'LL EXPLAIN LATER, BUT FIRST, I NEED TO CALL THE POLICE...
NO PROBLEMO! I HAVE THEIR NUMBER ON SPEED-DIAL ON MY CELL PHONE! BE MY GUEST!
Her call is forwarded to the Warden's office at the prison...
DAD? IT'S ME! THEY TURNED ME LOOSE, BUT YOU STILL HAVE TO KEEP LOOKING FOR THEM!
WHEN I LEFT, I THINK THEY WERE BEATING THE TAR OUT OF THE SPIRIT!
KEEP IT DOWN, MEN! THIS IS A LADY!
HEY, WE'VE SEEN THEM BEFORE!
JUST NOT WITHOUT TATTOOS ALL OVER THEM!

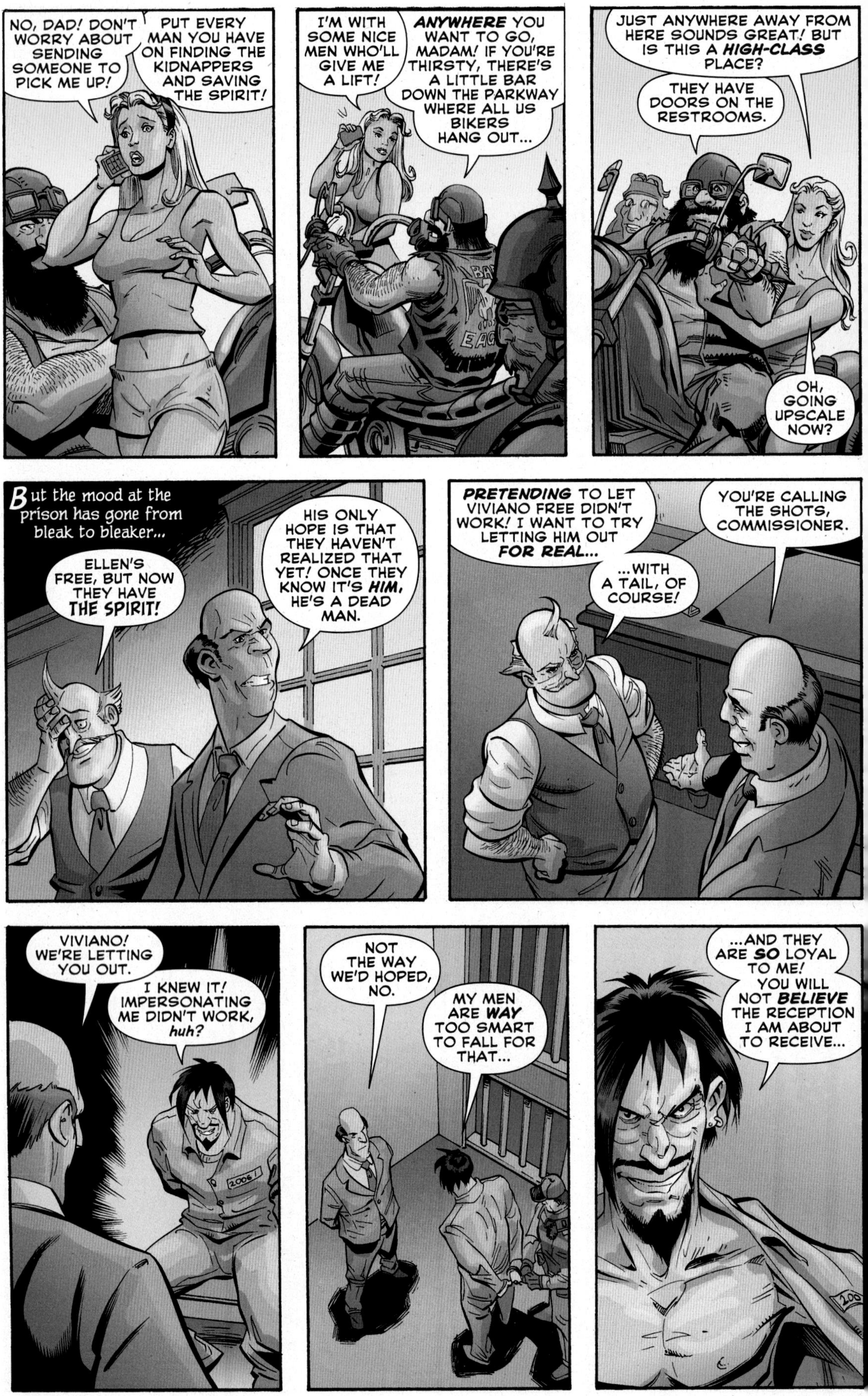
NO, DAD! DON'T WORRY ABOUT SENDING SOMEONE TO PICK ME UP!
PUT EVERY MAN YOU HAVE ON FINDING THE KIDNAPPERS AND SAVING THE SPIRIT!
I'M WITH SOME NICE MEN WHO'LL GIVE ME A LIFT!
ANYWHERE YOU WANT TO GO, MADAM! IF YOU'RE THIRSTY, THERE'S A LITTLE BAR DOWN THE PARKWAY WHERE ALL US BIKERS HANG OUT...
JUST ANYWHERE AWAY FROM HERE SOUNDS GREAT! BUT IS THIS A HIGH-CLASS PLACE?
THEY HAVE DOORS ON THE RESTROOMS.
OH, GOING UPSCALE NOW?
But the mood at the prison has gone from bleak to bleaker...
ELLEN'S FREE, BUT NOW THEY HAVE THE SPIRIT!
HIS ONLY HOPE IS THAT THEY HAVEN'T REALIZED THAT YET! ONCE THEY KNOW IT'S HIM, HE'S A DEAD MAN.
PRETENDING TO LET VIVIANO FREE DIDN'T WORK! I WANT TO TRY LETTING HIM OUT FOR REAL...
...WITH A TAIL, OF COURSE!
YOU'RE CALLING THE SHOTS, COMMISSIONER.
VIVIANO! WE'RE LETTING YOU OUT.
I KNEW IT! IMPERSONATING ME DIDN'T WORK, huh?
NOT THE WAY WE'D HOPED, NO.
MY MEN ARE WAY TOO SMART TO FALL FOR THAT...
...AND THEY ARE SO LOYAL TO ME! YOU WILL NOT BELIEVE THE RECEPTION I AM ABOUT TO RECEIVE...

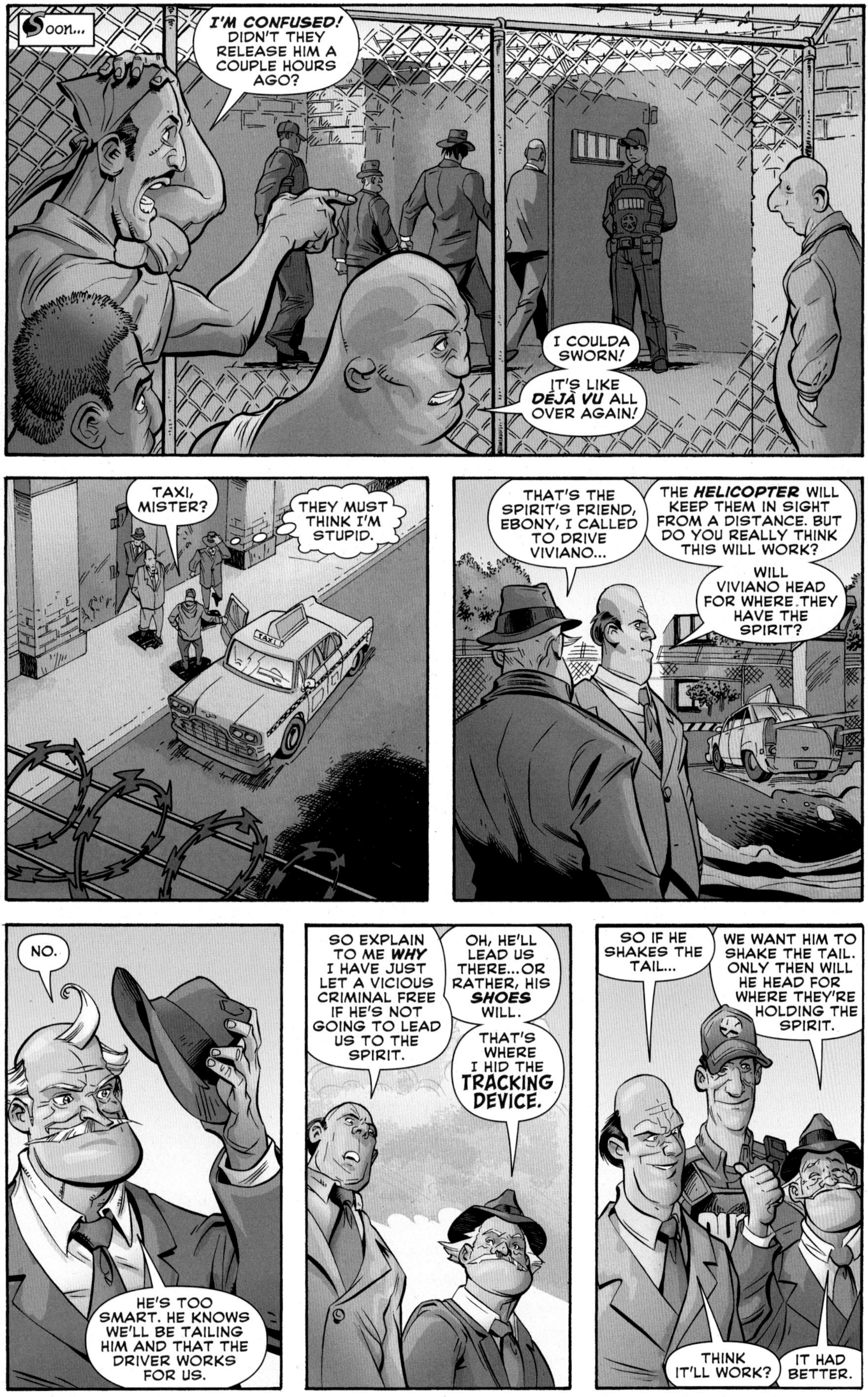
Soon...
I'M CONFUSED! DIDN'T THEY RELEASE HIM A COUPLE HOURS AGO?
I COULDA SWORN!
IT'S LIKE DÉJÀ VU ALL OVER AGAIN!
TAXI, MISTER?
THEY MUST THINK I'M STUPID.
THAT'S THE SPIRIT'S FRIEND, EBONY, I CALLED TO DRIVE VIVIANO...
THE HELICOPTER WILL KEEP THEM IN SIGHT FROM A DISTANCE. BUT DO YOU REALLY THINK THIS WILL WORK?
WILL VIVIANO HEAD FOR WHERE THEY HAVE THE SPIRIT?
NO.
HE'S TOO SMART. HE KNOWS WE'LL BE TAILING HIM AND THAT THE DRIVER WORKS FOR US.
SO EXPLAIN TO ME WHY I HAVE JUST LET A VICIOUS CRIMINAL FREE IF HE'S NOT GOING TO LEAD US TO THE SPIRIT.
OH, HE'LL LEAD US THERE...OR RATHER, HIS SHOES WILL.
THAT'S WHERE I HID THE TRACKING DEVICE.
SO IF HE SHAKES THE TAIL...
WE WANT HIM TO SHAKE THE TAIL. ONLY THEN WILL HE HEAD FOR WHERE THEY'RE HOLDING THE SPIRIT.
THINK IT'LL WORK?
IT HAD BETTER.

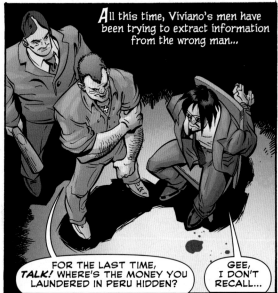

All this time, Viviano's men have been trying to extract information from the wrong man...

FOR THE LAST TIME, **TALK!** WHERE'S THE MONEY YOU LAUNDERED IN PERU HIDDEN?

GEE, I DON'T RECALL...

Y'KNOW, I'M ALMOST GLAD...

...ON ACCOUNT OF I'M REALLY ENJOYING BEATING YOU TO A PULP!

ALWAYS NICE TO SEE A MAN HAPPY IN HIS WORK!

TALK!

THIS IS FOR THAT TIME YOU DOUBLE-CROSSED ME IN CINCINNATI!

THIS IS FOR HOW YOU MOVED IN ON MY PAL LENNY'S BOOKMAKING RING!

HE'S OUT COLD AGAIN.

IT'S OKAY. I CAN WAIT. I GOT PLENTY OF TIME.

While a few miles away...

JUST LET ME OFF HERE.

"HERE"? I KNOW THIS BAR... IT'S **ROUGH!** NO ONE ADMITTED UNLESS ACCOMPANIED BY A TIRE IRON!

GAS
$5.99

DIESEL
$9

TAXI

BAR-EL MORO

BEER

MORE BEER

EVE

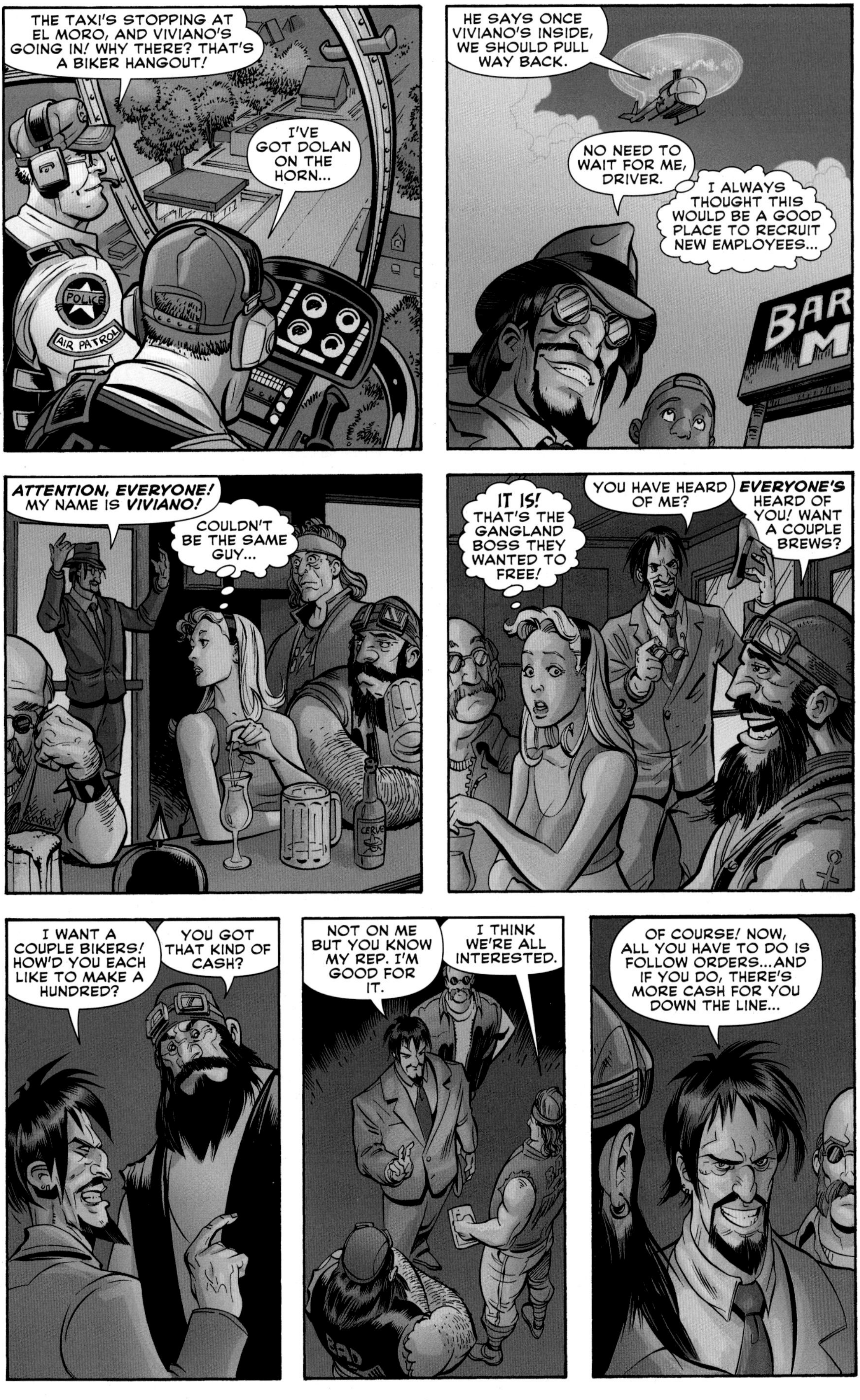

THE TAXI'S STOPPING AT EL MORO, AND VIVIANO'S GOING IN! WHY THERE? THAT'S A BIKER HANGOUT!
I'VE GOT DOLAN ON THE HORN...
POLICE
AIR PATROL
HE SAYS ONCE VIVIANO'S INSIDE, WE SHOULD PULL WAY BACK.
NO NEED TO WAIT FOR ME, DRIVER.
I ALWAYS THOUGHT THIS WOULD BE A GOOD PLACE TO RECRUIT NEW EMPLOYEES...
ATTENTION, EVERYONE! MY NAME IS VIVIANO!
COULDN'T BE THE SAME GUY...
IT IS! THAT'S THE GANGLAND BOSS THEY WANTED TO FREE!
YOU HAVE HEARD OF ME?
EVERYONE'S HEARD OF YOU! WANT A COUPLE BREWS?
I WANT A COUPLE BIKERS! HOW'D YOU EACH LIKE TO MAKE A HUNDRED?
YOU GOT THAT KIND OF CASH?
NOT ON ME BUT YOU KNOW MY REP. I'M GOOD FOR IT.
I THINK WE'RE ALL INTERESTED.
OF COURSE! NOW, ALL YOU HAVE TO DO IS FOLLOW ORDERS...AND IF YOU DO, THERE'S MORE CASH FOR YOU DOWN THE LINE...

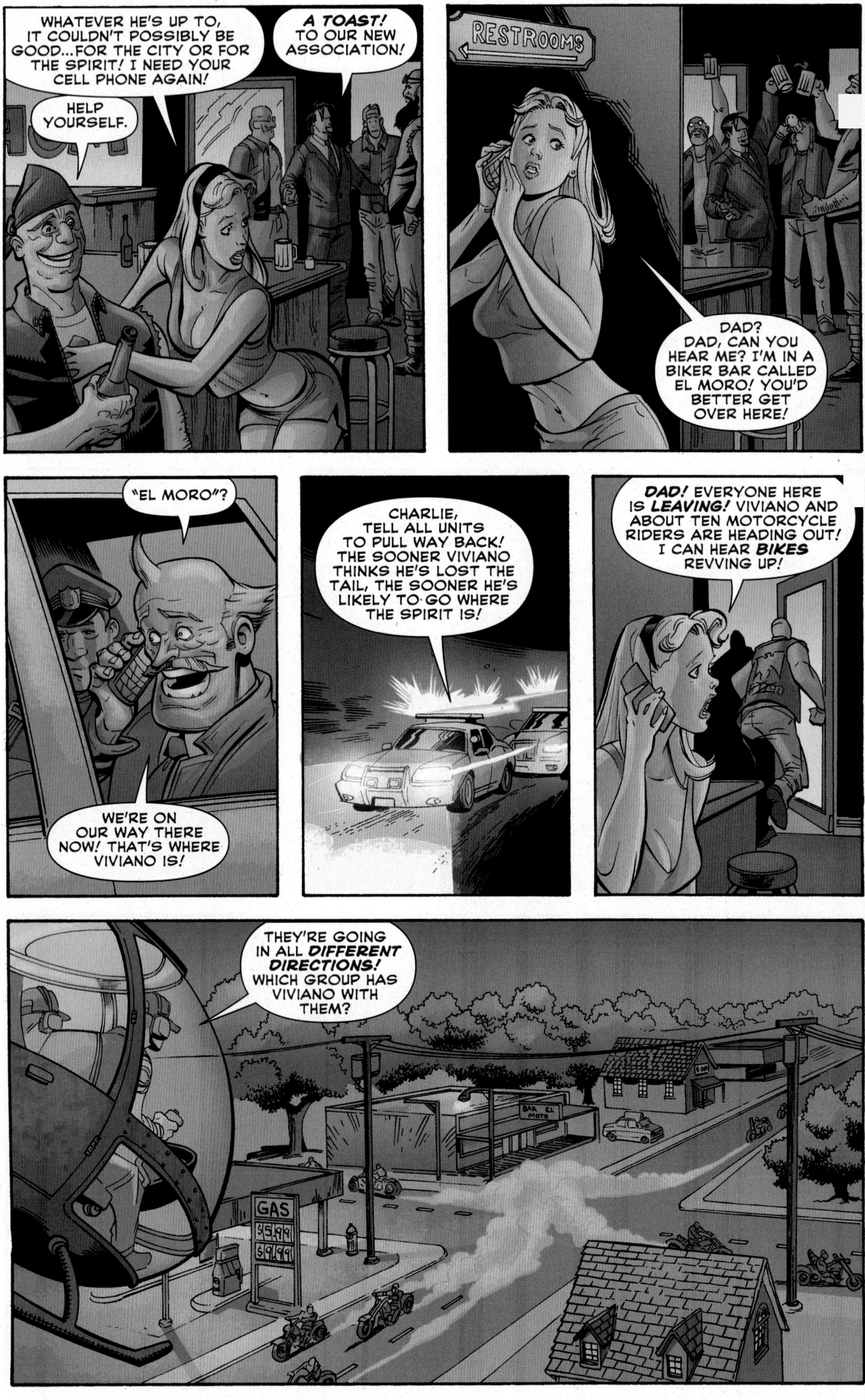
WHATEVER HE'S UP TO, IT COULDN'T POSSIBLY BE GOOD...FOR THE CITY OR FOR THE SPIRIT! I NEED YOUR CELL PHONE AGAIN!
HELP YOURSELF.
A TOAST! TO OUR NEW ASSOCIATION!
RESTROOMS
DAD? DAD, CAN YOU HEAR ME? I'M IN A BIKER BAR CALLED EL MORO! YOU'D BETTER GET OVER HERE!
"EL MORO"?
WE'RE ON OUR WAY THERE NOW! THAT'S WHERE VIVIANO IS!
CHARLIE, TELL ALL UNITS TO PULL WAY BACK! THE SOONER VIVIANO THINKS HE'S LOST THE TAIL, THE SOONER HE'S LIKELY TO GO WHERE THE SPIRIT IS!
DAD! EVERYONE HERE IS ***LEAVING!*** VIVIANO AND ABOUT TEN MOTORCYCLE RIDERS ARE HEADING OUT! I CAN HEAR ***BIKES*** REVVING UP!
THEY'RE GOING IN ALL ***DIFFERENT DIRECTIONS!*** WHICH GROUP HAS VIVIANO WITH THEM?
GAS

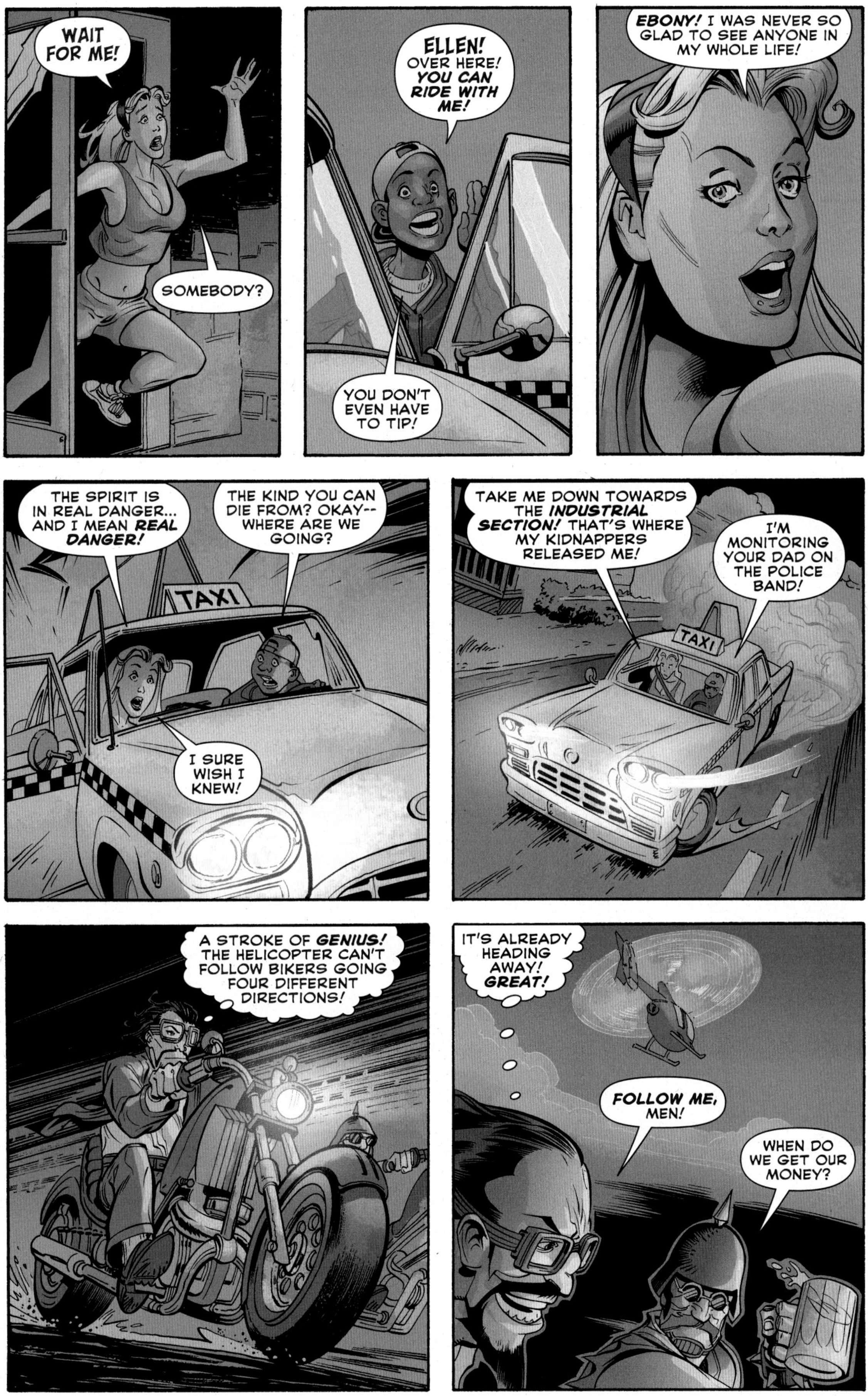
WAIT FOR ME!
SOMEBODY?
ELLEN! OVER HERE! YOU CAN RIDE WITH ME!
YOU DON'T EVEN HAVE TO TIP!
EBONY! I WAS NEVER SO GLAD TO SEE ANYONE IN MY WHOLE LIFE!
THE SPIRIT IS IN REAL DANGER... AND I MEAN REAL DANGER!
THE KIND YOU CAN DIE FROM? OKAY-- WHERE ARE WE GOING?
TAXI
I SURE WISH I KNEW!
TAKE ME DOWN TOWARDS THE INDUSTRIAL SECTION! THAT'S WHERE MY KIDNAPPERS RELEASED ME!
I'M MONITORING YOUR DAD ON THE POLICE BAND!
TAXI
A STROKE OF GENIUS! THE HELICOPTER CAN'T FOLLOW BIKERS GOING FOUR DIFFERENT DIRECTIONS!
IT'S ALREADY HEADING AWAY! GREAT!
FOLLOW ME, MEN!
WHEN DO WE GET OUR MONEY?

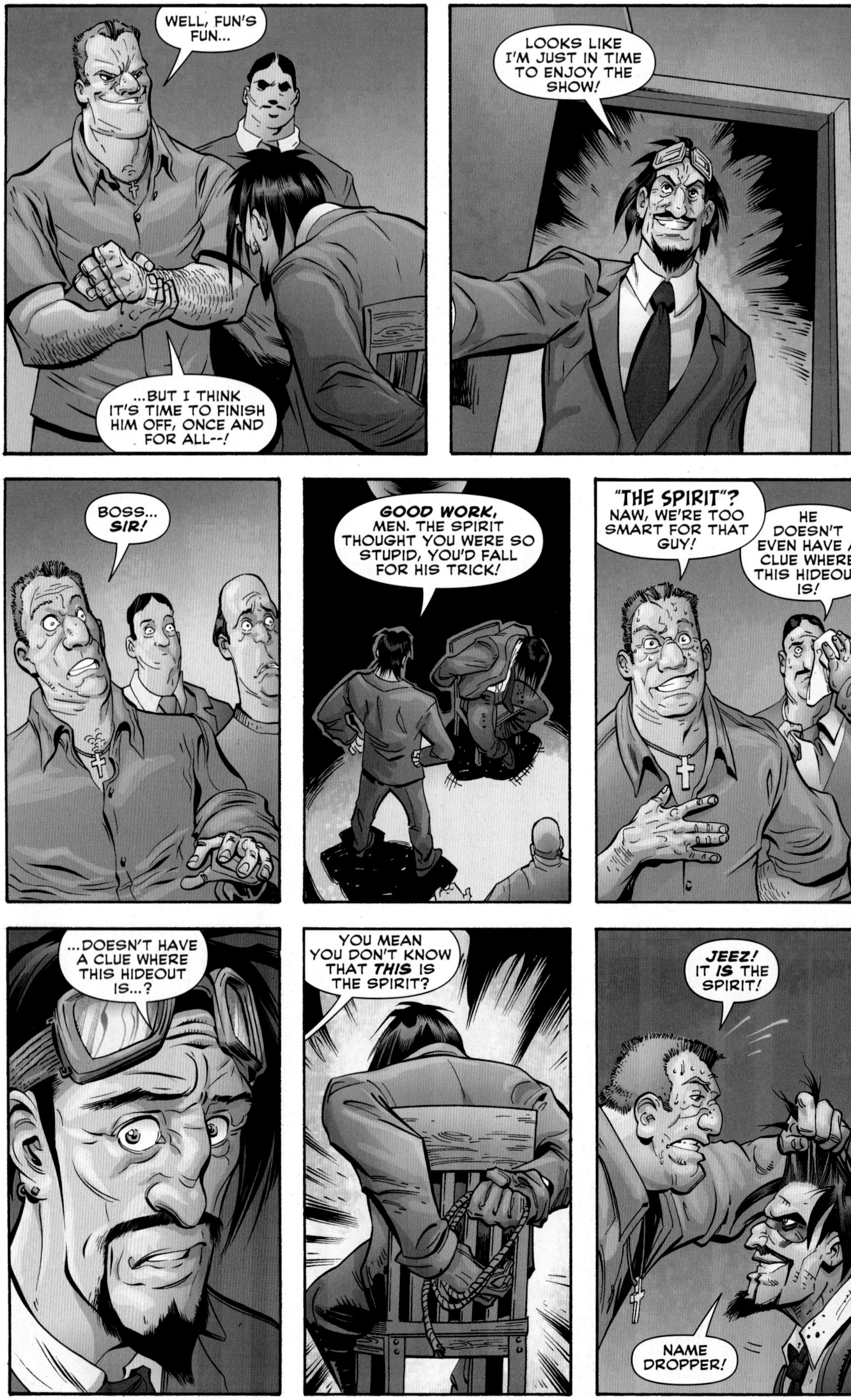

WELL, FUN'S FUN...
...BUT I THINK IT'S TIME TO FINISH HIM OFF, ONCE AND FOR ALL--!
LOOKS LIKE I'M JUST IN TIME TO ENJOY THE SHOW!
BOSS... SIR!
GOOD WORK, MEN. THE SPIRIT THOUGHT YOU WERE SO STUPID, YOU'D FALL FOR HIS TRICK!
"THE SPIRIT"? NAW, WE'RE TOO SMART FOR THAT GUY!
HE DOESN'T EVEN HAVE A CLUE WHERE THIS HIDEOUT IS!
...DOESN'T HAVE A CLUE WHERE THIS HIDEOUT IS...?
YOU MEAN YOU DON'T KNOW THAT THIS IS THE SPIRIT?
JEEZ! IT IS THE SPIRIT!
NAME DROPPER!

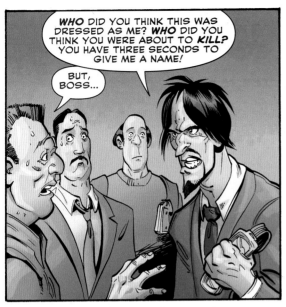

WHO DID YOU THINK THIS WAS DRESSED AS ME? WHO DID YOU THINK YOU WERE ABOUT TO KILL? YOU HAVE THREE SECONDS TO GIVE ME A NAME!

BUT, BOSS...

YOU THOUGHT IT WAS ME! YOU THOUGHT YOU'D KILL ME! YOU WERE PROBABLY BEHIND THE ATTEMPTS ON ME IN PRISON, TOO!

YOU CATCH ON FAST, BUZZ!

AFTER ALL I'VE DONE TO CUT YOU BOYS IN ON EVERYTHING, THIS IS HOW YOU REPAY ME?

"CUT US IN"? YOU MOVED IN ON OUR OPERATIONS, VIVIANO! THEN CUT US IN FOR TEN OR TWENTY PERCENT WHERE WE USED TO HAVE ONE HUNDRED!

I THINK THIS WOULD BE A GOOD TIME TO GET RID OF BOTH OF THEM!

GEE, I DON'T!

DON'T JUST STAND THERE, VIVIANO! IF THEY KILL ME, YOU'RE NEXT!

SHOTS BEING FIRED! WHAT DO YOU THINK THAT MEANS?

I THINK IT MEANS WE'RE NOT GOING TO GET OUR MONEY!

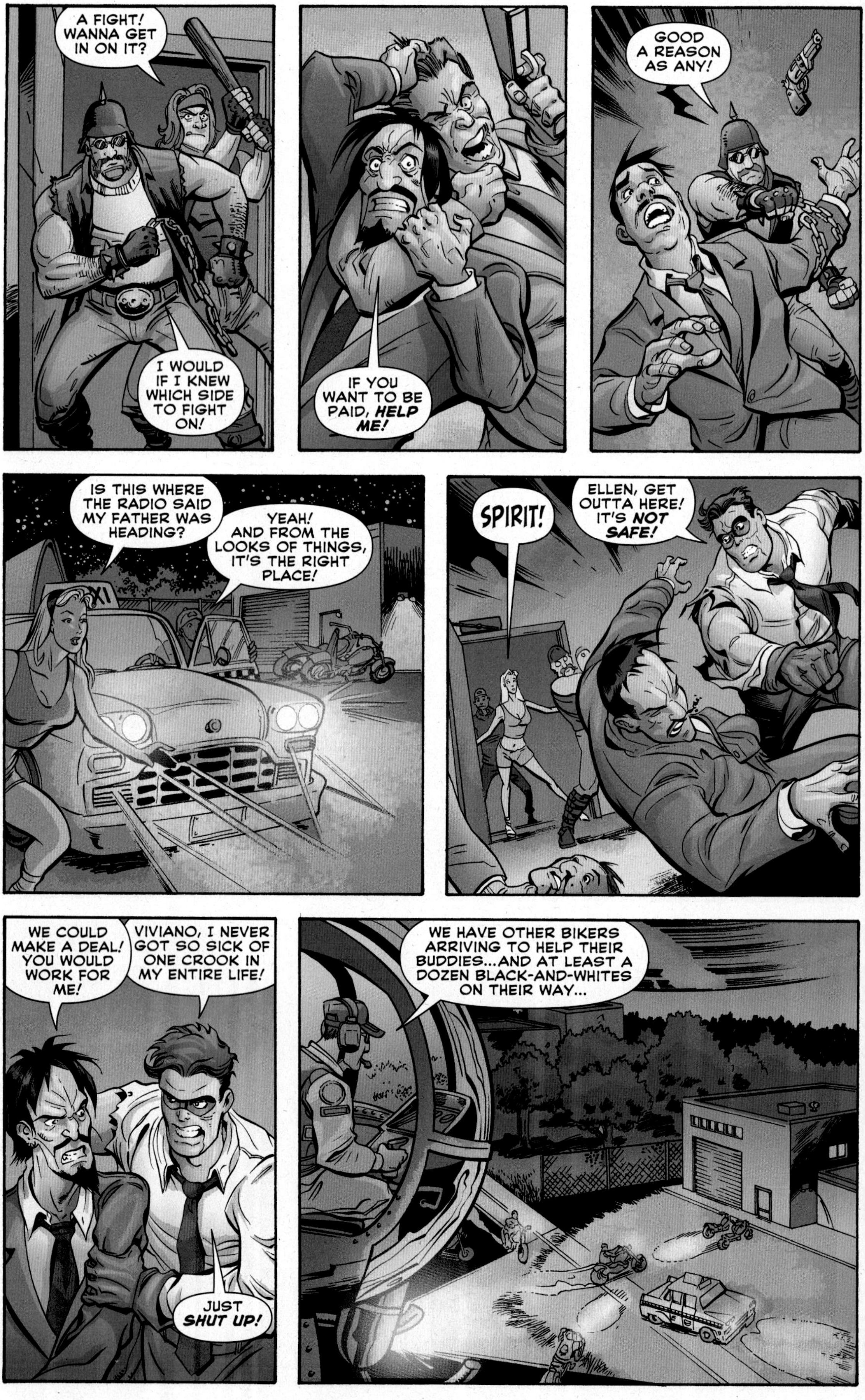
A FIGHT! WANNA GET IN ON IT?
I WOULD IF I KNEW WHICH SIDE TO FIGHT ON!
IF YOU WANT TO BE PAID, HELP ME!
GOOD A REASON AS ANY!
IS THIS WHERE THE RADIO SAID MY FATHER WAS HEADING?
YEAH! AND FROM THE LOOKS OF THINGS, IT'S THE RIGHT PLACE!
SPIRIT!
ELLEN, GET OUTTA HERE! IT'S NOT SAFE!
WE COULD MAKE A DEAL! YOU WOULD WORK FOR ME!
VIVIANO, I NEVER GOT SO SICK OF ONE CROOK IN MY ENTIRE LIFE!
JUST SHUT UP!
WE HAVE OTHER BIKERS ARRIVING TO HELP THEIR BUDDIES...AND AT LEAST A DOZEN BLACK-AND-WHITES ON THEIR WAY...

WHO ARE WE FIGHTING?

I DON'T CARE A WHOLE HEAP!

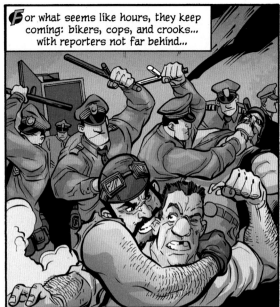

For what seems like hours, they keep coming: bikers, cops, and crooks... with reporters not far behind...

HI, DAD!

IF WE COULD GET A FEW CONSTRUCTION WORKERS HERE, THIS WOULD LOOK LIKE A VILLAGE PEOPLE CONVENTION!

STOP!

JUST ARREST *EVERYONE!* WE CAN SORT IT OUT LATER AT THE STATION!

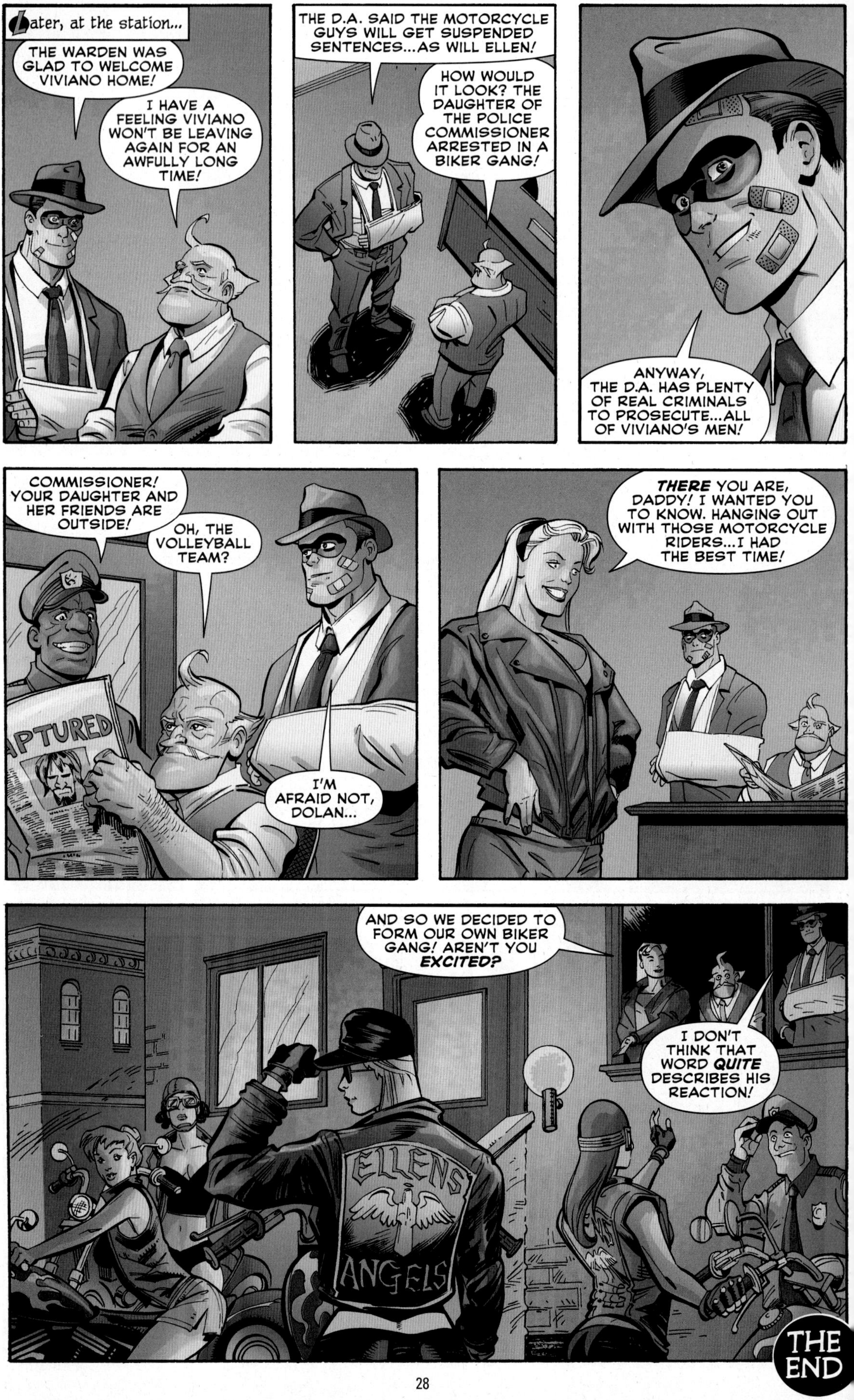
Later, at the station...
THE WARDEN WAS GLAD TO WELCOME VIVIANO HOME!
I HAVE A FEELING VIVIANO WON'T BE LEAVING AGAIN FOR AN AWFULLY LONG TIME!
THE D.A. SAID THE MOTORCYCLE GUYS WILL GET SUSPENDED SENTENCES...AS WILL ELLEN!
HOW WOULD IT LOOK? THE DAUGHTER OF THE POLICE COMMISSIONER ARRESTED IN A BIKER GANG!
ANYWAY, THE D.A. HAS PLENTY OF REAL CRIMINALS TO PROSECUTE...ALL OF VIVIANO'S MEN!
COMMISSIONER! YOUR DAUGHTER AND HER FRIENDS ARE OUTSIDE!
OH, THE VOLLEYBALL TEAM?
APTURED
I'M AFRAID NOT, DOLAN...
THERE YOU ARE, DADDY! I WANTED YOU TO KNOW. HANGING OUT WITH THOSE MOTORCYCLE RIDERS...I HAD THE BEST TIME!
AND SO WE DECIDED TO FORM OUR OWN BIKER GANG! AREN'T YOU EXCITED?
I DON'T THINK THAT WORD QUITE DESCRIBES HIS REACTION!
ELLENS
ANGELS
THE END

2

ACTION · Mystery · ADVENTURE

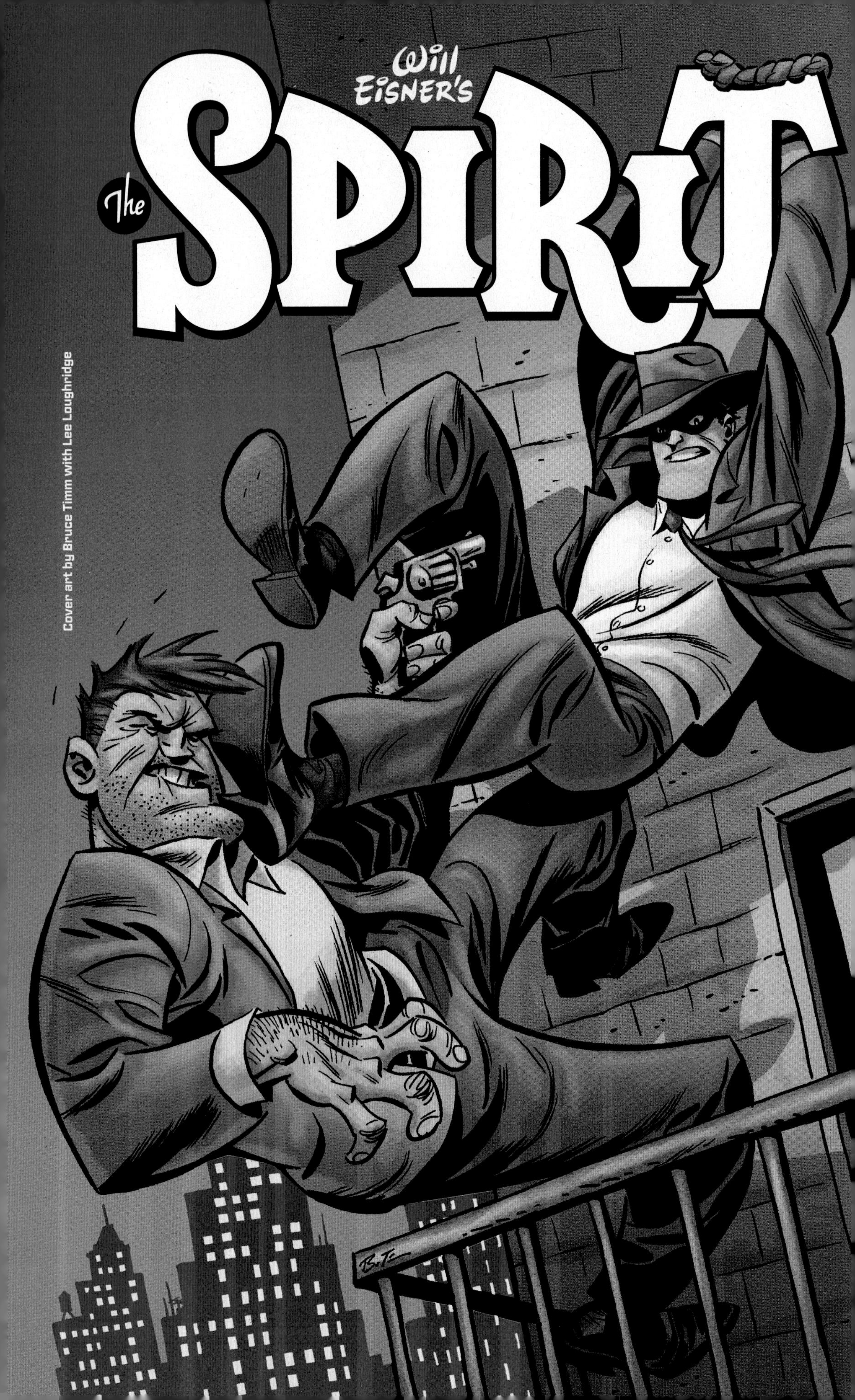
Will Eisner's
The SPIRIT

Cover art by Bruce Timm with Lee Loughridge

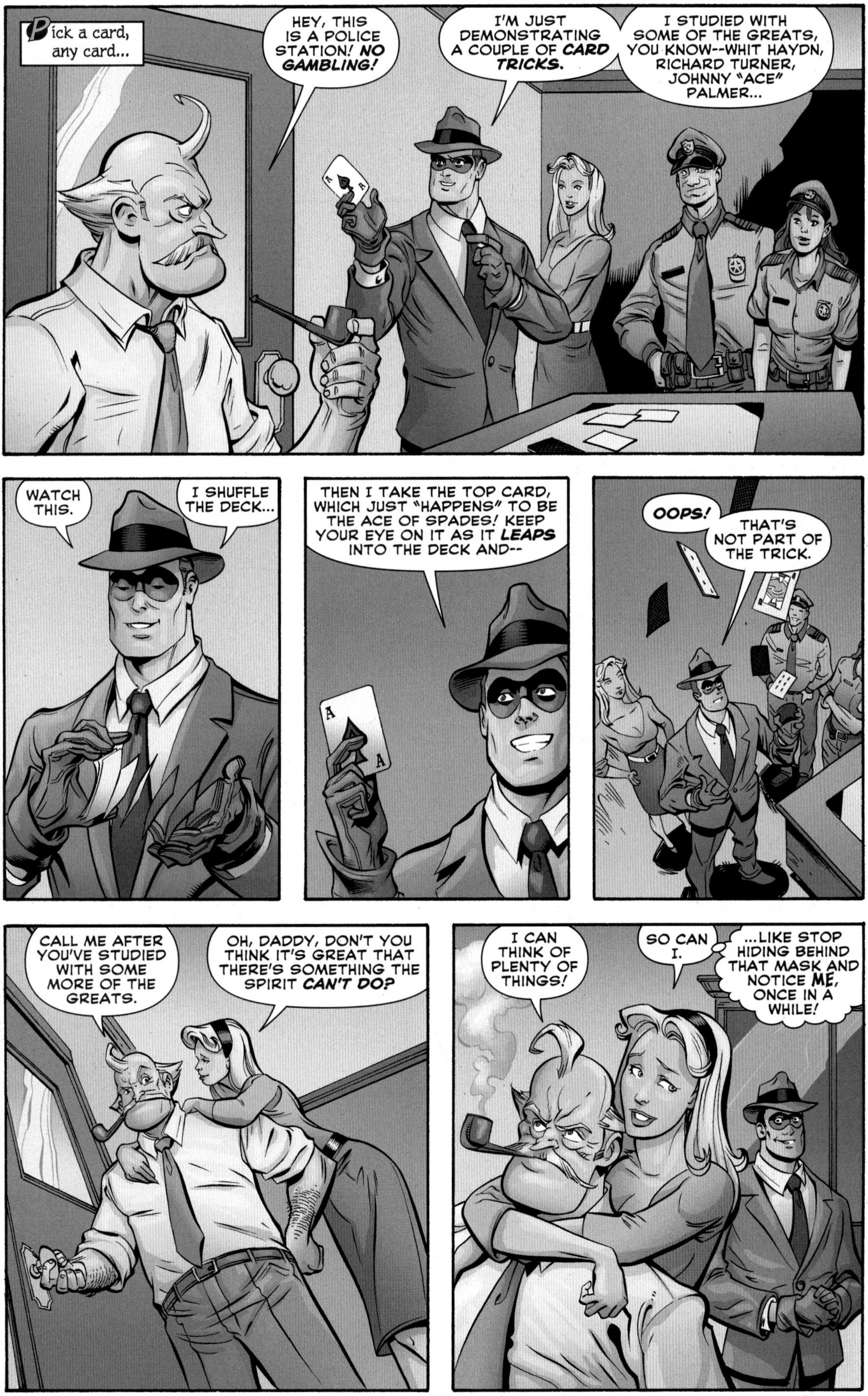
Pick a card, any card...
HEY, THIS IS A POLICE STATION! NO GAMBLING!
I'M JUST DEMONSTRATING A COUPLE OF CARD TRICKS.
I STUDIED WITH SOME OF THE GREATS, YOU KNOW--WHIT HAYDN, RICHARD TURNER, JOHNNY "ACE" PALMER...
WATCH THIS.
I SHUFFLE THE DECK...
THEN I TAKE THE TOP CARD, WHICH JUST "HAPPENS" TO BE THE ACE OF SPADES! KEEP YOUR EYE ON IT AS IT LEAPS INTO THE DECK AND--
OOPS!
THAT'S NOT PART OF THE TRICK.
CALL ME AFTER YOU'VE STUDIED WITH SOME MORE OF THE GREATS.
OH, DADDY, DON'T YOU THINK IT'S GREAT THAT THERE'S SOMETHING THE SPIRIT CAN'T DO?
I CAN THINK OF PLENTY OF THINGS!
SO CAN I.
...LIKE STOP HIDING BEHIND THAT MASK AND NOTICE ME, ONCE IN A WHILE!

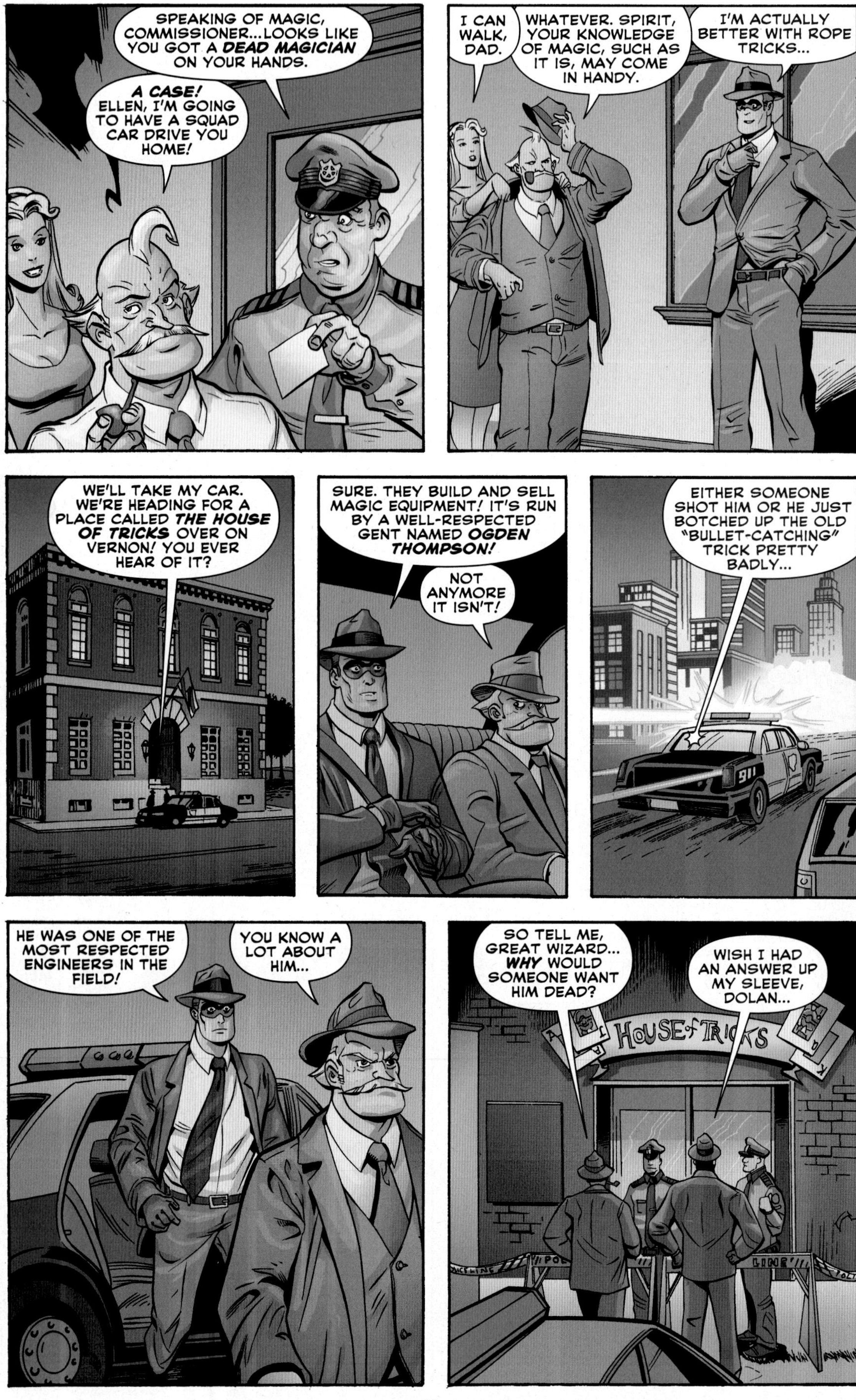
SPEAKING OF MAGIC, COMMISSIONER...LOOKS LIKE YOU GOT A DEAD MAGICIAN ON YOUR HANDS.
A CASE! ELLEN, I'M GOING TO HAVE A SQUAD CAR DRIVE YOU HOME!
I CAN WALK, DAD.
WHATEVER. SPIRIT, YOUR KNOWLEDGE OF MAGIC, SUCH AS IT IS, MAY COME IN HANDY.
I'M ACTUALLY BETTER WITH ROPE TRICKS...
WE'LL TAKE MY CAR. WE'RE HEADING FOR A PLACE CALLED THE HOUSE OF TRICKS OVER ON VERNON! YOU EVER HEAR OF IT?
SURE. THEY BUILD AND SELL MAGIC EQUIPMENT! IT'S RUN BY A WELL-RESPECTED GENT NAMED OGDEN THOMPSON!
NOT ANYMORE IT ISN'T!
EITHER SOMEONE SHOT HIM OR HE JUST BOTCHED UP THE OLD "BULLET-CATCHING" TRICK PRETTY BADLY...
911
HE WAS ONE OF THE MOST RESPECTED ENGINEERS IN THE FIELD!
YOU KNOW A LOT ABOUT HIM...
SO TELL ME, GREAT WIZARD... WHY WOULD SOMEONE WANT HIM DEAD?
WISH I HAD AN ANSWER UP MY SLEEVE, DOLAN...
HOUSE of TRICKS

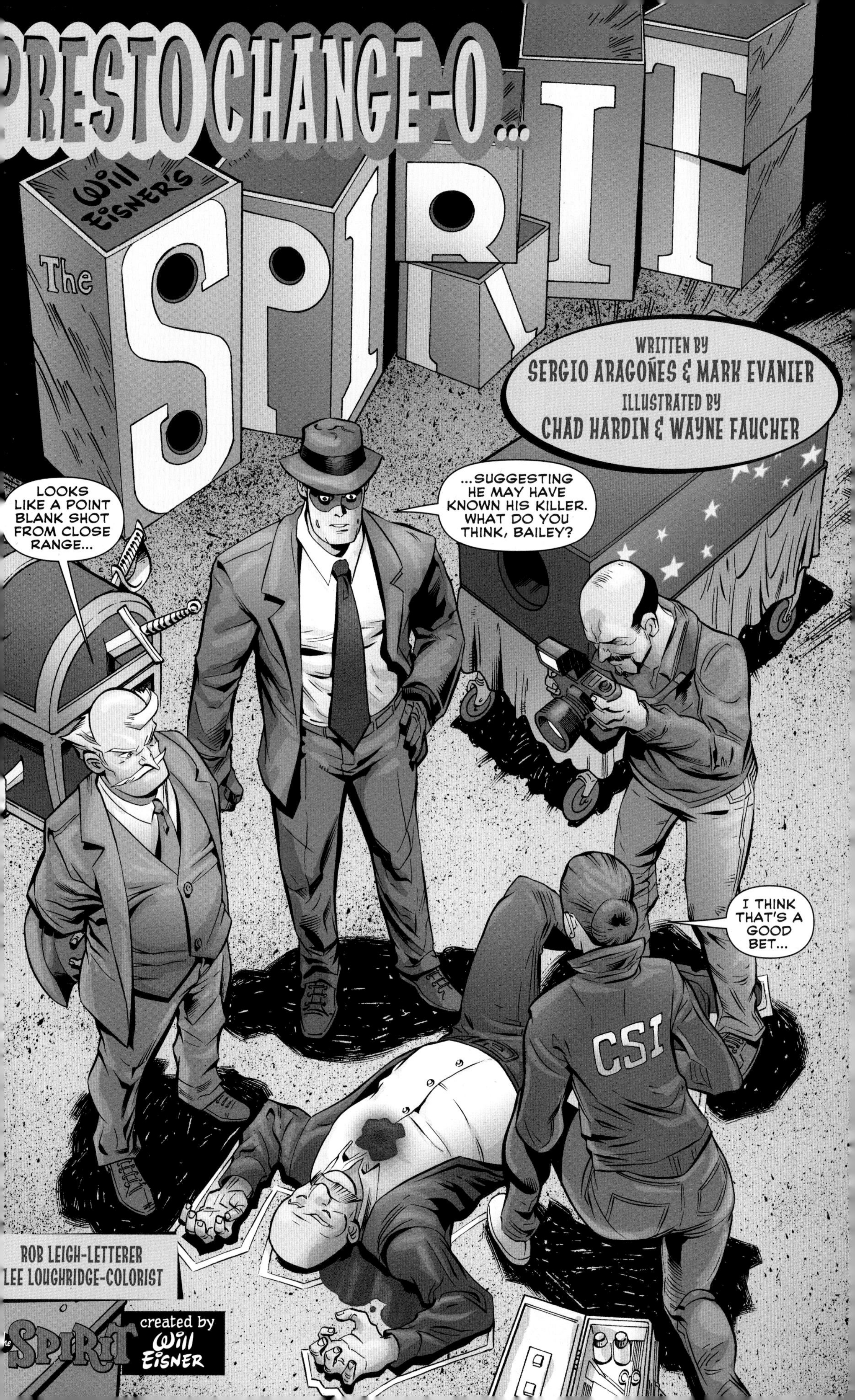
PRESTO CHANGE-O...
WILL EISNER'S
The SPIRIT
WRITTEN BY
SERGIO ARAGOÑES & MARK EVANIER
ILLUSTRATED BY
CHAD HARDIN & WAYNE FAUCHER
LOOKS LIKE A POINT BLANK SHOT FROM CLOSE RANGE...
...SUGGESTING HE MAY HAVE KNOWN HIS KILLER. WHAT DO YOU THINK, BAILEY?
I THINK THAT'S A GOOD BET...
CSI
ROB LEIGH-LETTERER
LEE LOUGHRIDGE-COLORIST
The SPIRIT created by WILL EISNER

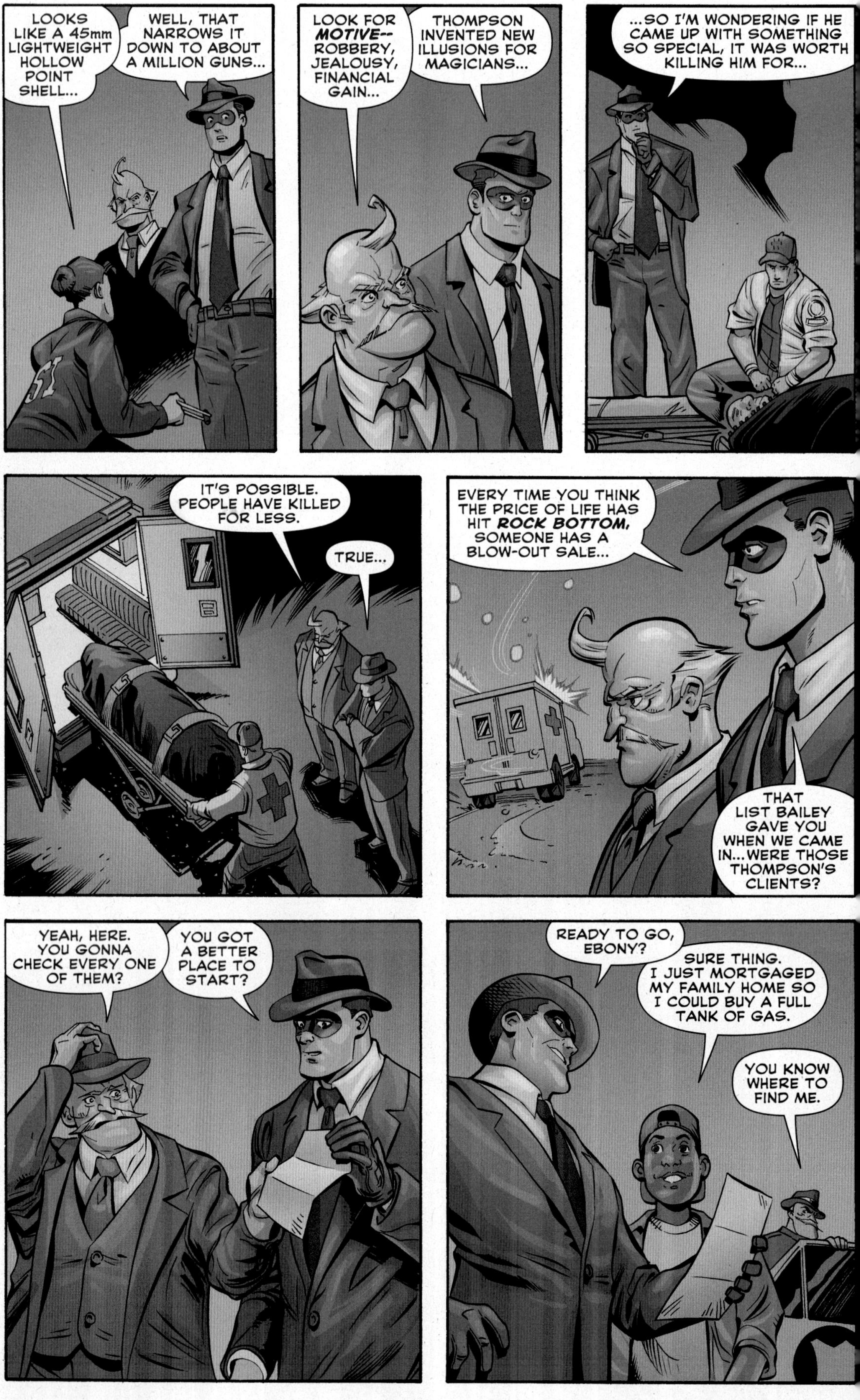
LOOKS LIKE A 45mm LIGHTWEIGHT HOLLOW POINT SHELL...
WELL, THAT NARROWS IT DOWN TO ABOUT A MILLION GUNS...
LOOK FOR *MOTIVE*-- ROBBERY, JEALOUSY, FINANCIAL GAIN...
THOMPSON INVENTED NEW ILLUSIONS FOR MAGICIANS...
...SO I'M WONDERING IF HE CAME UP WITH SOMETHING SO SPECIAL, IT WAS WORTH KILLING HIM FOR...
IT'S POSSIBLE. PEOPLE HAVE KILLED FOR LESS.
TRUE...
EVERY TIME YOU THINK THE PRICE OF LIFE HAS HIT ***ROCK BOTTOM,*** SOMEONE HAS A BLOW-OUT SALE...
THAT LIST BAILEY GAVE YOU WHEN WE CAME IN...WERE THOSE THOMPSON'S CLIENTS?
YEAH, HERE. YOU GONNA CHECK EVERY ONE OF THEM?
YOU GOT A BETTER PLACE TO START?
READY TO GO, EBONY?
SURE THING. I JUST MORTGAGED MY FAMILY HOME SO I COULD BUY A FULL TANK OF GAS.
YOU KNOW WHERE TO FIND ME.

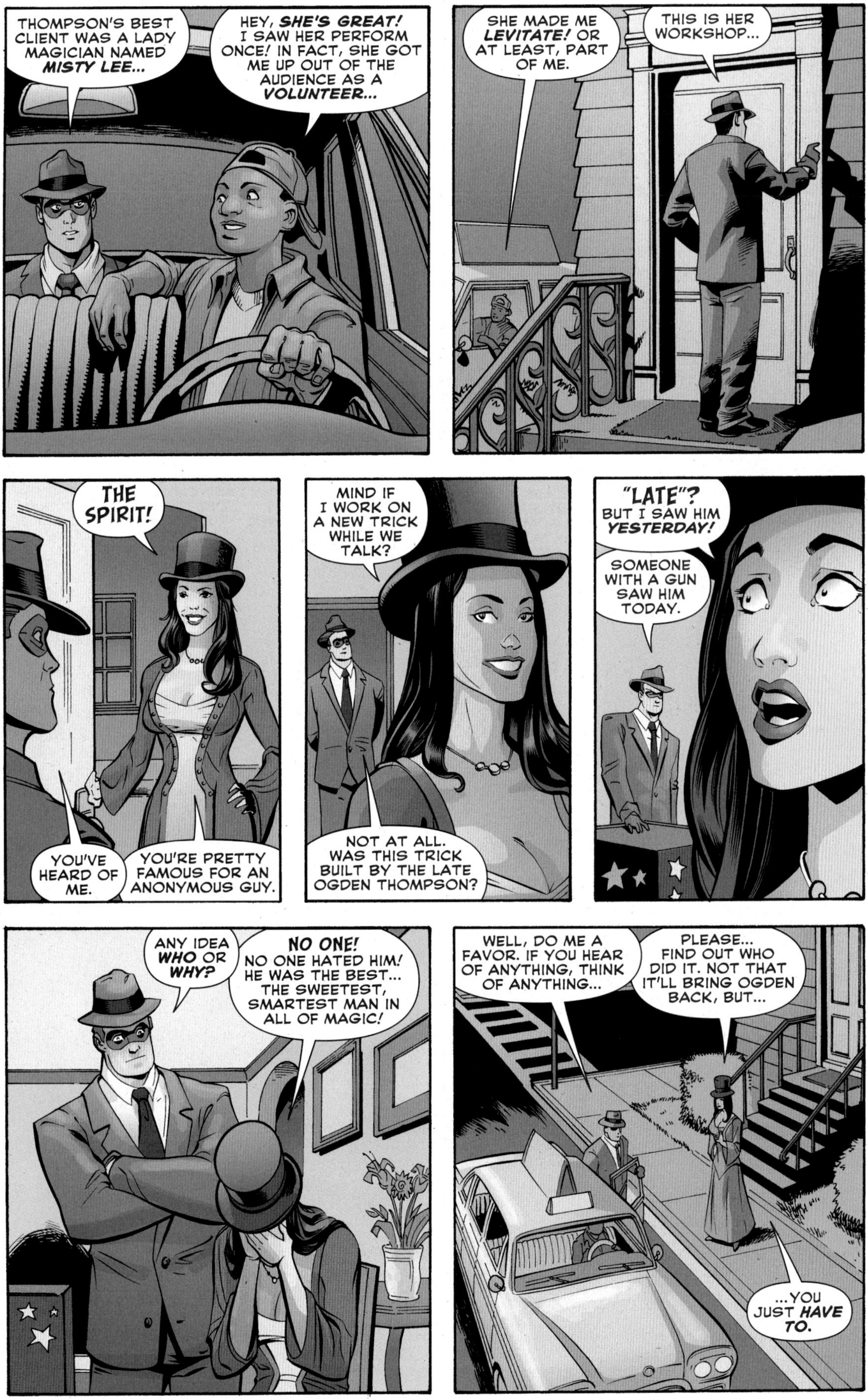
THOMPSON'S BEST CLIENT WAS A LADY MAGICIAN NAMED MISTY LEE...
HEY, SHE'S GREAT! I SAW HER PERFORM ONCE! IN FACT, SHE GOT ME UP OUT OF THE AUDIENCE AS A VOLUNTEER...
SHE MADE ME LEVITATE! OR AT LEAST, PART OF ME.
THIS IS HER WORKSHOP...
THE SPIRIT!
YOU'VE HEARD OF ME.
YOU'RE PRETTY FAMOUS FOR AN ANONYMOUS GUY.
MIND IF I WORK ON A NEW TRICK WHILE WE TALK?
NOT AT ALL. WAS THIS TRICK BUILT BY THE LATE OGDEN THOMPSON?
"LATE"? BUT I SAW HIM YESTERDAY!
SOMEONE WITH A GUN SAW HIM TODAY.
ANY IDEA WHO OR WHY?
NO ONE! NO ONE HATED HIM! HE WAS THE BEST... THE SWEETEST, SMARTEST MAN IN ALL OF MAGIC!
WELL, DO ME A FAVOR. IF YOU HEAR OF ANYTHING, THINK OF ANYTHING...
PLEASE... FIND OUT WHO DID IT. NOT THAT IT'LL BRING OGDEN BACK, BUT...
...YOU JUST HAVE TO.

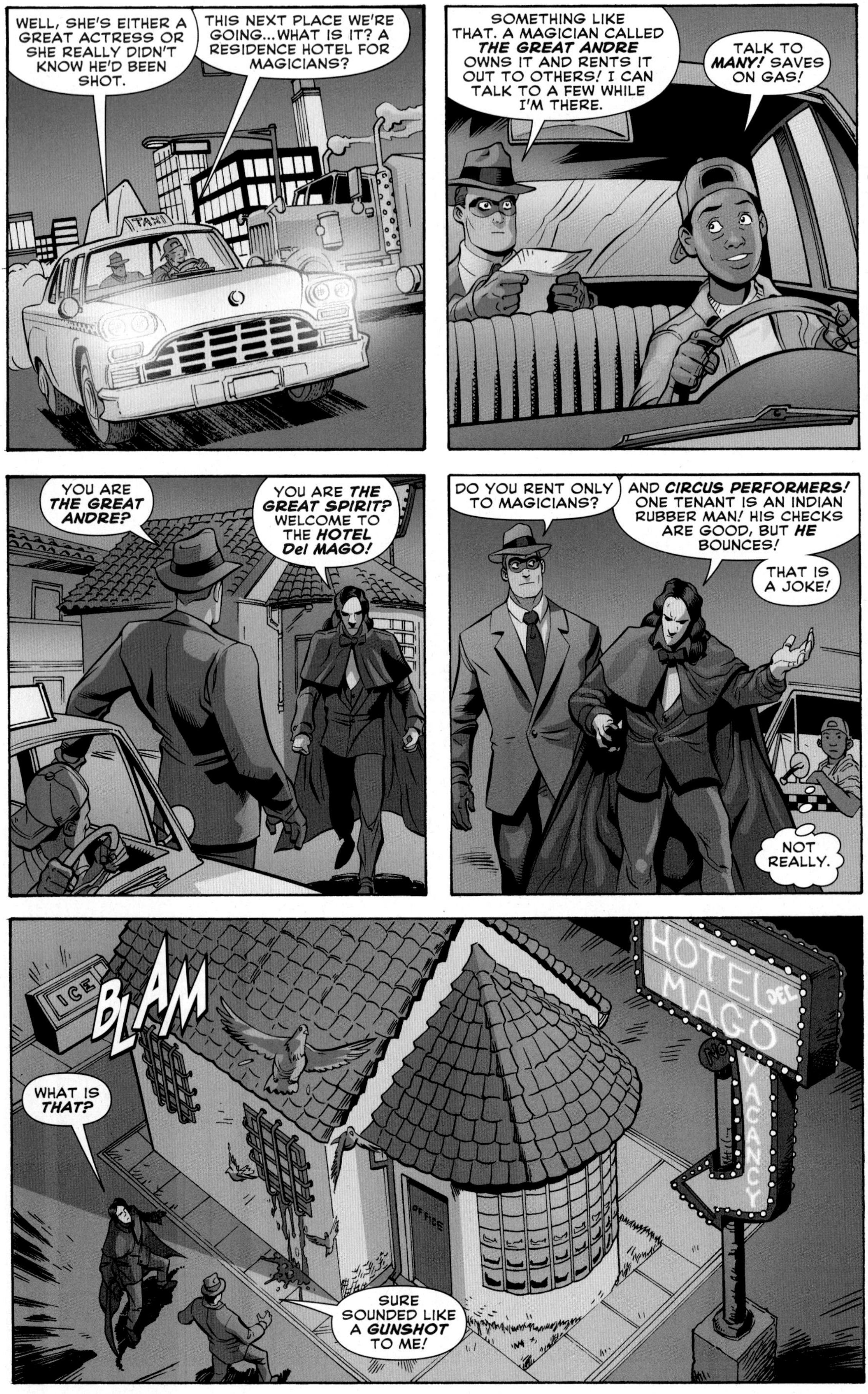
WELL, SHE'S EITHER A GREAT ACTRESS OR SHE REALLY DIDN'T KNOW HE'D BEEN SHOT.
THIS NEXT PLACE WE'RE GOING...WHAT IS IT? A RESIDENCE HOTEL FOR MAGICIANS?
TAXI
SOMETHING LIKE THAT. A MAGICIAN CALLED THE GREAT ANDRE OWNS IT AND RENTS IT OUT TO OTHERS! I CAN TALK TO A FEW WHILE I'M THERE.
TALK TO MANY! SAVES ON GAS!
YOU ARE THE GREAT ANDRE?
YOU ARE THE GREAT SPIRIT? WELCOME TO THE HOTEL Del MAGO!
DO YOU RENT ONLY TO MAGICIANS?
AND CIRCUS PERFORMERS! ONE TENANT IS AN INDIAN RUBBER MAN! HIS CHECKS ARE GOOD, BUT HE BOUNCES!
THAT IS A JOKE!
NOT REALLY.
ICE
BLAM
HOTEL DEL MAGO
NO VACANCY
WHAT IS THAT?
OFFICE
SURE SOUNDED LIKE A GUNSHOT TO ME!

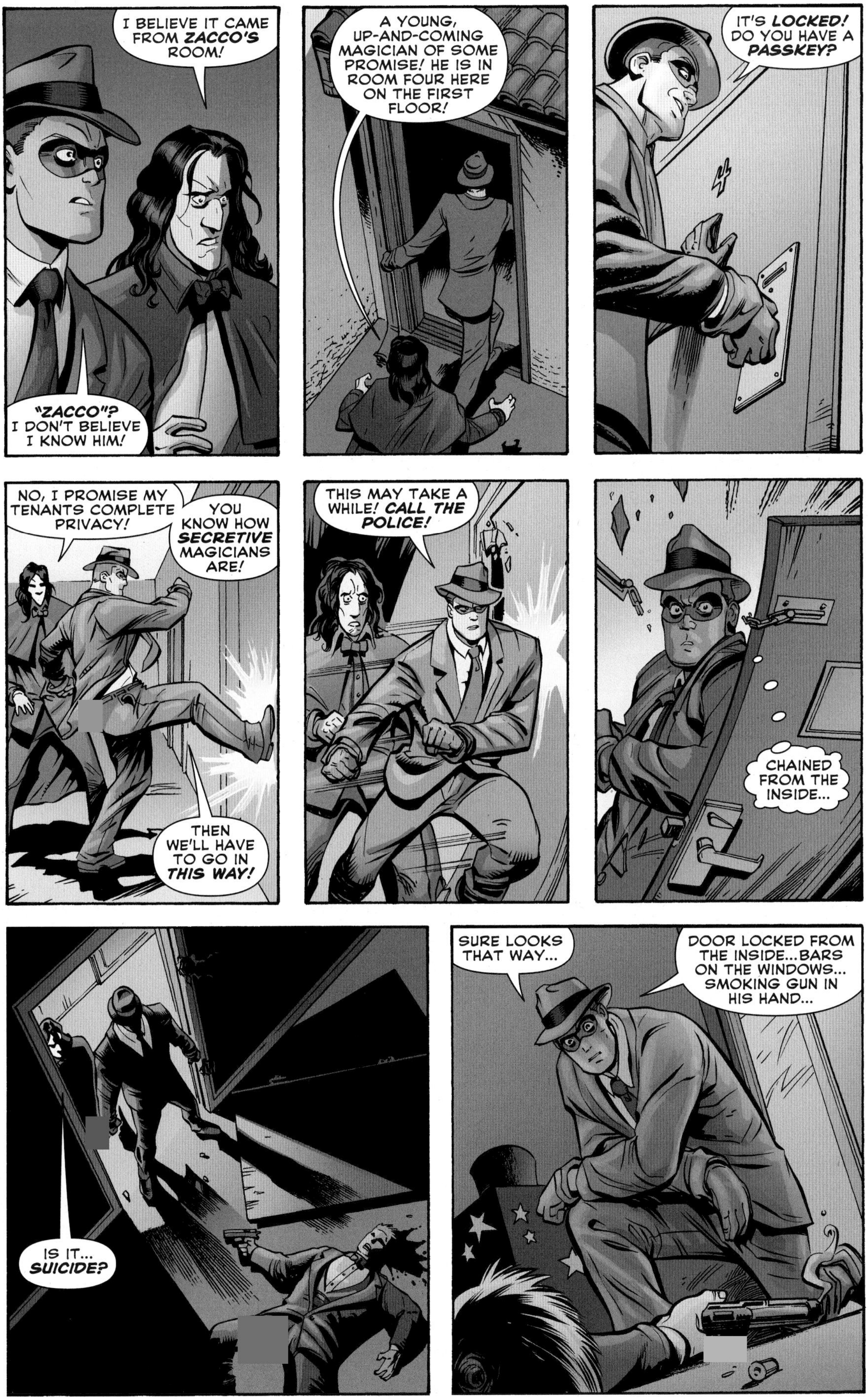
I BELIEVE IT CAME FROM ZACCO'S ROOM!
"ZACCO"? I DON'T BELIEVE I KNOW HIM!
A YOUNG, UP-AND-COMING MAGICIAN OF SOME PROMISE! HE IS IN ROOM FOUR HERE ON THE FIRST FLOOR!
4
IT'S LOCKED! DO YOU HAVE A PASSKEY?
NO, I PROMISE MY TENANTS COMPLETE PRIVACY!
YOU KNOW HOW SECRETIVE MAGICIANS ARE!
THEN WE'LL HAVE TO GO IN THIS WAY!
THIS MAY TAKE A WHILE! CALL THE POLICE!
CHAINED FROM THE INSIDE...
IS IT... SUICIDE?
SURE LOOKS THAT WAY...
DOOR LOCKED FROM THE INSIDE...BARS ON THE WINDOWS... SMOKING GUN IN HIS HAND...

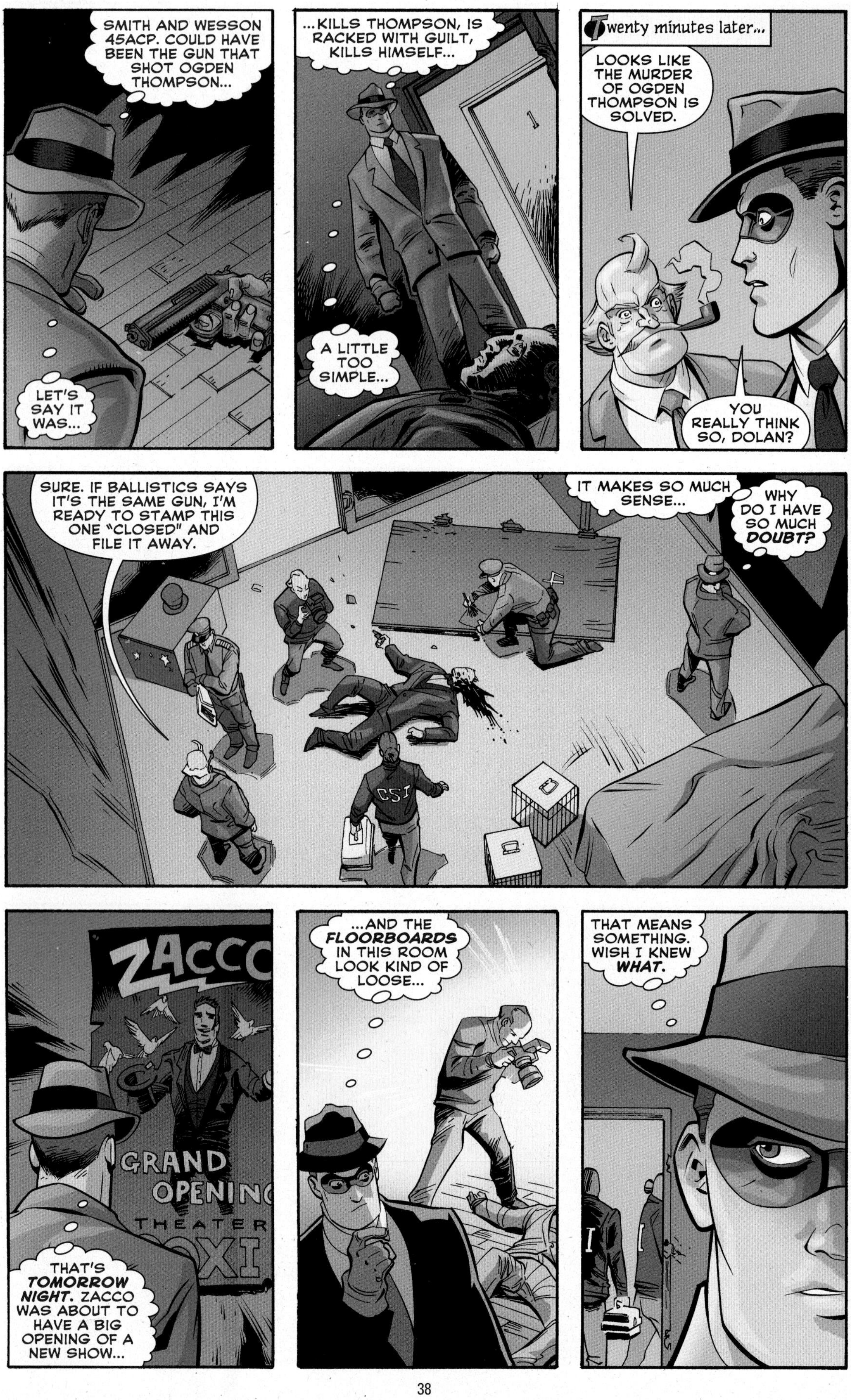
SMITH AND WESSON 45ACP. COULD HAVE BEEN THE GUN THAT SHOT OGDEN THOMPSON...
LET'S SAY IT WAS...
...KILLS THOMPSON, IS RACKED WITH GUILT, KILLS HIMSELF...
A LITTLE TOO SIMPLE...
Twenty minutes later...
LOOKS LIKE THE MURDER OF OGDEN THOMPSON IS SOLVED.
YOU REALLY THINK SO, DOLAN?
SURE. IF BALLISTICS SAYS IT'S THE SAME GUN, I'M READY TO STAMP THIS ONE "CLOSED" AND FILE IT AWAY.
IT MAKES SO MUCH SENSE...
WHY DO I HAVE SO MUCH DOUBT?
CSI
ZACCO
GRAND OPENING
THEATER
THAT'S TOMORROW NIGHT. ZACCO WAS ABOUT TO HAVE A BIG OPENING OF A NEW SHOW...
...AND THE FLOORBOARDS IN THIS ROOM LOOK KIND OF LOOSE...
THAT MEANS SOMETHING. WISH I KNEW WHAT.

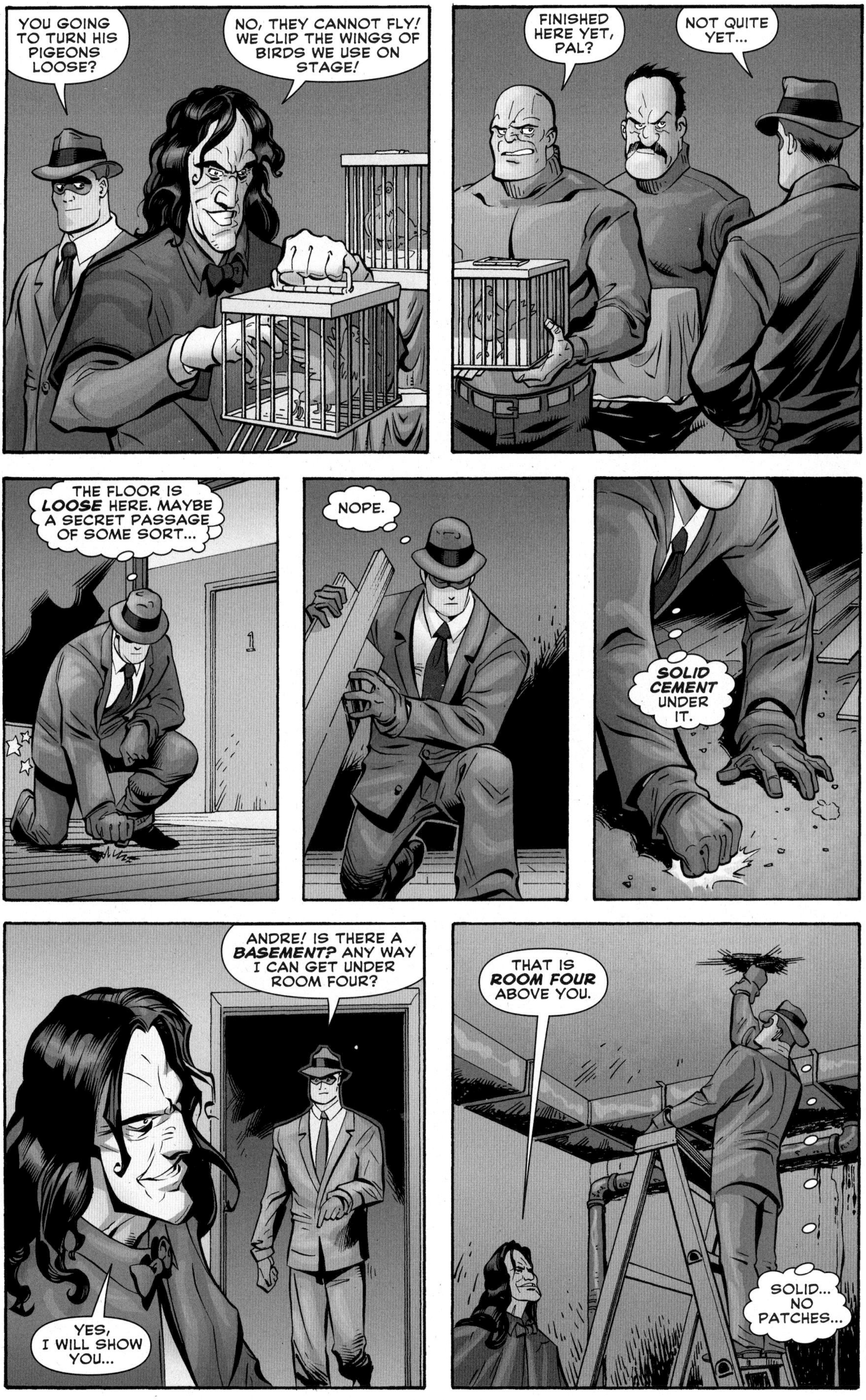
YOU GOING TO TURN HIS PIGEONS LOOSE?
NO, THEY CANNOT FLY! WE CLIP THE WINGS OF BIRDS WE USE ON STAGE!
FINISHED HERE YET, PAL?
NOT QUITE YET...
THE FLOOR IS LOOSE HERE. MAYBE A SECRET PASSAGE OF SOME SORT...
1
NOPE.
SOLID CEMENT UNDER IT.
ANDRE! IS THERE A BASEMENT? ANY WAY I CAN GET UNDER ROOM FOUR?
YES, I WILL SHOW YOU...
THAT IS ROOM FOUR ABOVE YOU.
SOLID... NO PATCHES...

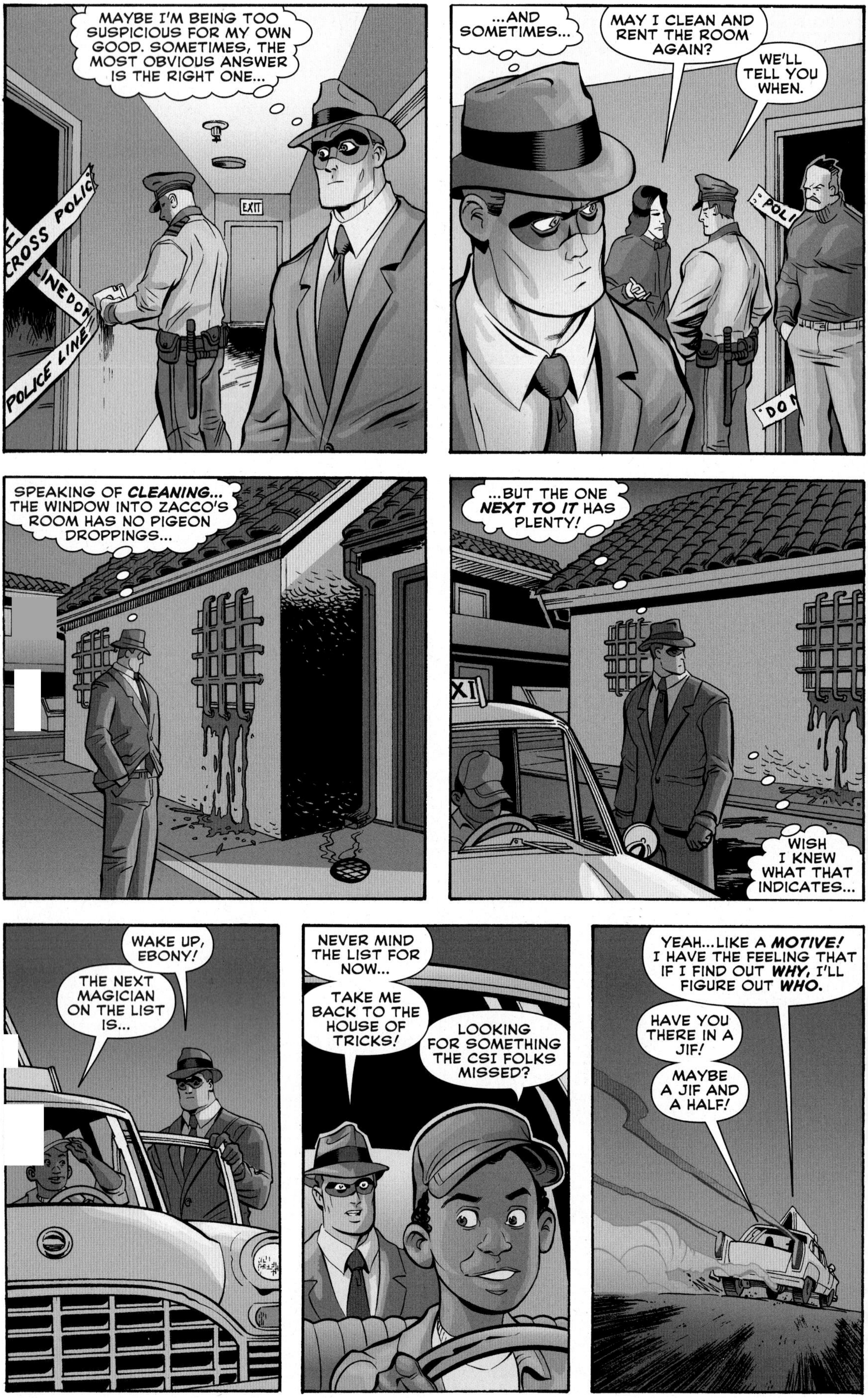

MAYBE I'M BEING TOO SUSPICIOUS FOR MY OWN GOOD. SOMETIMES, THE MOST OBVIOUS ANSWER IS THE RIGHT ONE...
CROSS POLIC
LINE DO
POLICE LINE
EXIT
...AND SOMETIMES...
MAY I CLEAN AND RENT THE ROOM AGAIN?
WE'LL TELL YOU WHEN.
POLI
DO N
SPEAKING OF CLEANING... THE WINDOW INTO ZACCO'S ROOM HAS NO PIGEON DROPPINGS...
...BUT THE ONE NEXT TO IT HAS PLENTY!
WISH I KNEW WHAT THAT INDICATES...
WAKE UP, EBONY!
THE NEXT MAGICIAN ON THE LIST IS...
NEVER MIND THE LIST FOR NOW...
TAKE ME BACK TO THE HOUSE OF TRICKS!
LOOKING FOR SOMETHING THE CSI FOLKS MISSED?
YEAH...LIKE A MOTIVE! I HAVE THE FEELING THAT IF I FIND OUT WHY, I'LL FIGURE OUT WHO.
HAVE YOU THERE IN A JIF!
MAYBE A JIF AND A HALF!

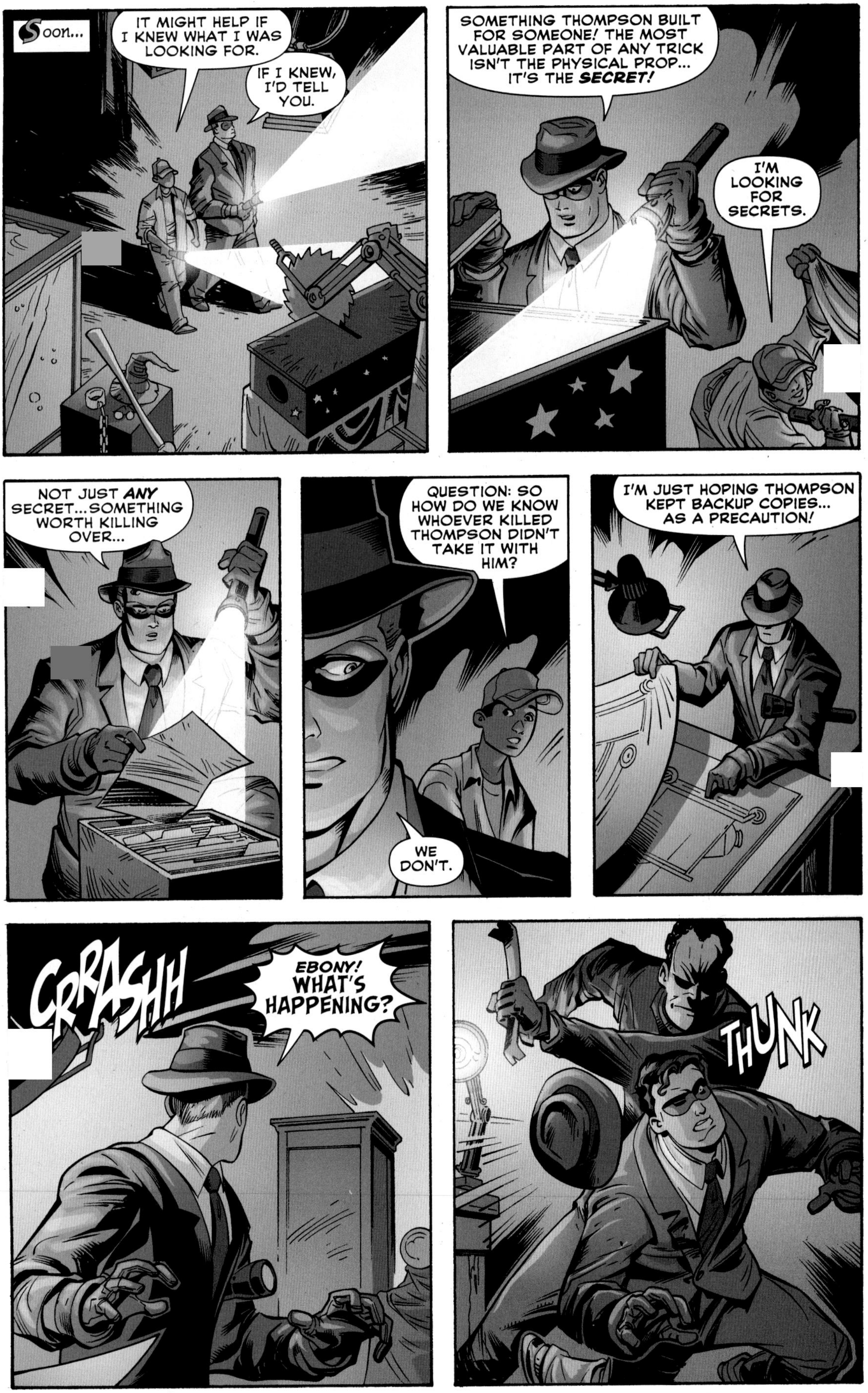
Soon...
IT MIGHT HELP IF I KNEW WHAT I WAS LOOKING FOR.
IF I KNEW, I'D TELL YOU.
SOMETHING THOMPSON BUILT FOR SOMEONE! THE MOST VALUABLE PART OF ANY TRICK ISN'T THE PHYSICAL PROP... IT'S THE SECRET!
I'M LOOKING FOR SECRETS.
NOT JUST ANY SECRET...SOMETHING WORTH KILLING OVER...
QUESTION: SO HOW DO WE KNOW WHOEVER KILLED THOMPSON DIDN'T TAKE IT WITH HIM?
WE DON'T.
I'M JUST HOPING THOMPSON KEPT BACKUP COPIES... AS A PRECAUTION!
CRRASHH
EBONY! WHAT'S HAPPENING?
THUNK

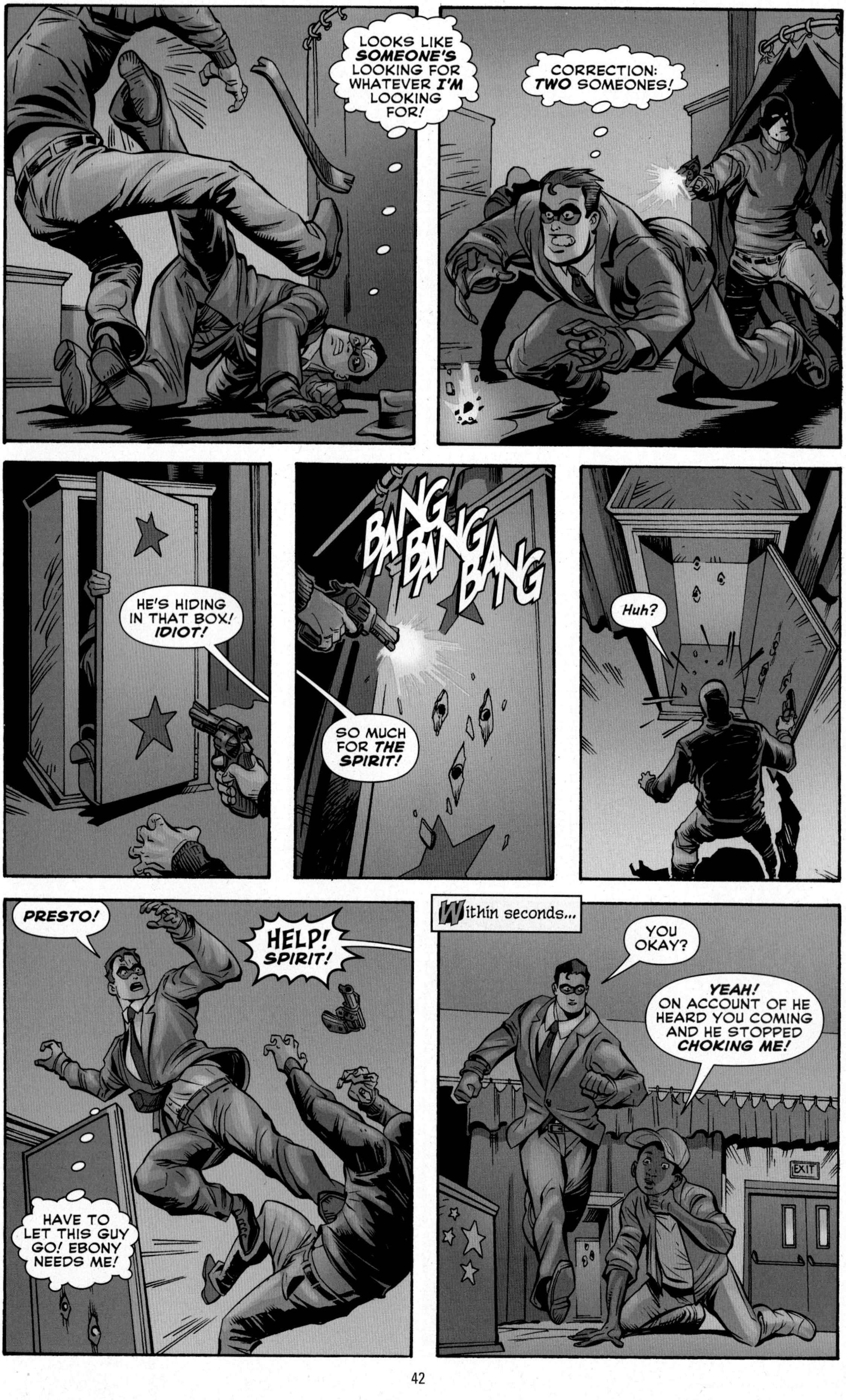

LOOKS LIKE SOMEONE'S LOOKING FOR WHATEVER I'M LOOKING FOR!
CORRECTION: TWO SOMEONES!
HE'S HIDING IN THAT BOX! IDIOT!
BANG BANG BANG
SO MUCH FOR THE SPIRIT!
Huh?
PRESTO!
HELP! SPIRIT!
HAVE TO LET THIS GUY GO! EBONY NEEDS ME!
Within seconds...
YOU OKAY?
YEAH! ON ACCOUNT OF HE HEARD YOU COMING AND HE STOPPED CHOKING ME!
EXIT

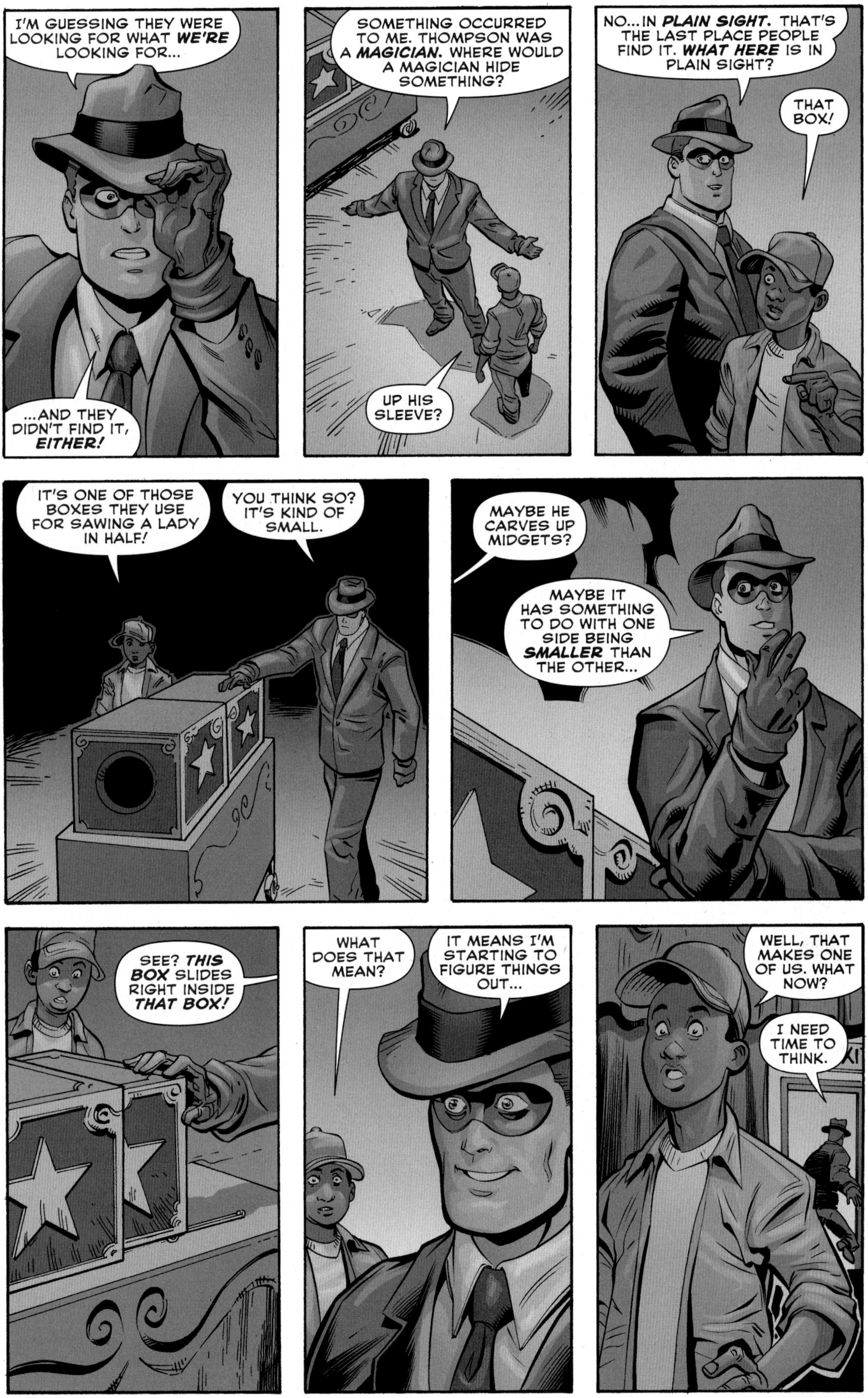
I'M GUESSING THEY WERE LOOKING FOR WHAT **WE'RE** LOOKING FOR...
...AND THEY DIDN'T FIND IT, **EITHER!**
SOMETHING OCCURRED TO ME. THOMPSON WAS A **MAGICIAN.** WHERE WOULD A MAGICIAN HIDE SOMETHING?
UP HIS SLEEVE?
NO...IN **PLAIN SIGHT.** THAT'S THE LAST PLACE PEOPLE FIND IT. **WHAT HERE** IS IN PLAIN SIGHT?
THAT BOX!
IT'S ONE OF THOSE BOXES THEY USE FOR SAWING A LADY IN HALF!
YOU THINK SO? IT'S KIND OF SMALL.
MAYBE HE CARVES UP MIDGETS?
MAYBE IT HAS SOMETHING TO DO WITH ONE SIDE BEING **SMALLER** THAN THE OTHER...
SEE? **THIS BOX** SLIDES RIGHT INSIDE **THAT BOX!**
WHAT DOES THAT MEAN?
IT MEANS I'M STARTING TO FIGURE THINGS OUT...
WELL, THAT MAKES ONE OF US. WHAT NOW?
I NEED TIME TO THINK.

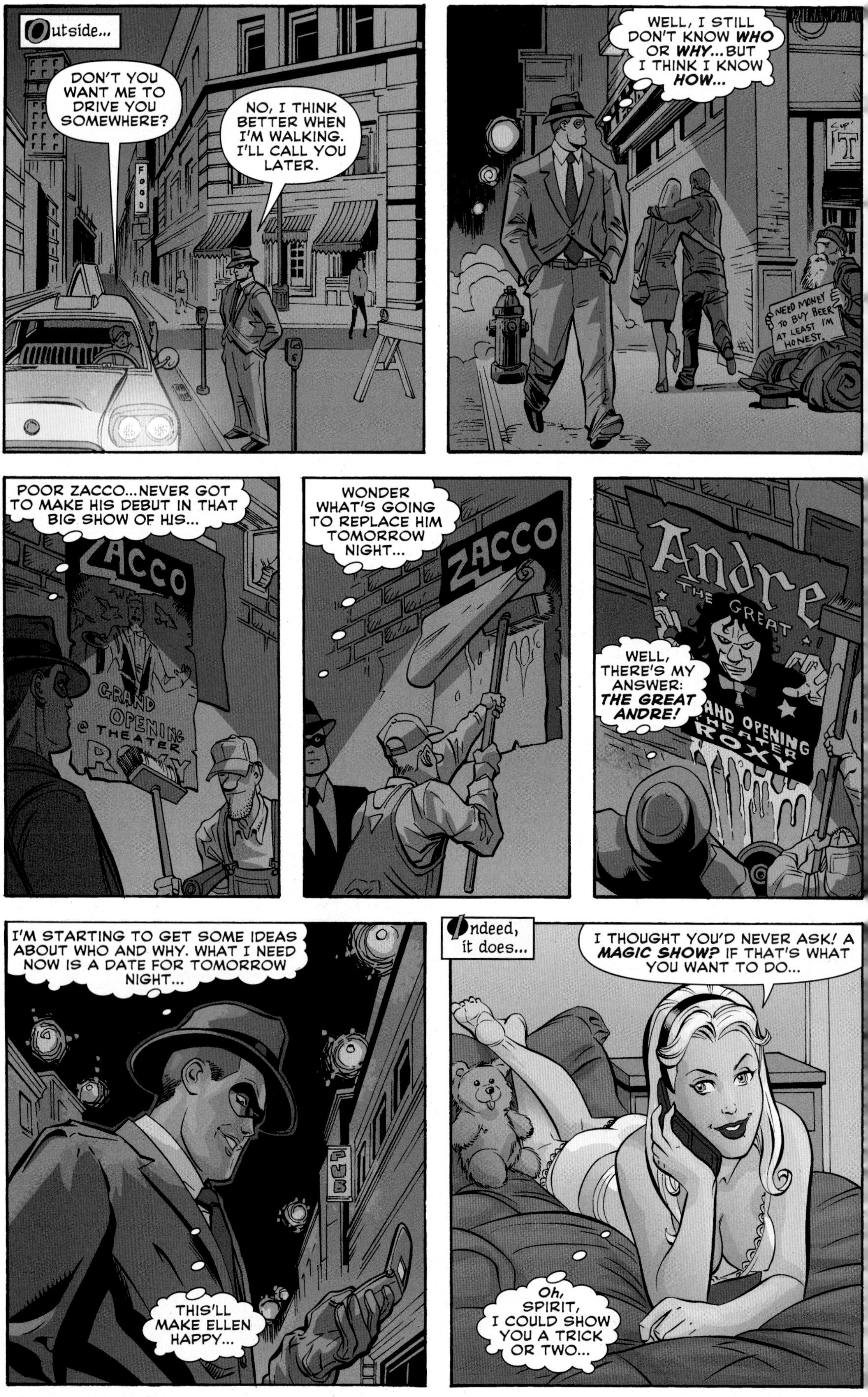

Outside...
DON'T YOU WANT ME TO DRIVE YOU SOMEWHERE?
NO, I THINK BETTER WHEN I'M WALKING. I'LL CALL YOU LATER.
FOOD
WELL, I STILL DON'T KNOW **WHO** OR **WHY**... BUT I THINK I KNOW **HOW**...
NEED MONEY TO BUY BEER AT LEAST I'M HONEST.
POOR ZACCO... NEVER GOT TO MAKE HIS DEBUT IN THAT BIG SHOW OF HIS...
ZACCO
GRAND OPENING @ THEATER ROXY
WONDER WHAT'S GOING TO REPLACE HIM TOMORROW NIGHT...
ZACCO
Andre THE GREAT
WELL, THERE'S MY ANSWER: **THE GREAT ANDRE!**
GRAND OPENING THEATER ROXY
I'M STARTING TO GET SOME IDEAS ABOUT WHO AND WHY. WHAT I NEED NOW IS A DATE FOR TOMORROW NIGHT...
PUB
THIS'LL MAKE ELLEN HAPPY...
Indeed, it does...
I THOUGHT YOU'D NEVER ASK! A **MAGIC SHOW?** IF THAT'S WHAT YOU WANT TO DO...
Oh, SPIRIT, I COULD SHOW YOU A TRICK OR TWO...

ROXY
ANDRE THE GREAT TONIGHT

I'M GLAD YOU WERE FREE TONIGHT.

I CANCELLED SOME PRETTY BIG PLANS FOR THIS...

I'M JUST GLAD I HAVE THE OPPORTUNITY TO TAKE YOUR MIND OFF *WORK* FOR A LITTLE WHILE...

THERE WERE NO FINGERPRINTS IN ZACCO'S ROOM...

THIS IS A VERY FAMOUS TRICK CALLED "METAMORPHOSIS!"

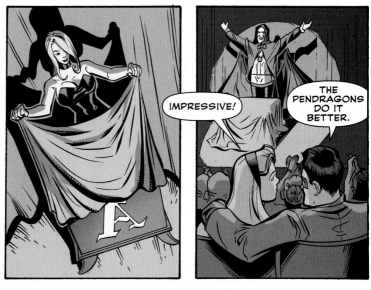

IMPRESSIVE!

THE PENDRAGONS DO IT BETTER.

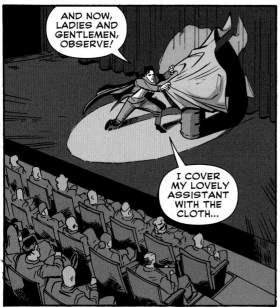

AND NOW, LADIES AND GENTLEMEN, OBSERVE!

I COVER MY LOVELY ASSISTANT WITH THE CLOTH...

...VOILÀ!

OKAY, I THINK I HAVE IT FIGURED OUT...

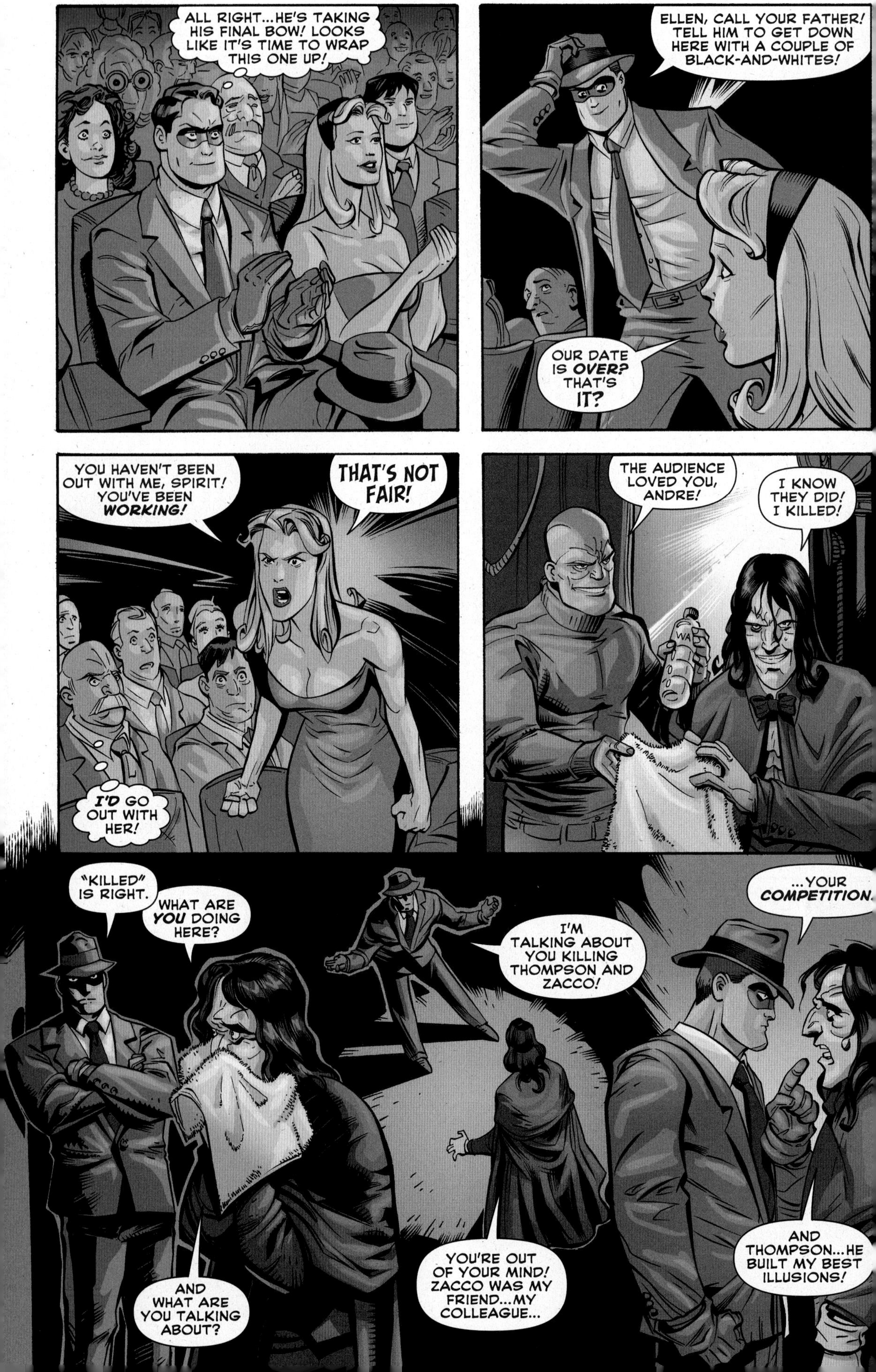
ALL RIGHT...HE'S TAKING HIS FINAL BOW! LOOKS LIKE IT'S TIME TO WRAP THIS ONE UP!
ELLEN, CALL YOUR FATHER! TELL HIM TO GET DOWN HERE WITH A COUPLE OF BLACK-AND-WHITES!
OUR DATE IS OVER? THAT'S IT?
YOU HAVEN'T BEEN OUT WITH ME, SPIRIT! YOU'VE BEEN WORKING!
THAT'S NOT FAIR!
I'D GO OUT WITH HER!
THE AUDIENCE LOVED YOU, ANDRE!
I KNOW THEY DID! I KILLED!
"KILLED" IS RIGHT.
WHAT ARE YOU DOING HERE?
AND WHAT ARE YOU TALKING ABOUT?
I'M TALKING ABOUT YOU KILLING THOMPSON AND ZACCO!
YOU'RE OUT OF YOUR MIND! ZACCO WAS MY FRIEND...MY COLLEAGUE...
...YOUR COMPETITION.
AND THOMPSON...HE BUILT MY BEST ILLUSIONS!

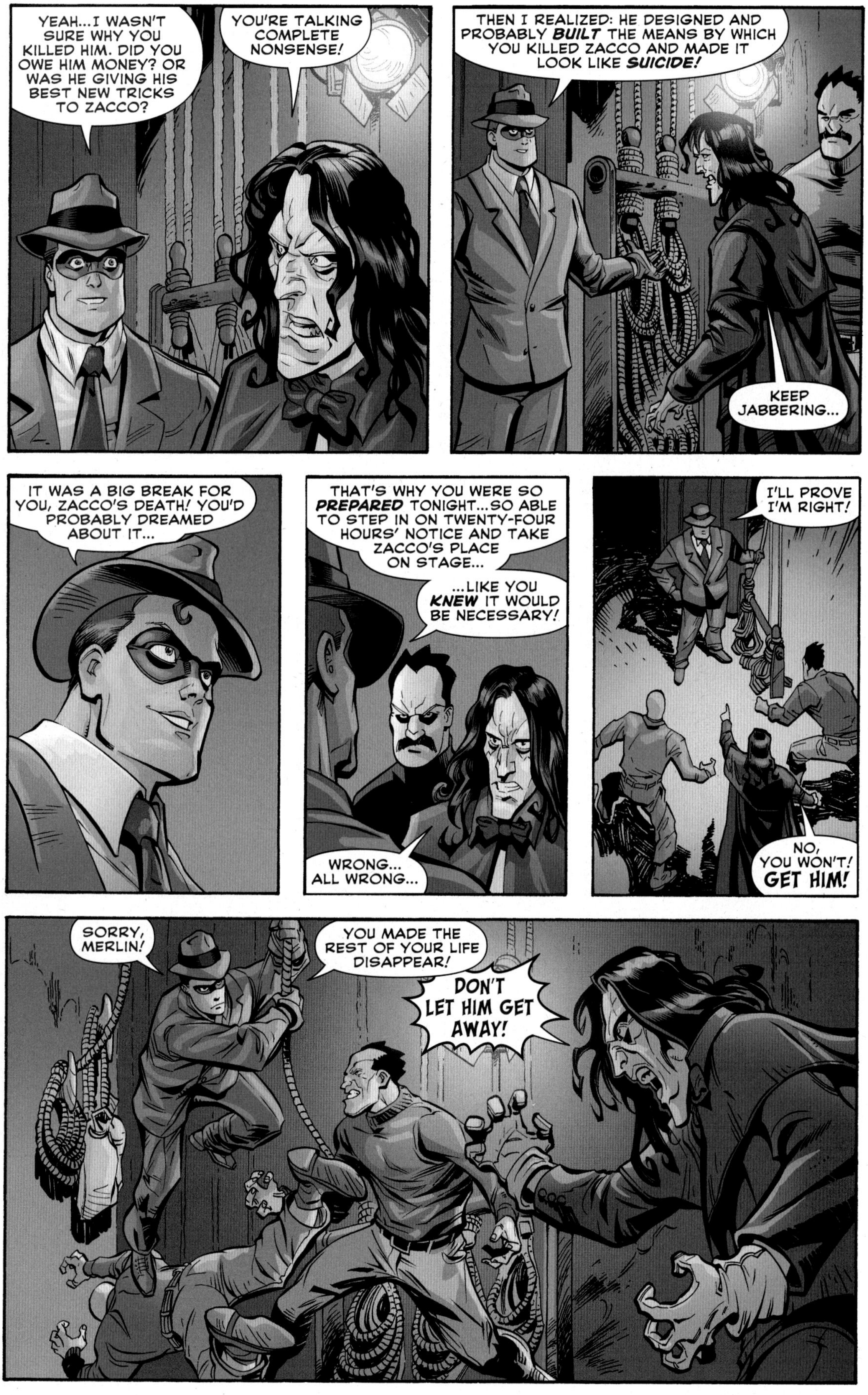
YEAH...I WASN'T SURE WHY YOU KILLED HIM. DID YOU OWE HIM MONEY? OR WAS HE GIVING HIS BEST NEW TRICKS TO ZACCO?
YOU'RE TALKING COMPLETE NONSENSE!
THEN I REALIZED: HE DESIGNED AND PROBABLY BUILT THE MEANS BY WHICH YOU KILLED ZACCO AND MADE IT LOOK LIKE SUICIDE!
KEEP JABBERING...
IT WAS A BIG BREAK FOR YOU, ZACCO'S DEATH! YOU'D PROBABLY DREAMED ABOUT IT...
THAT'S WHY YOU WERE SO PREPARED TONIGHT...SO ABLE TO STEP IN ON TWENTY-FOUR HOURS' NOTICE AND TAKE ZACCO'S PLACE ON STAGE...
...LIKE YOU KNEW IT WOULD BE NECESSARY!
WRONG... ALL WRONG...
I'LL PROVE I'M RIGHT!
NO, YOU WON'T! GET HIM!
SORRY, MERLIN!
YOU MADE THE REST OF YOUR LIFE DISAPPEAR!
DON'T LET HIM GET AWAY!

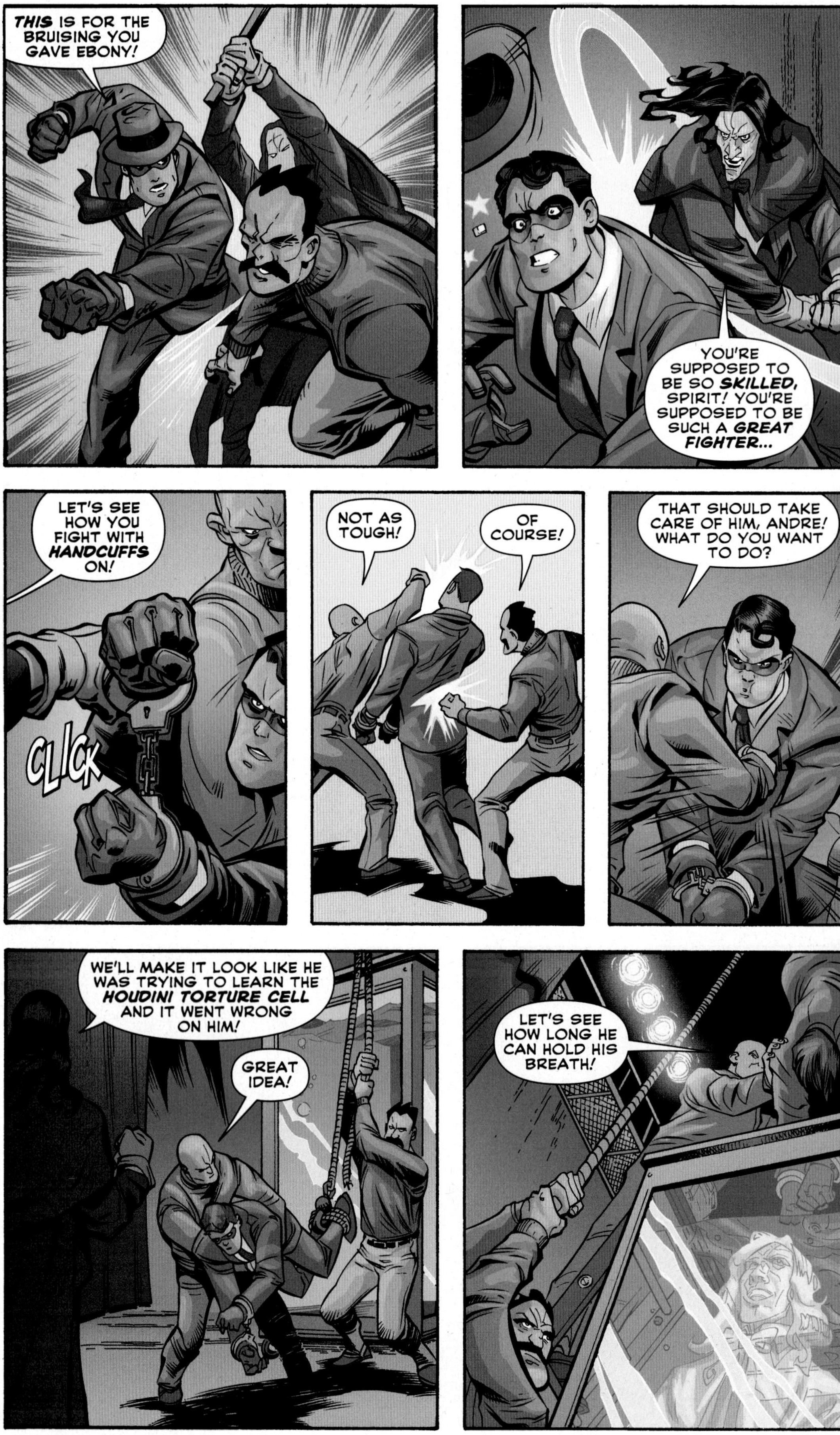
THIS IS FOR THE BRUISING YOU GAVE EBONY!
YOU'RE SUPPOSED TO BE SO SKILLED, SPIRIT! YOU'RE SUPPOSED TO BE SUCH A GREAT FIGHTER...
LET'S SEE HOW YOU FIGHT WITH HANDCUFFS ON!
CLICK
NOT AS TOUGH!
OF COURSE!
THAT SHOULD TAKE CARE OF HIM, ANDRE! WHAT DO YOU WANT TO DO?
WE'LL MAKE IT LOOK LIKE HE WAS TRYING TO LEARN THE HOUDINI TORTURE CELL AND IT WENT WRONG ON HIM!
GREAT IDEA!
LET'S SEE HOW LONG HE CAN HOLD HIS BREATH!

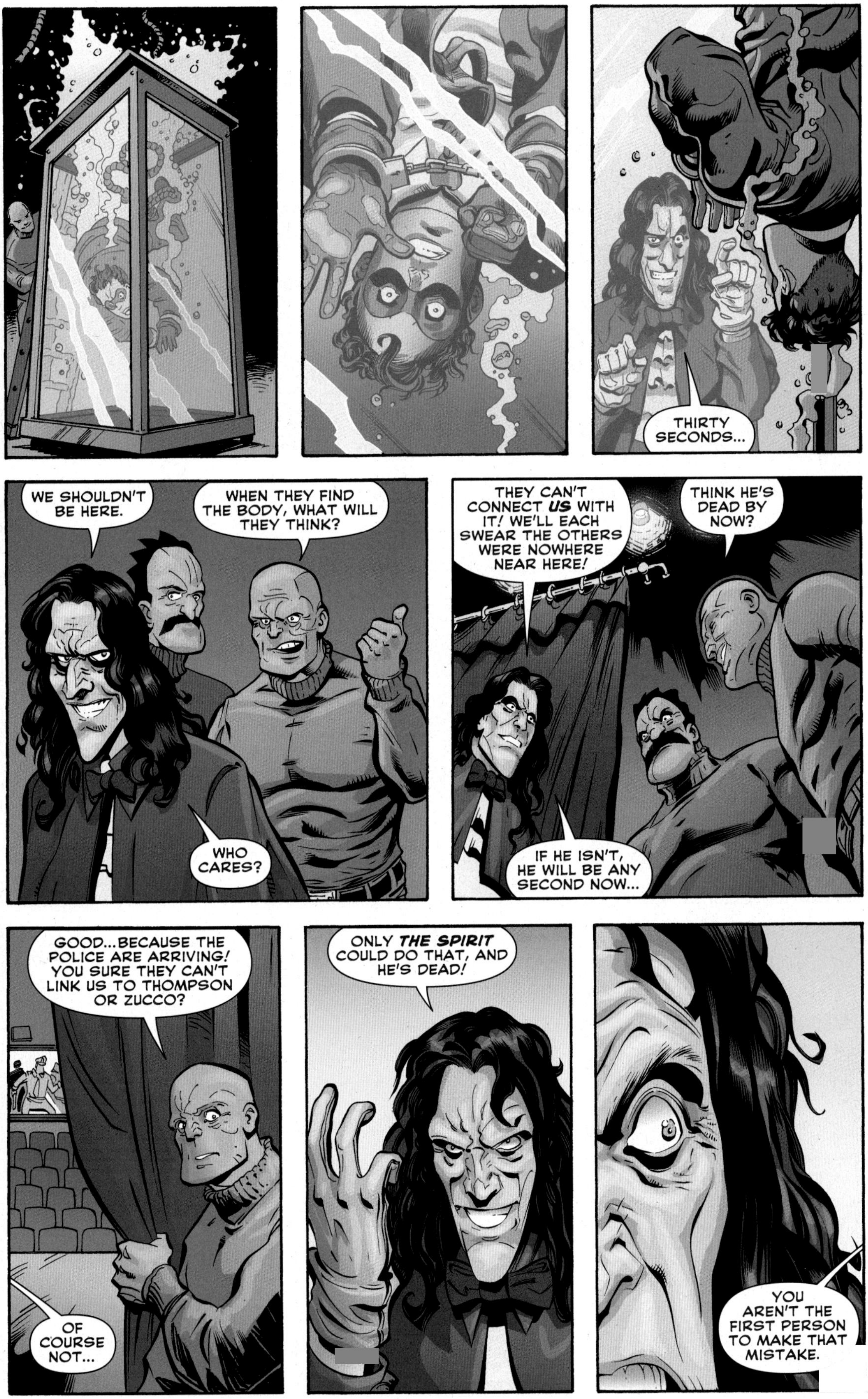
THIRTY SECONDS...
WE SHOULDN'T BE HERE.
WHEN THEY FIND THE BODY, WHAT WILL THEY THINK?
WHO CARES?
THEY CAN'T CONNECT **US** WITH IT! WE'LL EACH SWEAR THE OTHERS WERE NOWHERE NEAR HERE!
THINK HE'S DEAD BY NOW?
IF HE ISN'T, HE WILL BE ANY SECOND NOW...
GOOD...BECAUSE THE POLICE ARE ARRIVING! YOU SURE THEY CAN'T LINK US TO THOMPSON OR ZUCCO?
OF COURSE NOT...
ONLY ***THE SPIRIT*** COULD DO THAT, AND HE'S DEAD!
YOU AREN'T THE FIRST PERSON TO MAKE THAT MISTAKE.

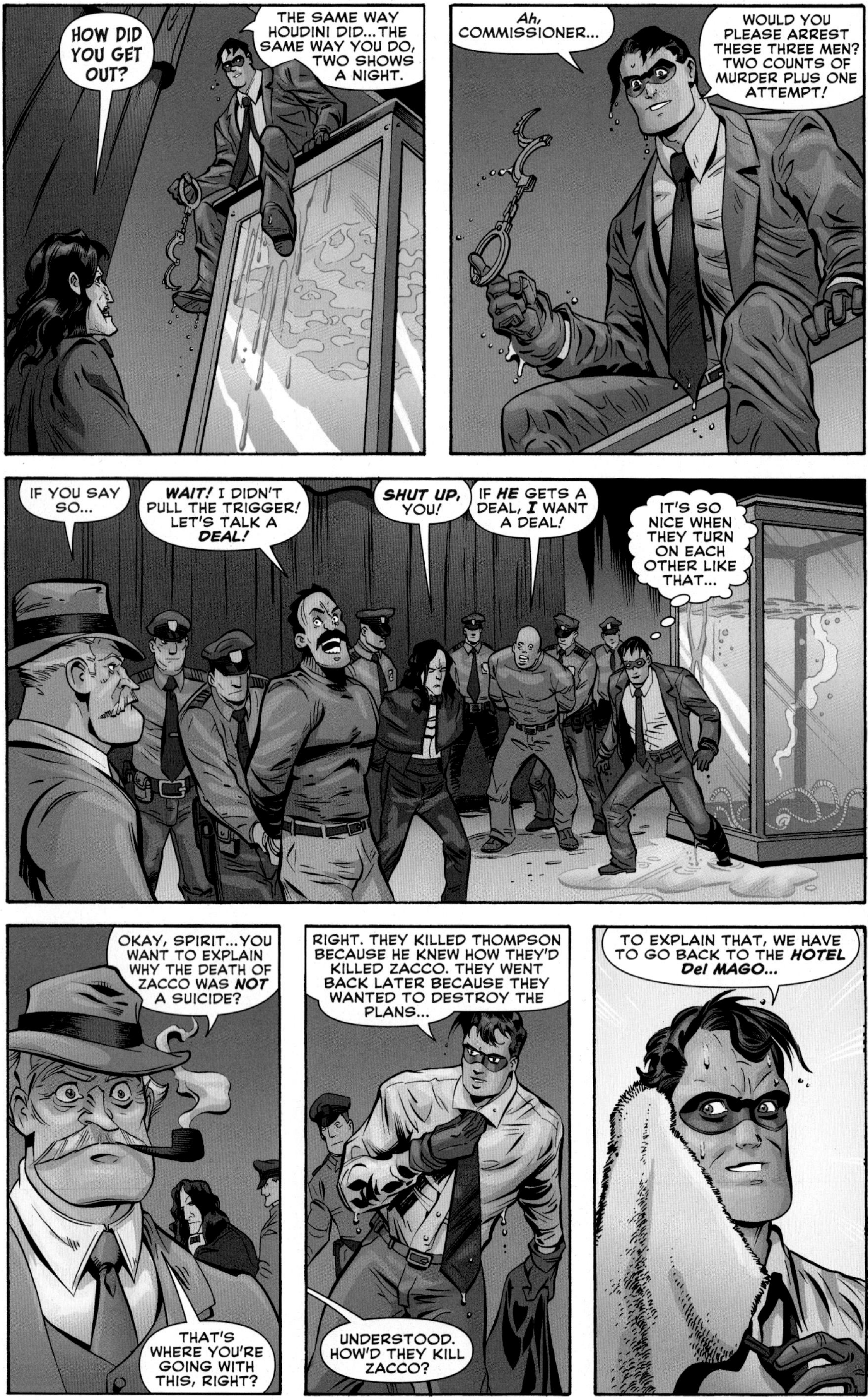
HOW DID YOU GET OUT?
THE SAME WAY HOUDINI DID...THE SAME WAY YOU DO, TWO SHOWS A NIGHT.
Ah, COMMISSIONER...
WOULD YOU PLEASE ARREST THESE THREE MEN? TWO COUNTS OF MURDER PLUS ONE ATTEMPT!
IF YOU SAY SO...
WAIT! I DIDN'T PULL THE TRIGGER! LET'S TALK A DEAL!
SHUT UP, YOU!
IF HE GETS A DEAL, I WANT A DEAL!
IT'S SO NICE WHEN THEY TURN ON EACH OTHER LIKE THAT...
OKAY, SPIRIT...YOU WANT TO EXPLAIN WHY THE DEATH OF ZACCO WAS NOT A SUICIDE?
THAT'S WHERE YOU'RE GOING WITH THIS, RIGHT?
RIGHT. THEY KILLED THOMPSON BECAUSE HE KNEW HOW THEY'D KILLED ZACCO. THEY WENT BACK LATER BECAUSE THEY WANTED TO DESTROY THE PLANS...
UNDERSTOOD. HOW'D THEY KILL ZACCO?
TO EXPLAIN THAT, WE HAVE TO GO BACK TO THE HOTEL Del MAGO...

Shortly...

AS YOU CAN SEE, THE WINDOW OF **ROOM 3** IS COVERED WITH PIGEON DROPPINGS...NOT **ROOM 4**, WHICH IS WHERE ZACCO LIVED WITH HIS PIGEONS...

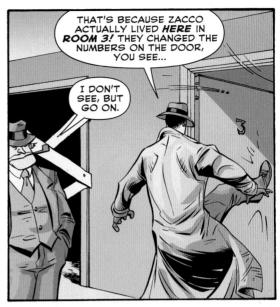

THAT'S BECAUSE ZACCO ACTUALLY LIVED **HERE** IN **ROOM 3!** THEY CHANGED THE NUMBERS ON THE DOOR, YOU SEE...

I DON'T SEE, BUT GO ON.

THERE'S A HOLE HERE IN THE FLOOR OF ROOM 3. IT GOES DOWN TO THE BASEMENT...

THEY GOT IN THROUGH THE HOLE, SHOT ZACCO AND THEN, WITH A SYSTEM OF PULLEYS THAT THOMPSON DEVISED, PULLED ROOM 3 OVER SO IT WAS **INSIDE** ROOM 4...

SO WHY DIDN'T WE SPOT THIS HOLE?

BECAUSE WE WERE LOOKING FOR IT UNDER THE **WRONG ROOM!** THEN, SINCE THE WALLS IN ROOM 4 WERE BARRED AND THE DOOR WAS LOCKED...

I GET IT.

ANDRE MAY BE PSYCHOTIC, BUT HE'S A PRETTY CRAFTY MAGICIAN!

KEEP THAT IN MIND WHEN YOU PICK OUT HIS CELL.

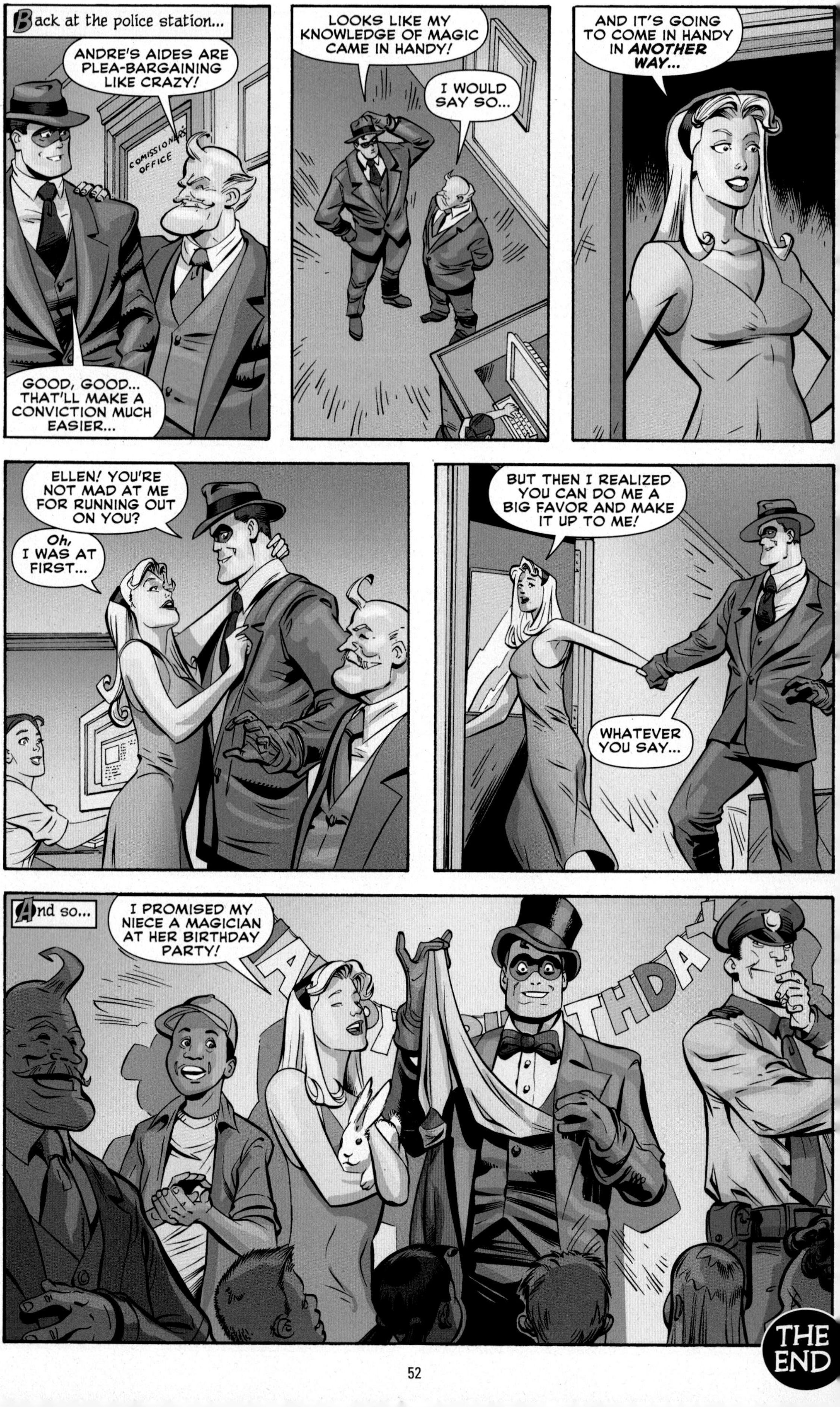

Back at the police station...
ANDRE'S AIDES ARE PLEA-BARGAINING LIKE CRAZY!
COMMISSIONER'S OFFICE
GOOD, GOOD... THAT'LL MAKE A CONVICTION MUCH EASIER...
LOOKS LIKE MY KNOWLEDGE OF MAGIC CAME IN HANDY!
I WOULD SAY SO...
AND IT'S GOING TO COME IN HANDY IN ANOTHER WAY...
ELLEN! YOU'RE NOT MAD AT ME FOR RUNNING OUT ON YOU?
Oh, I WAS AT FIRST...
BUT THEN I REALIZED YOU CAN DO ME A BIG FAVOR AND MAKE IT UP TO ME!
WHATEVER YOU SAY...
And so...
I PROMISED MY NIECE A MAGICIAN AT HER BIRTHDAY PARTY!
THE END

3

ACTION • Mystery • ADVENTURE

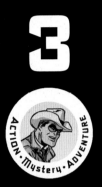

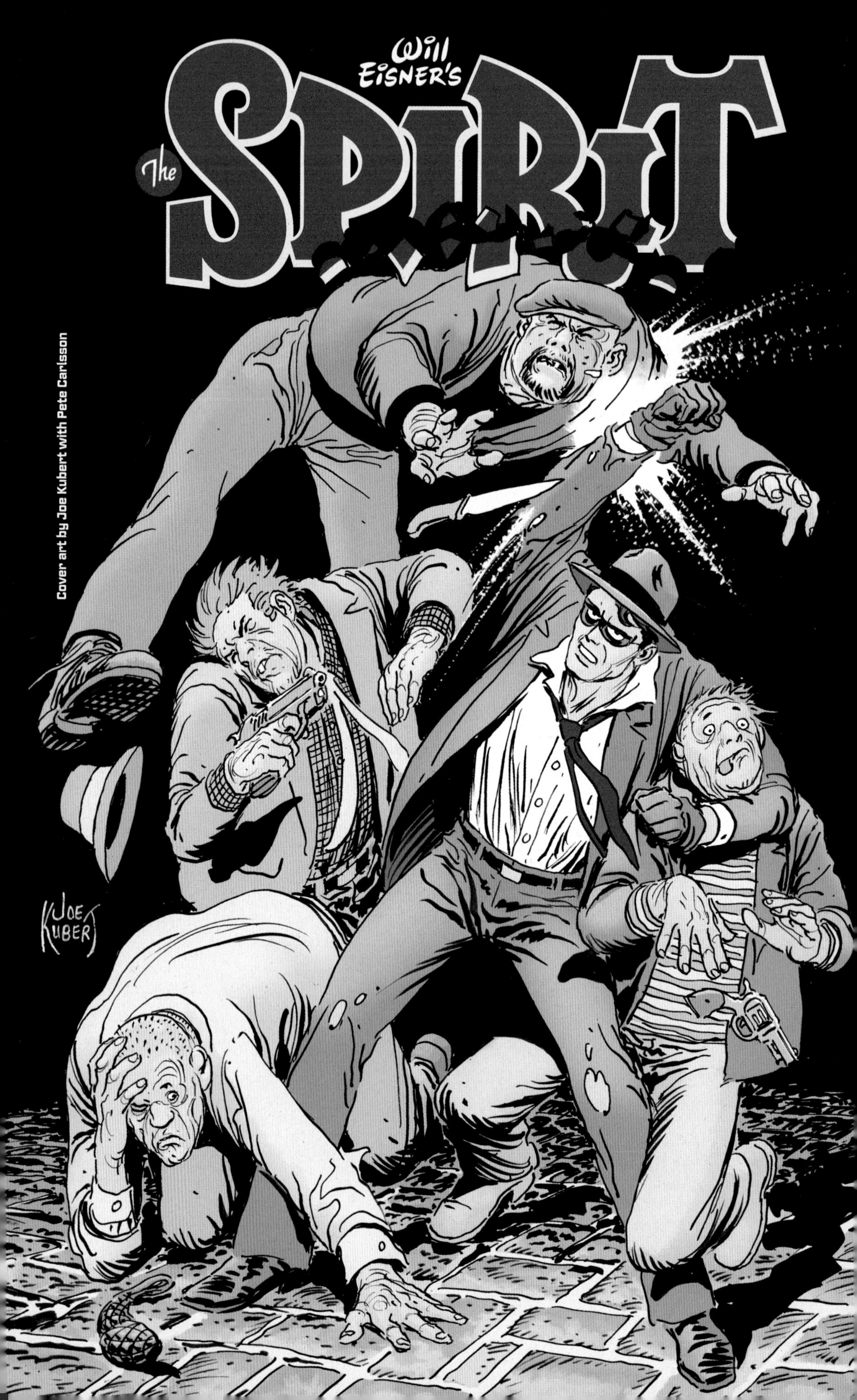
Will Eisner's
The SPIRIT
JOE KUBERT
Cover art by Joe Kubert with Pete Carlsson

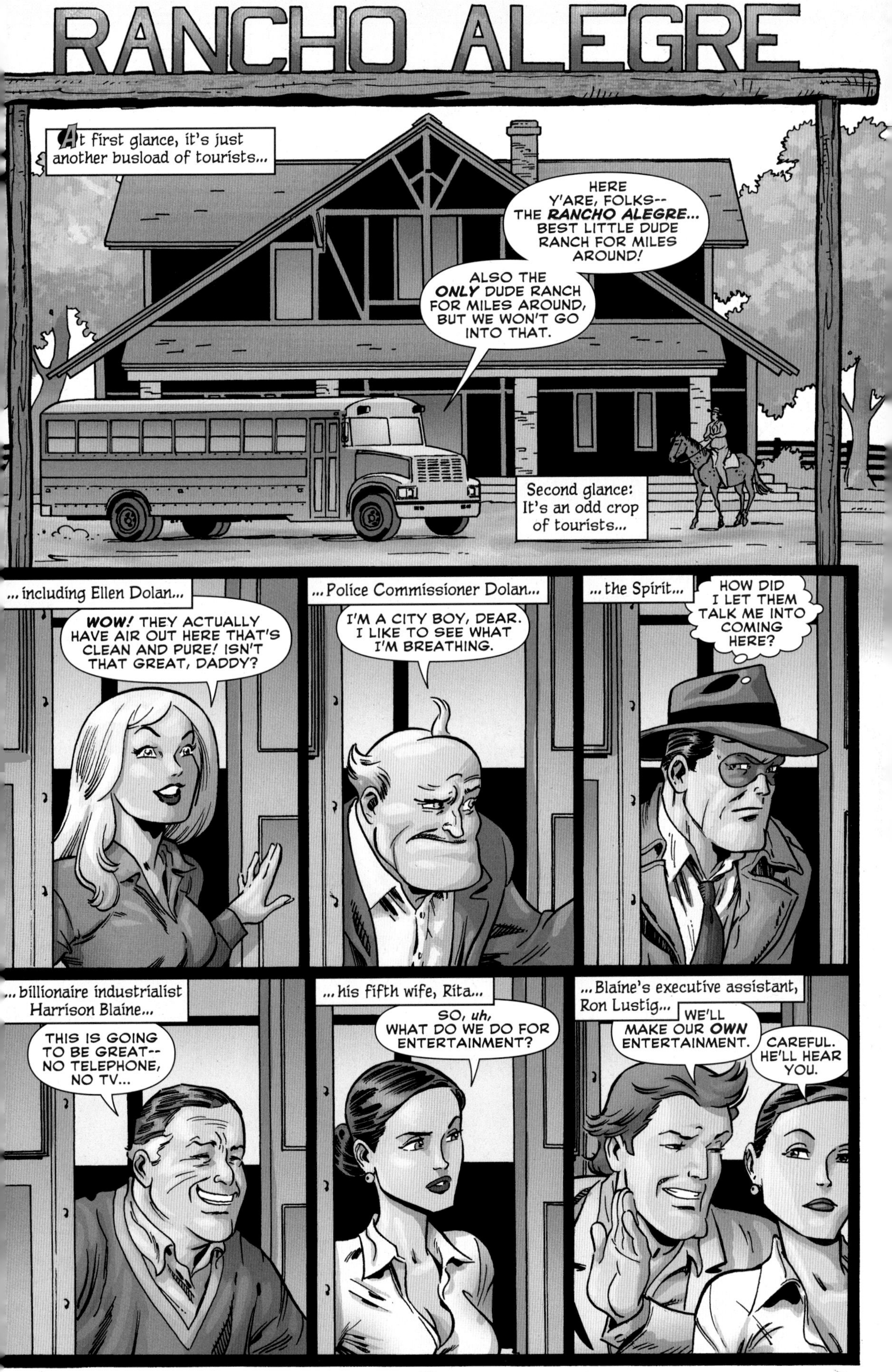
RANCHO ALEGRE
At first glance, it's just another busload of tourists...
HERE Y'ARE, FOLKS-- THE RANCHO ALEGRE... BEST LITTLE DUDE RANCH FOR MILES AROUND!
ALSO THE ONLY DUDE RANCH FOR MILES AROUND, BUT WE WON'T GO INTO THAT.
Second glance: It's an odd crop of tourists...
...including Ellen Dolan...
WOW! THEY ACTUALLY HAVE AIR OUT HERE THAT'S CLEAN AND PURE! ISN'T THAT GREAT, DADDY?
...Police Commissioner Dolan...
I'M A CITY BOY, DEAR. I LIKE TO SEE WHAT I'M BREATHING.
...the Spirit...
HOW DID I LET THEM TALK ME INTO COMING HERE?
...billionaire industrialist Harrison Blaine...
THIS IS GOING TO BE GREAT-- NO TELEPHONE, NO TV...
...his fifth wife, Rita...
SO, uh, WHAT DO WE DO FOR ENTERTAINMENT?
...Blaine's executive assistant, Ron Lustig...
WE'LL MAKE OUR OWN ENTERTAINMENT.
CAREFUL. HE'LL HEAR YOU.

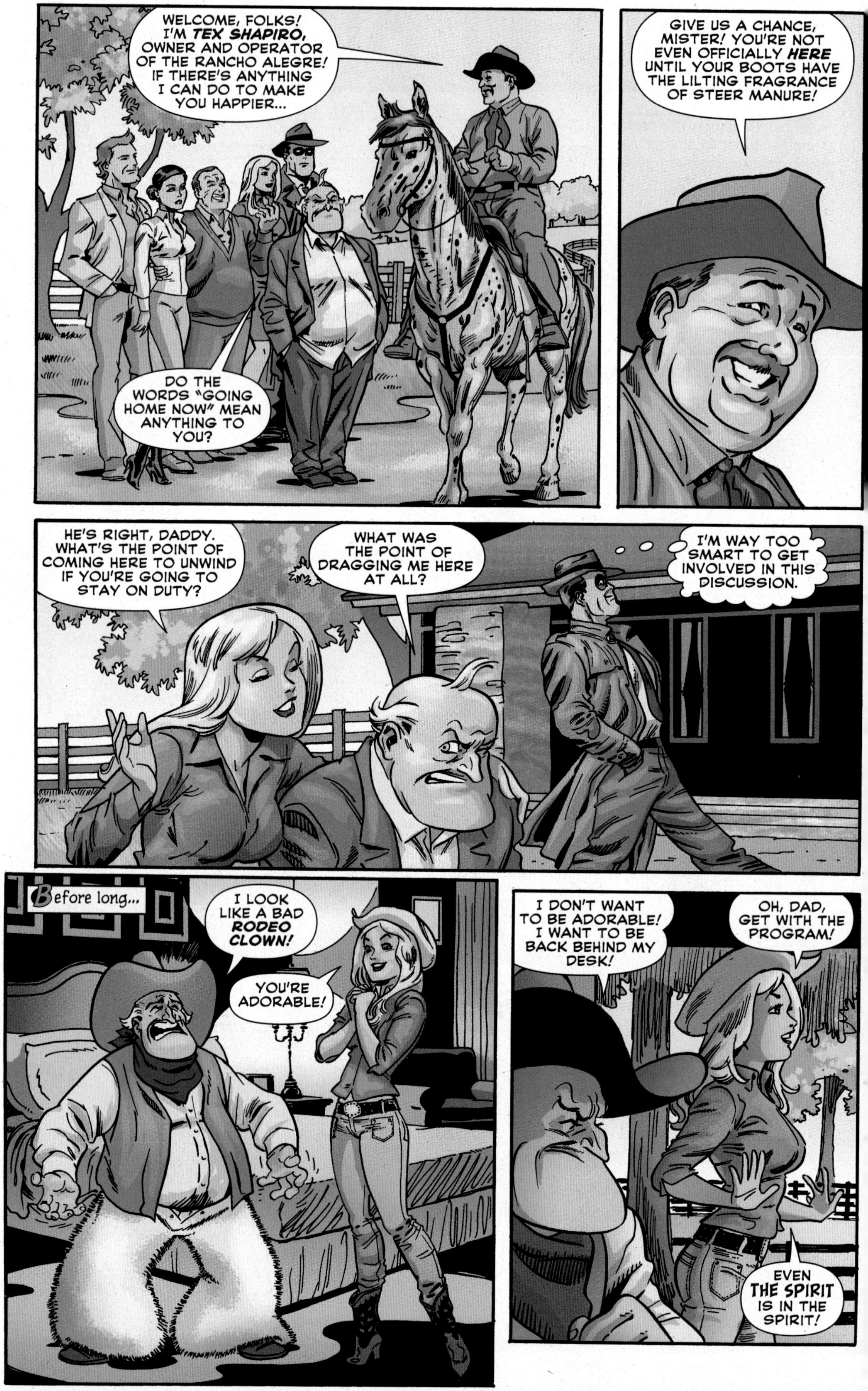
WELCOME, FOLKS! I'M TEX SHAPIRO, OWNER AND OPERATOR OF THE RANCHO ALEGRE! IF THERE'S ANYTHING I CAN DO TO MAKE YOU HAPPIER...
DO THE WORDS "GOING HOME NOW" MEAN ANYTHING TO YOU?
GIVE US A CHANCE, MISTER! YOU'RE NOT EVEN OFFICIALLY HERE UNTIL YOUR BOOTS HAVE THE LILTING FRAGRANCE OF STEER MANURE!
HE'S RIGHT, DADDY. WHAT'S THE POINT OF COMING HERE TO UNWIND IF YOU'RE GOING TO STAY ON DUTY?
WHAT WAS THE POINT OF DRAGGING ME HERE AT ALL?
I'M WAY TOO SMART TO GET INVOLVED IN THIS DISCUSSION.
Before long...
I LOOK LIKE A BAD RODEO CLOWN!
YOU'RE ADORABLE!
I DON'T WANT TO BE ADORABLE! I WANT TO BE BACK BEHIND MY DESK!
OH, DAD, GET WITH THE PROGRAM!
EVEN THE SPIRIT IS IN THE SPIRIT!

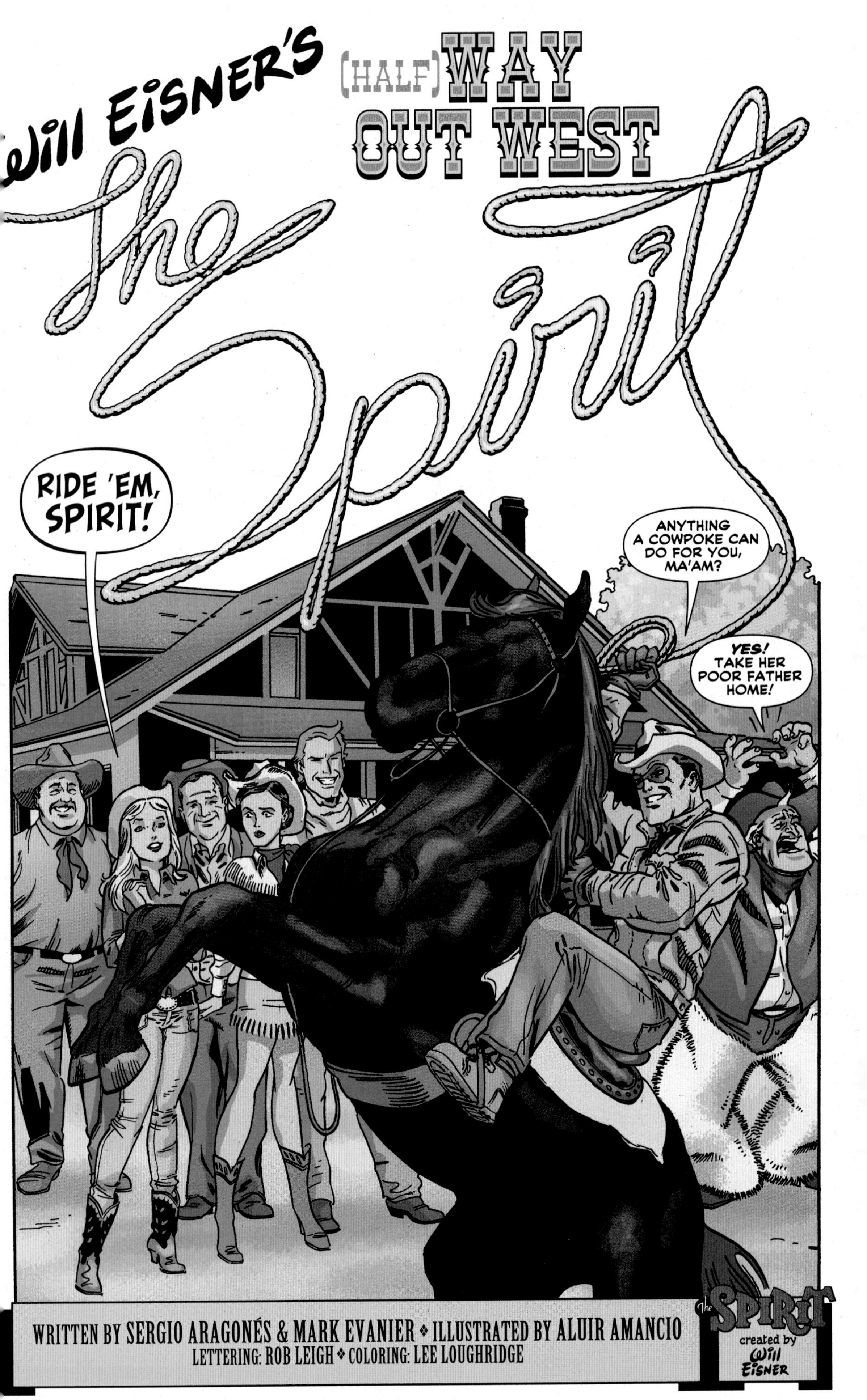
Will Eisner's
The Spirit
(HALF) WAY OUT WEST
RIDE 'EM, SPIRIT!
ANYTHING A COWPOKE CAN DO FOR YOU, MA'AM?
YES! TAKE HER POOR FATHER HOME!

WRITTEN BY SERGIO ARAGONÉS & MARK EVANIER ❖ ILLUSTRATED BY ALUIR AMANCIO
LETTERING: ROB LEIGH ❖ COLORING: LEE LOUGHRIDGE

The SPIRIT created by Will Eisner

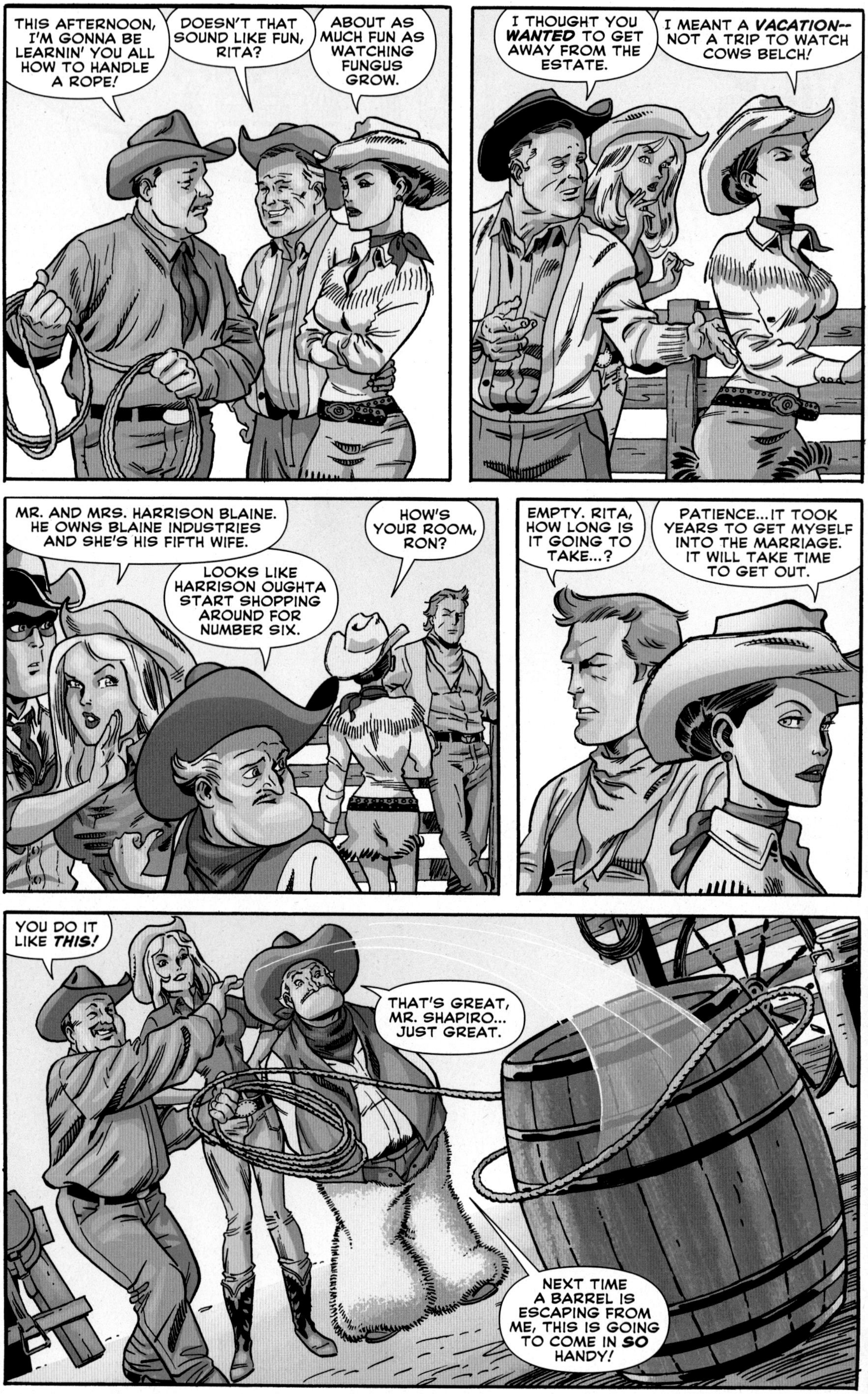
THIS AFTERNOON, I'M GONNA BE LEARNIN' YOU ALL HOW TO HANDLE A ROPE!
DOESN'T THAT SOUND LIKE FUN, RITA?
ABOUT AS MUCH FUN AS WATCHING FUNGUS GROW.
I THOUGHT YOU *WANTED* TO GET AWAY FROM THE ESTATE.
I MEANT A *VACATION*-- NOT A TRIP TO WATCH COWS BELCH!
MR. AND MRS. HARRISON BLAINE. HE OWNS BLAINE INDUSTRIES AND SHE'S HIS FIFTH WIFE.
LOOKS LIKE HARRISON OUGHTA START SHOPPING AROUND FOR NUMBER SIX.
HOW'S YOUR ROOM, RON?
EMPTY. RITA, HOW LONG IS IT GOING TO TAKE...?
PATIENCE...IT TOOK YEARS TO GET MYSELF INTO THE MARRIAGE. IT WILL TAKE TIME TO GET OUT.
YOU DO IT LIKE *THIS!*
THAT'S GREAT, MR. SHAPIRO... JUST GREAT.
NEXT TIME A BARREL IS ESCAPING FROM ME, THIS IS GOING TO COME IN *SO* HANDY!

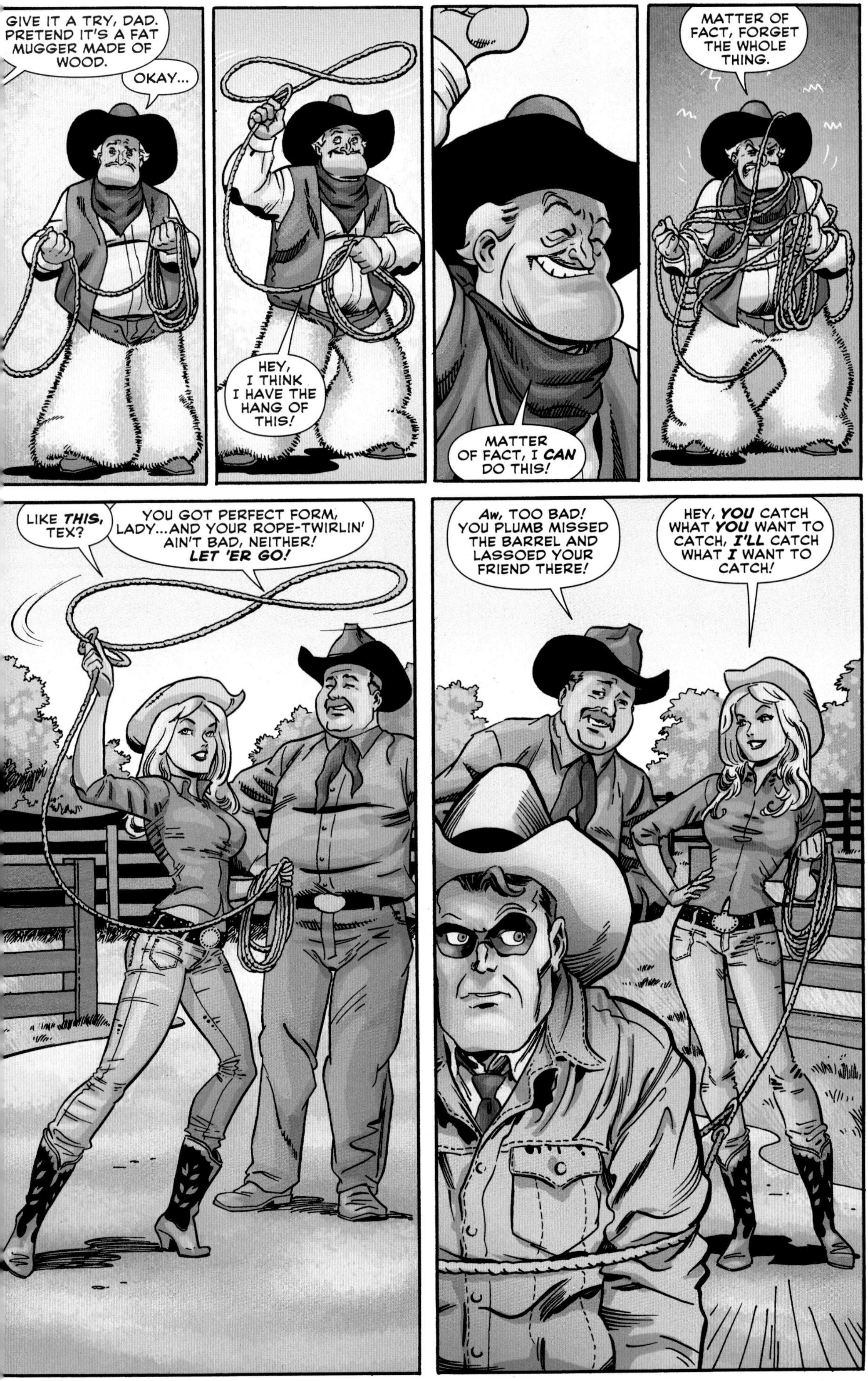

GIVE IT A TRY, DAD. PRETEND IT'S A FAT MUGGER MADE OF WOOD.
OKAY...
HEY, I THINK I HAVE THE HANG OF THIS!
MATTER OF FACT, I CAN DO THIS!
MATTER OF FACT, FORGET THE WHOLE THING.
LIKE THIS, TEX?
YOU GOT PERFECT FORM, LADY...AND YOUR ROPE-TWIRLIN' AIN'T BAD, NEITHER! LET 'ER GO!
AW, TOO BAD! YOU PLUMB MISSED THE BARREL AND LASSOED YOUR FRIEND THERE!
HEY, YOU CATCH WHAT YOU WANT TO CATCH, I'LL CATCH WHAT I WANT TO CATCH!

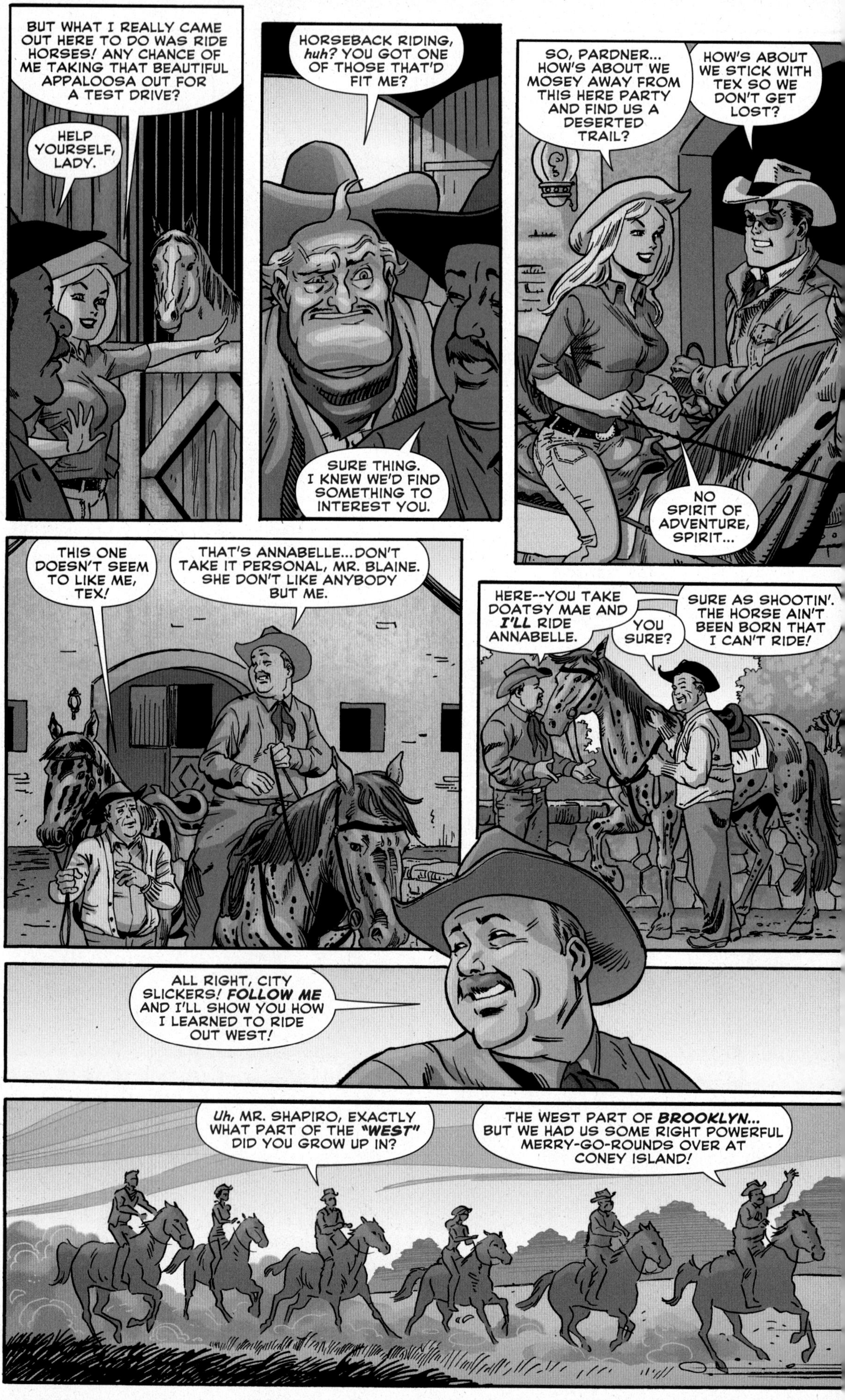
BUT WHAT I REALLY CAME OUT HERE TO DO WAS RIDE HORSES! ANY CHANCE OF ME TAKING THAT BEAUTIFUL APPALOOSA OUT FOR A TEST DRIVE?
HELP YOURSELF, LADY.
HORSEBACK RIDING, *huh?* YOU GOT ONE OF THOSE THAT'D FIT ME?
SURE THING. I KNEW WE'D FIND SOMETHING TO INTEREST YOU.
SO, PARDNER... HOW'S ABOUT WE MOSEY AWAY FROM THIS HERE PARTY AND FIND US A DESERTED TRAIL?
HOW'S ABOUT WE STICK WITH TEX SO WE DON'T GET LOST?
NO SPIRIT OF ADVENTURE, SPIRIT...
THIS ONE DOESN'T SEEM TO LIKE ME, TEX!
THAT'S ANNABELLE...DON'T TAKE IT PERSONAL, MR. BLAINE. SHE DON'T LIKE ANYBODY BUT ME.
HERE--YOU TAKE DOATSY MAE AND ***I'LL*** RIDE ANNABELLE.
YOU SURE?
SURE AS SHOOTIN'. THE HORSE AIN'T BEEN BORN THAT I CAN'T RIDE!
ALL RIGHT, CITY SLICKERS! ***FOLLOW ME*** AND I'LL SHOW YOU HOW I LEARNED TO RIDE OUT WEST!
Uh, MR. SHAPIRO, EXACTLY WHAT PART OF THE ***"WEST"*** DID YOU GROW UP IN?
THE WEST PART OF **BROOKLYN...** BUT WE HAD US SOME RIGHT POWERFUL MERRY-GO-ROUNDS OVER AT CONEY ISLAND!

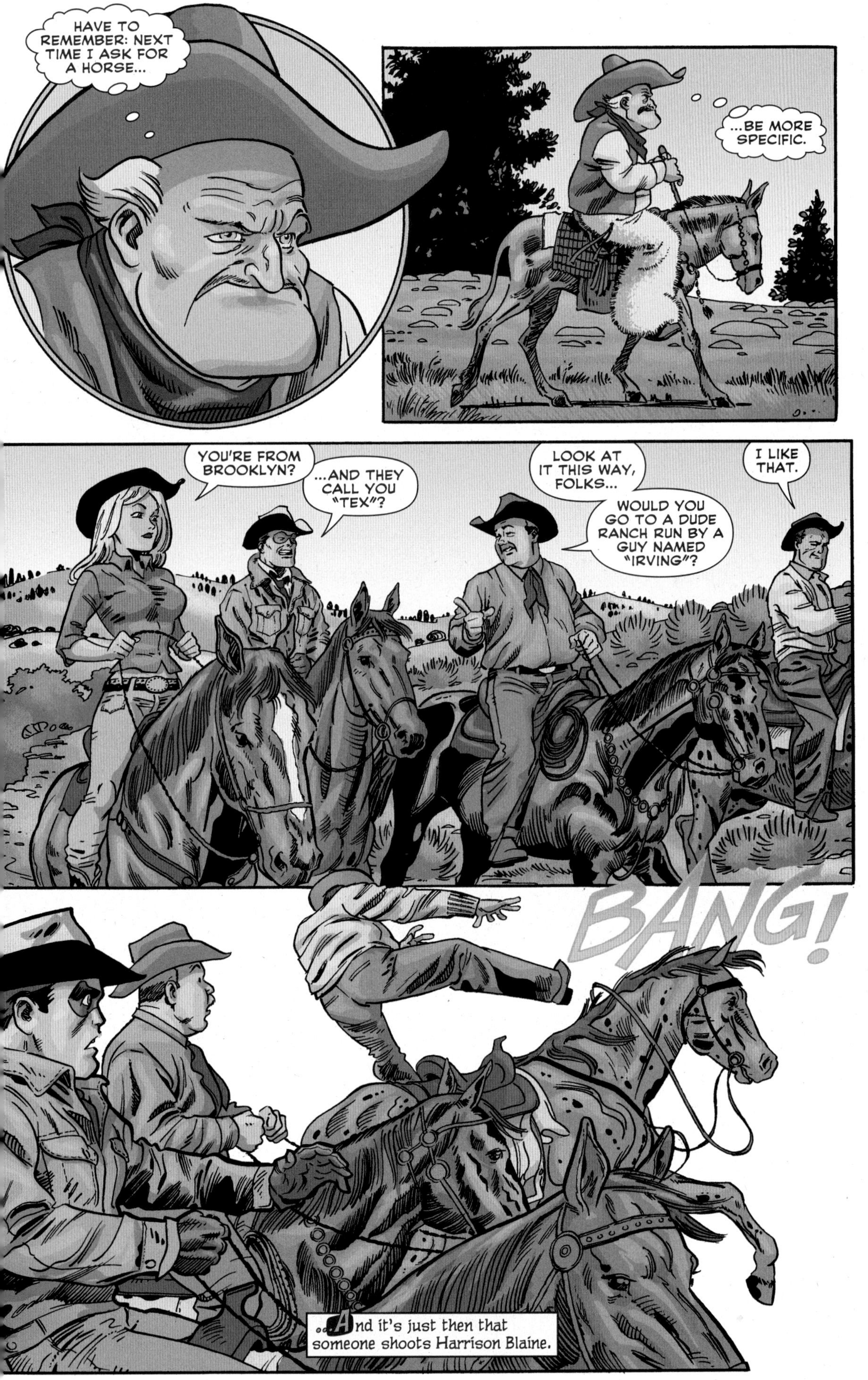
HAVE TO REMEMBER: NEXT TIME I ASK FOR A HORSE...
...BE MORE SPECIFIC.
YOU'RE FROM BROOKLYN?
...AND THEY CALL YOU "TEX"?
LOOK AT IT THIS WAY, FOLKS...
WOULD YOU GO TO A DUDE RANCH RUN BY A GUY NAMED "IRVING"?
I LIKE THAT.
BANG!
...And it's just then that someone shoots Harrison Blaine.

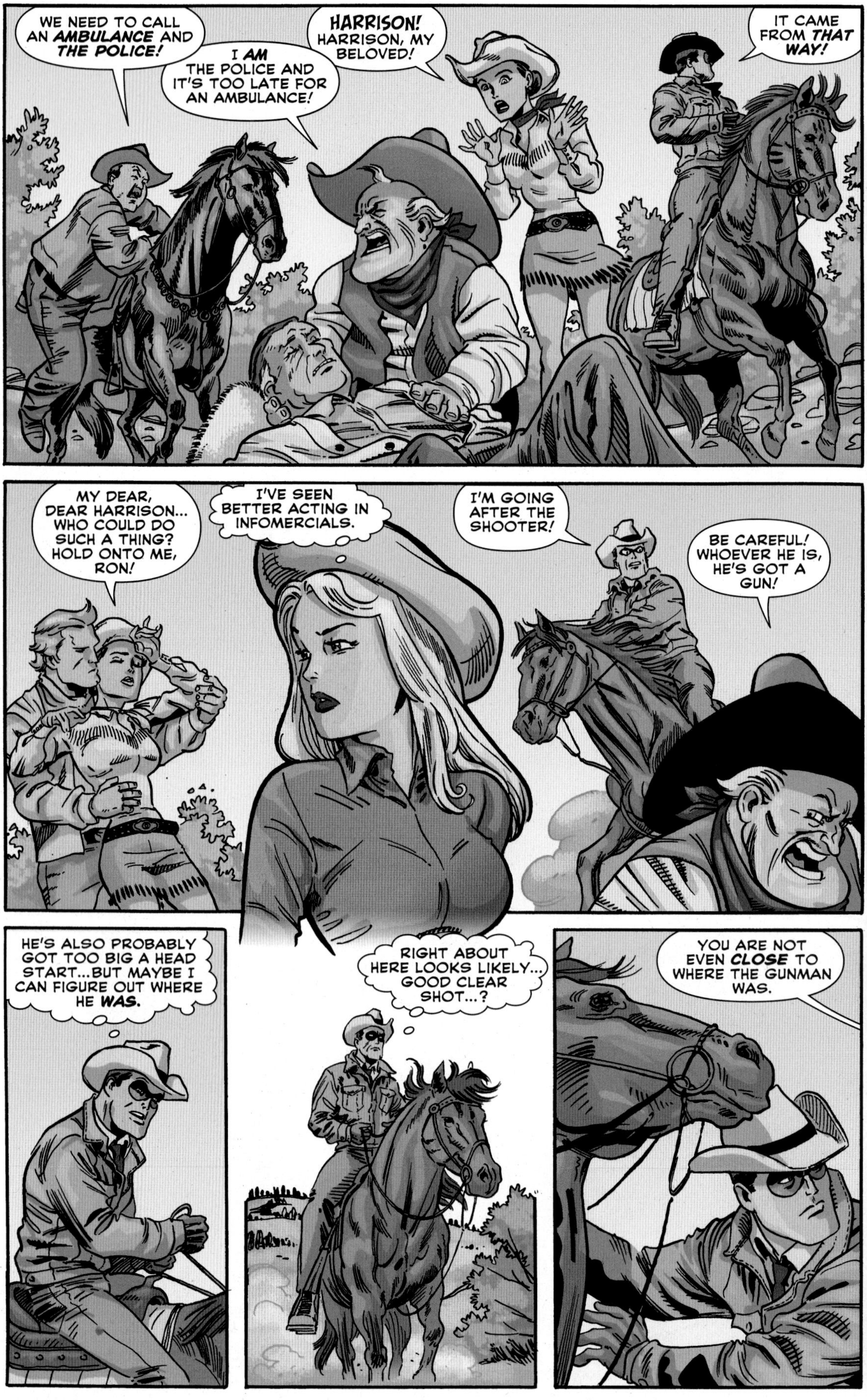
WE NEED TO CALL AN AMBULANCE AND THE POLICE!
I AM THE POLICE AND IT'S TOO LATE FOR AN AMBULANCE!
HARRISON! HARRISON, MY BELOVED!
IT CAME FROM THAT WAY!
MY DEAR, DEAR HARRISON... WHO COULD DO SUCH A THING? HOLD ONTO ME, RON!
I'VE SEEN BETTER ACTING IN INFOMERCIALS.
I'M GOING AFTER THE SHOOTER!
BE CAREFUL! WHOEVER HE IS, HE'S GOT A GUN!
HE'S ALSO PROBABLY GOT TOO BIG A HEAD START...BUT MAYBE I CAN FIGURE OUT WHERE HE WAS.
RIGHT ABOUT HERE LOOKS LIKELY... GOOD CLEAR SHOT...?
YOU ARE NOT EVEN CLOSE TO WHERE THE GUNMAN WAS.

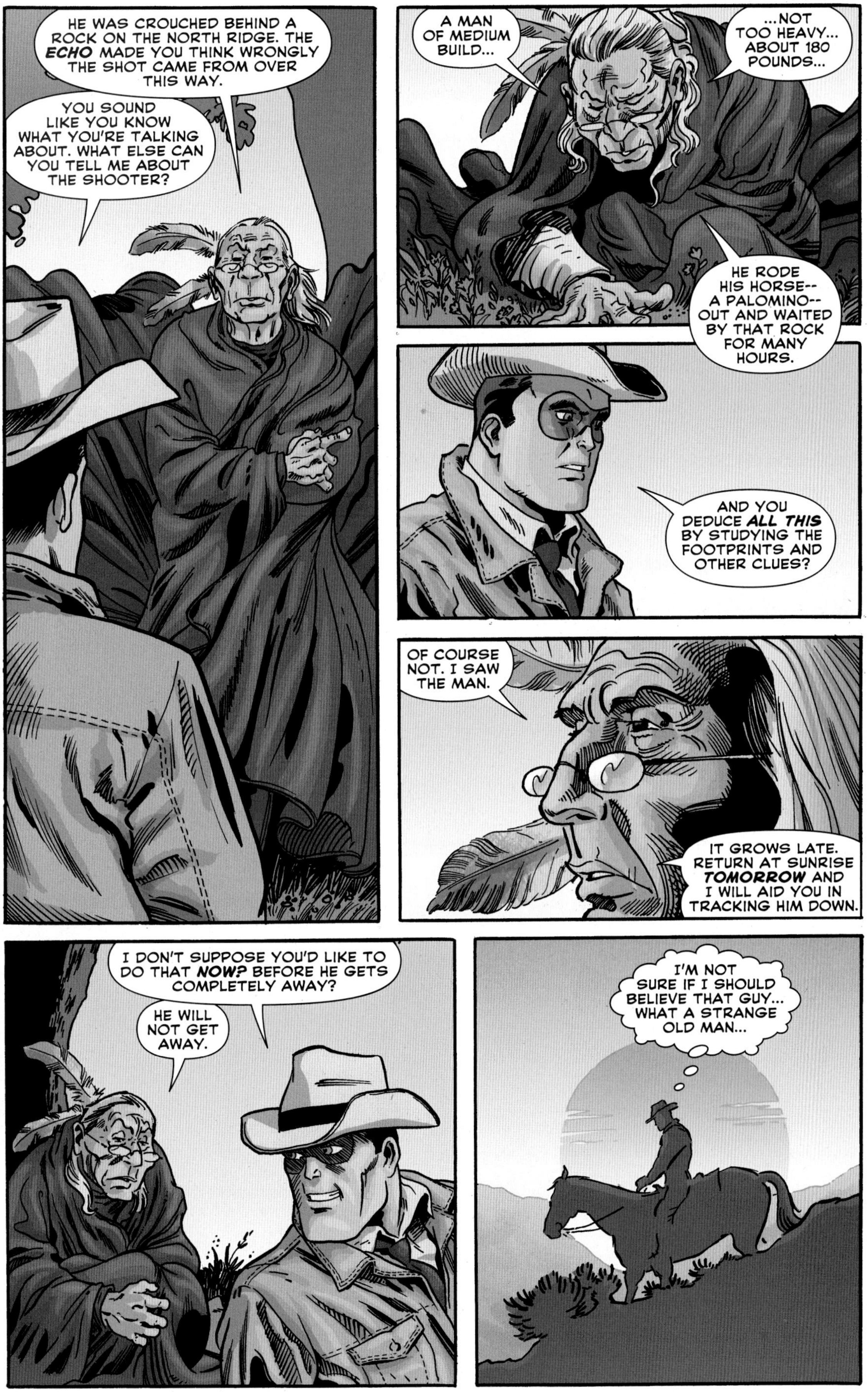
HE WAS CROUCHED BEHIND A ROCK ON THE NORTH RIDGE. THE ECHO MADE YOU THINK WRONGLY THE SHOT CAME FROM OVER THIS WAY.
YOU SOUND LIKE YOU KNOW WHAT YOU'RE TALKING ABOUT. WHAT ELSE CAN YOU TELL ME ABOUT THE SHOOTER?
A MAN OF MEDIUM BUILD...
...NOT TOO HEAVY... ABOUT 180 POUNDS...
HE RODE HIS HORSE-- A PALOMINO-- OUT AND WAITED BY THAT ROCK FOR MANY HOURS.
AND YOU DEDUCE ALL THIS BY STUDYING THE FOOTPRINTS AND OTHER CLUES?
OF COURSE NOT. I SAW THE MAN.
IT GROWS LATE. RETURN AT SUNRISE TOMORROW AND I WILL AID YOU IN TRACKING HIM DOWN.
I DON'T SUPPOSE YOU'D LIKE TO DO THAT NOW? BEFORE HE GETS COMPLETELY AWAY?
HE WILL NOT GET AWAY.
I'M NOT SURE IF I SHOULD BELIEVE THAT GUY... WHAT A STRANGE OLD MAN...

WHY IS THE AMBULANCE IN SUCH A *HURRY?* IT'S NOT LIKE BLAINE MIGHT GET EVEN DEADER!

SPIRIT? MEET *SHERIFF LIM!* HE'S INVESTIGATING!

GOD HELP US.

ANYTHING WE CAN DO TO HELP, SHERIFF?

SURE THING. YOU CAN STAY THE HECK OUTTA MY WAY, YOU TWO! THIS IS MY COUNTY AND MY CASE!

YOU GOT THAT?

NOW, LISTEN HERE, LIM! I HAVE YEARS OF EXPERIENCE ON THE FORCE AND THE SPIRIT. HERE--

YOU DIDN'T HEAR ME. FAR AS I'M CONCERNED, YOU'RE JUST TWO GREENHORN TOURISTS...

...BUT I'LL DO YOU A FAVOR AND FILL YOU IN... *AFTER* I SOLVE THE CASE.

IDIOT.

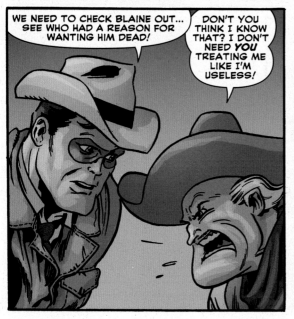

WE NEED TO CHECK BLAINE OUT... SEE WHO HAD A REASON FOR WANTING HIM DEAD!

DON'T YOU THINK I KNOW THAT? I DON'T NEED *YOU* TREATING ME LIKE I'M USELESS!

I JUST GOT A BELLYFUL OF THAT FROM A GUY WHO WEARS A TEN-GALLON HAT ON A TWO-GALLON HEAD!

YOU FIND ANY LEADS OUT THERE?

ONE POSSIBLE...ONLY I CAN'T FOLLOW UP ON IT 'TIL MORNING. DON'T ASK ME WHY.

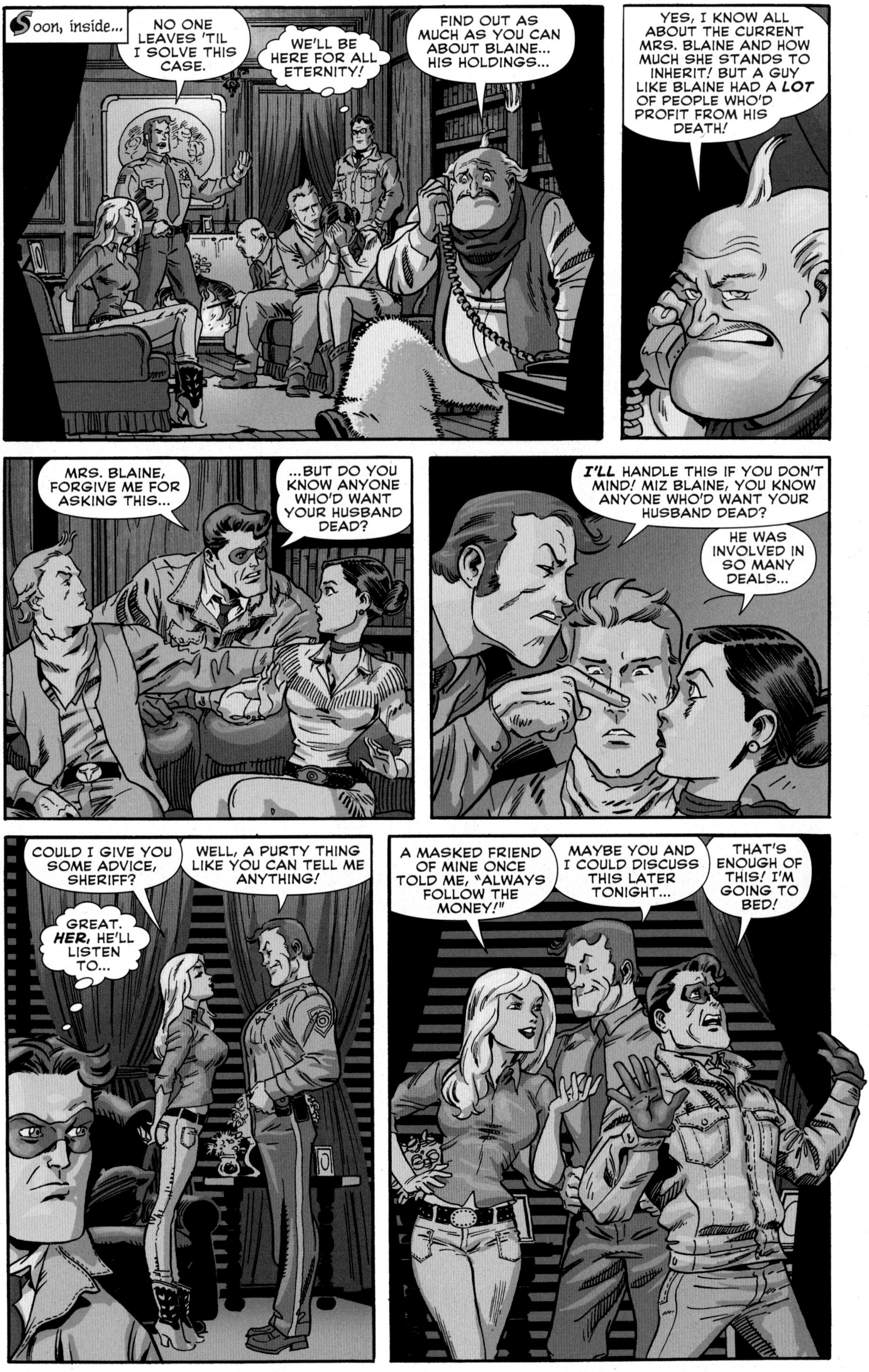
Soon, inside...
NO ONE LEAVES 'TIL I SOLVE THIS CASE.
WE'LL BE HERE FOR ALL ETERNITY!
FIND OUT AS MUCH AS YOU CAN ABOUT BLAINE... HIS HOLDINGS...
YES, I KNOW ALL ABOUT THE CURRENT MRS. BLAINE AND HOW MUCH SHE STANDS TO INHERIT! BUT A GUY LIKE BLAINE HAD A LOT OF PEOPLE WHO'D PROFIT FROM HIS DEATH!
MRS. BLAINE, FORGIVE ME FOR ASKING THIS...
...BUT DO YOU KNOW ANYONE WHO'D WANT YOUR HUSBAND DEAD?
I'LL HANDLE THIS IF YOU DON'T MIND! MIZ BLAINE, YOU KNOW ANYONE WHO'D WANT YOUR HUSBAND DEAD?
HE WAS INVOLVED IN SO MANY DEALS...
COULD I GIVE YOU SOME ADVICE, SHERIFF?
WELL, A PURTY THING LIKE YOU CAN TELL ME ANYTHING!
GREAT. HER, HE'LL LISTEN TO...
A MASKED FRIEND OF MINE ONCE TOLD ME, "ALWAYS FOLLOW THE MONEY!"
MAYBE YOU AND I COULD DISCUSS THIS LATER TONIGHT...
THAT'S ENOUGH OF THIS! I'M GOING TO BED!

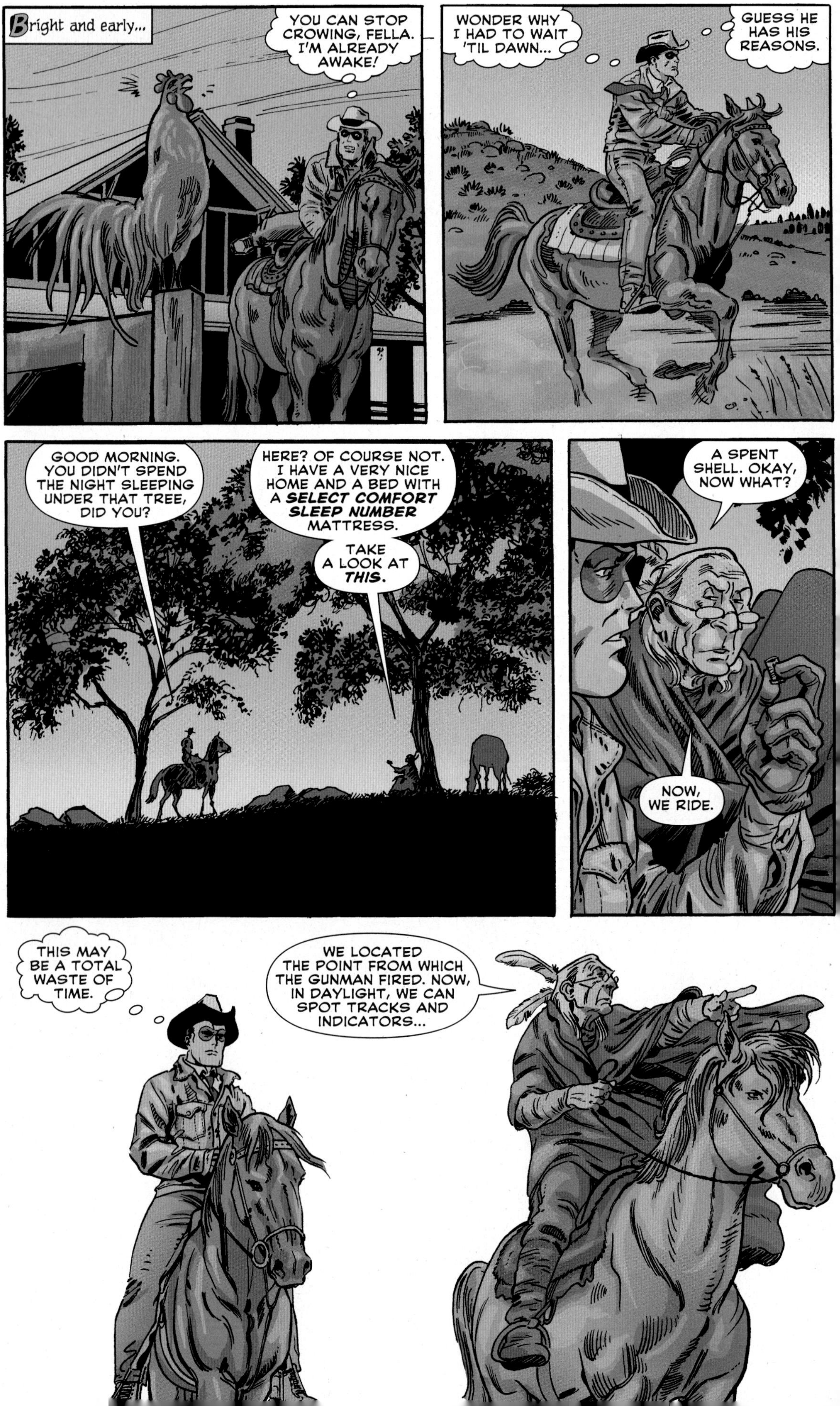
Bright and early...
YOU CAN STOP CROWING, FELLA. I'M ALREADY AWAKE!
WONDER WHY I HAD TO WAIT 'TIL DAWN...
GUESS HE HAS HIS REASONS.
GOOD MORNING. YOU DIDN'T SPEND THE NIGHT SLEEPING UNDER THAT TREE, DID YOU?
HERE? OF COURSE NOT. I HAVE A VERY NICE HOME AND A BED WITH A SELECT COMFORT SLEEP NUMBER MATTRESS.
TAKE A LOOK AT THIS.
A SPENT SHELL. OKAY, NOW WHAT?
NOW, WE RIDE.
THIS MAY BE A TOTAL WASTE OF TIME.
WE LOCATED THE POINT FROM WHICH THE GUNMAN FIRED. NOW, IN DAYLIGHT, WE CAN SPOT TRACKS AND INDICATORS...

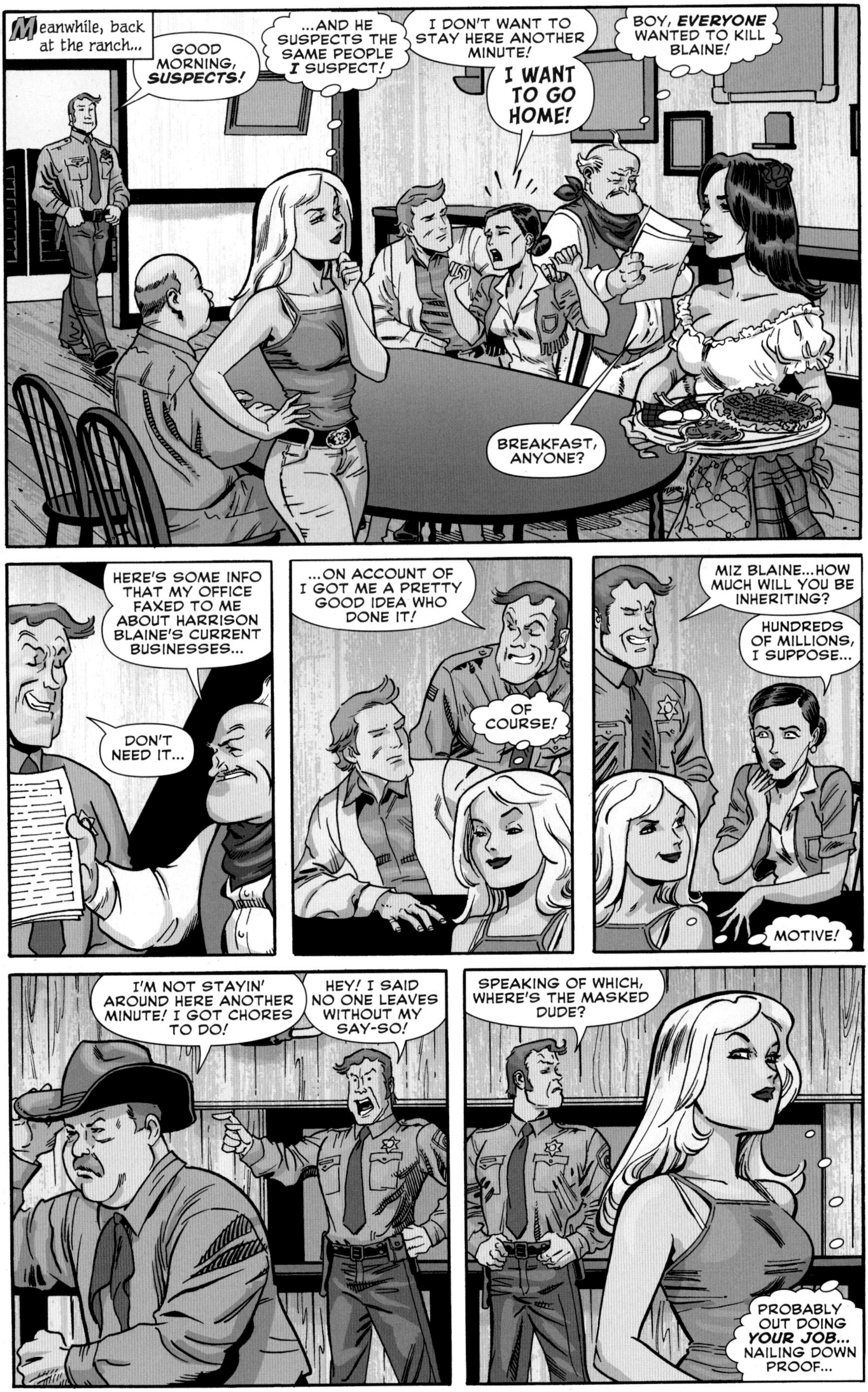
Meanwhile, back at the ranch...
GOOD MORNING, SUSPECTS!
...AND HE SUSPECTS THE SAME PEOPLE I SUSPECT!
I DON'T WANT TO STAY HERE ANOTHER MINUTE!
I WANT TO GO HOME!
BOY, EVERYONE WANTED TO KILL BLAINE!
BREAKFAST, ANYONE?
HERE'S SOME INFO THAT MY OFFICE FAXED TO ME ABOUT HARRISON BLAINE'S CURRENT BUSINESSES...
DON'T NEED IT...
...ON ACCOUNT OF I GOT ME A PRETTY GOOD IDEA WHO DONE IT!
OF COURSE!
MIZ BLAINE...HOW MUCH WILL YOU BE INHERITING?
HUNDREDS OF MILLIONS, I SUPPOSE...
MOTIVE!
I'M NOT STAYIN' AROUND HERE ANOTHER MINUTE! I GOT CHORES TO DO!
HEY! I SAID NO ONE LEAVES WITHOUT MY SAY-SO!
SPEAKING OF WHICH, WHERE'S THE MASKED DUDE?
PROBABLY OUT DOING YOUR JOB... NAILING DOWN PROOF...

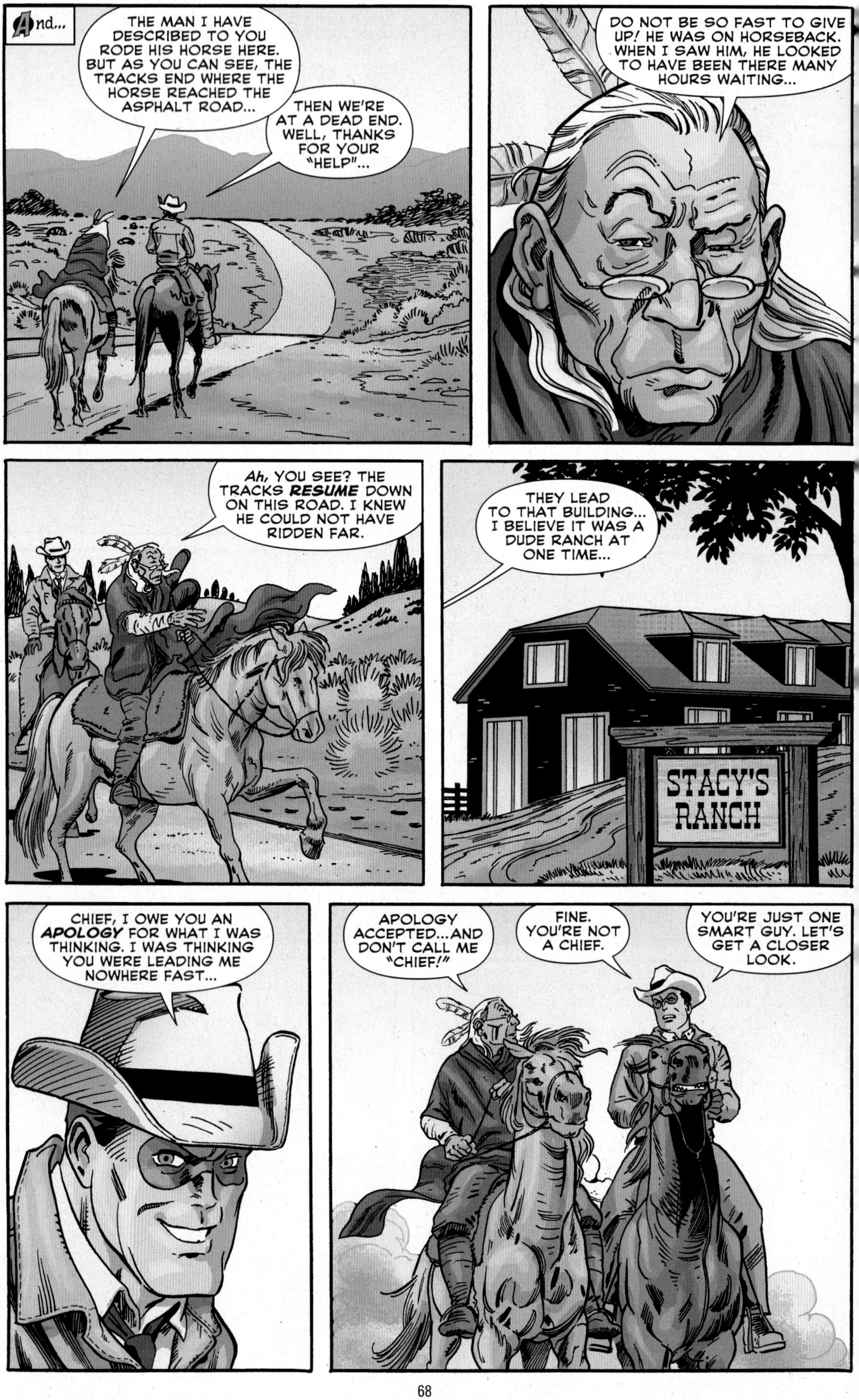
And...
THE MAN I HAVE DESCRIBED TO YOU RODE HIS HORSE HERE. BUT AS YOU CAN SEE, THE TRACKS END WHERE THE HORSE REACHED THE ASPHALT ROAD...
THEN WE'RE AT A DEAD END. WELL, THANKS FOR YOUR "HELP"...
DO NOT BE SO FAST TO GIVE UP! HE WAS ON HORSEBACK. WHEN I SAW HIM, HE LOOKED TO HAVE BEEN THERE MANY HOURS WAITING...
Ah, YOU SEE? THE TRACKS RESUME DOWN ON THIS ROAD. I KNEW HE COULD NOT HAVE RIDDEN FAR.
THEY LEAD TO THAT BUILDING... I BELIEVE IT WAS A DUDE RANCH AT ONE TIME...
STACY'S RANCH
CHIEF, I OWE YOU AN APOLOGY FOR WHAT I WAS THINKING. I WAS THINKING YOU WERE LEADING ME NOWHERE FAST...
APOLOGY ACCEPTED...AND DON'T CALL ME "CHIEF!"
FINE. YOU'RE NOT A CHIEF.
YOU'RE JUST ONE SMART GUY. LET'S GET A CLOSER LOOK.

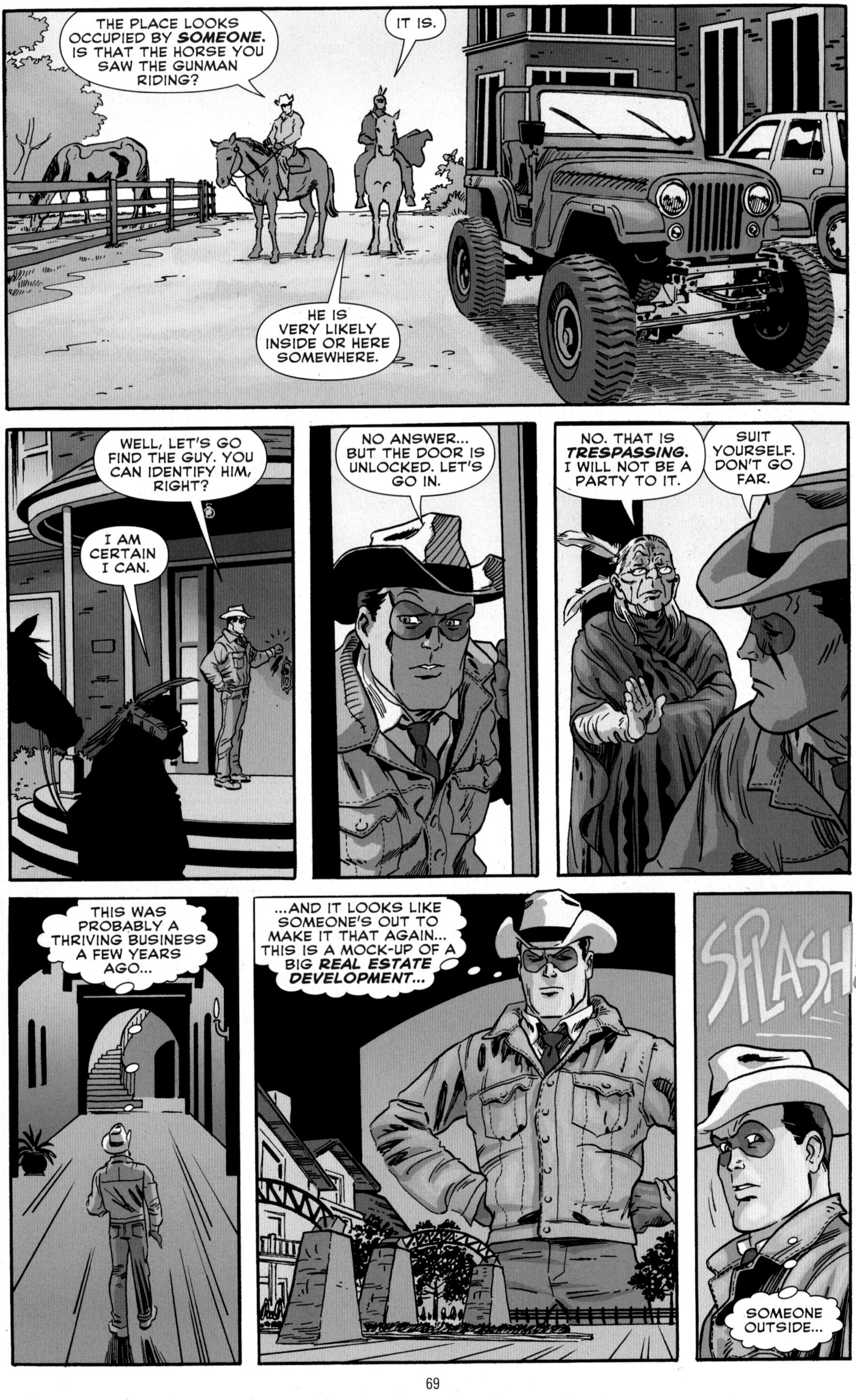
THE PLACE LOOKS OCCUPIED BY SOMEONE. IS THAT THE HORSE YOU SAW THE GUNMAN RIDING?
IT IS.
HE IS VERY LIKELY INSIDE OR HERE SOMEWHERE.
WELL, LET'S GO FIND THE GUY. YOU CAN IDENTIFY HIM, RIGHT?
I AM CERTAIN I CAN.
NO ANSWER... BUT THE DOOR IS UNLOCKED. LET'S GO IN.
NO. THAT IS TRESPASSING. I WILL NOT BE A PARTY TO IT.
SUIT YOURSELF. DON'T GO FAR.
THIS WAS PROBABLY A THRIVING BUSINESS A FEW YEARS AGO...
...AND IT LOOKS LIKE SOMEONE'S OUT TO MAKE IT THAT AGAIN... THIS IS A MOCK-UP OF A BIG REAL ESTATE DEVELOPMENT...
SPLASH!
SOMEONE OUTSIDE...

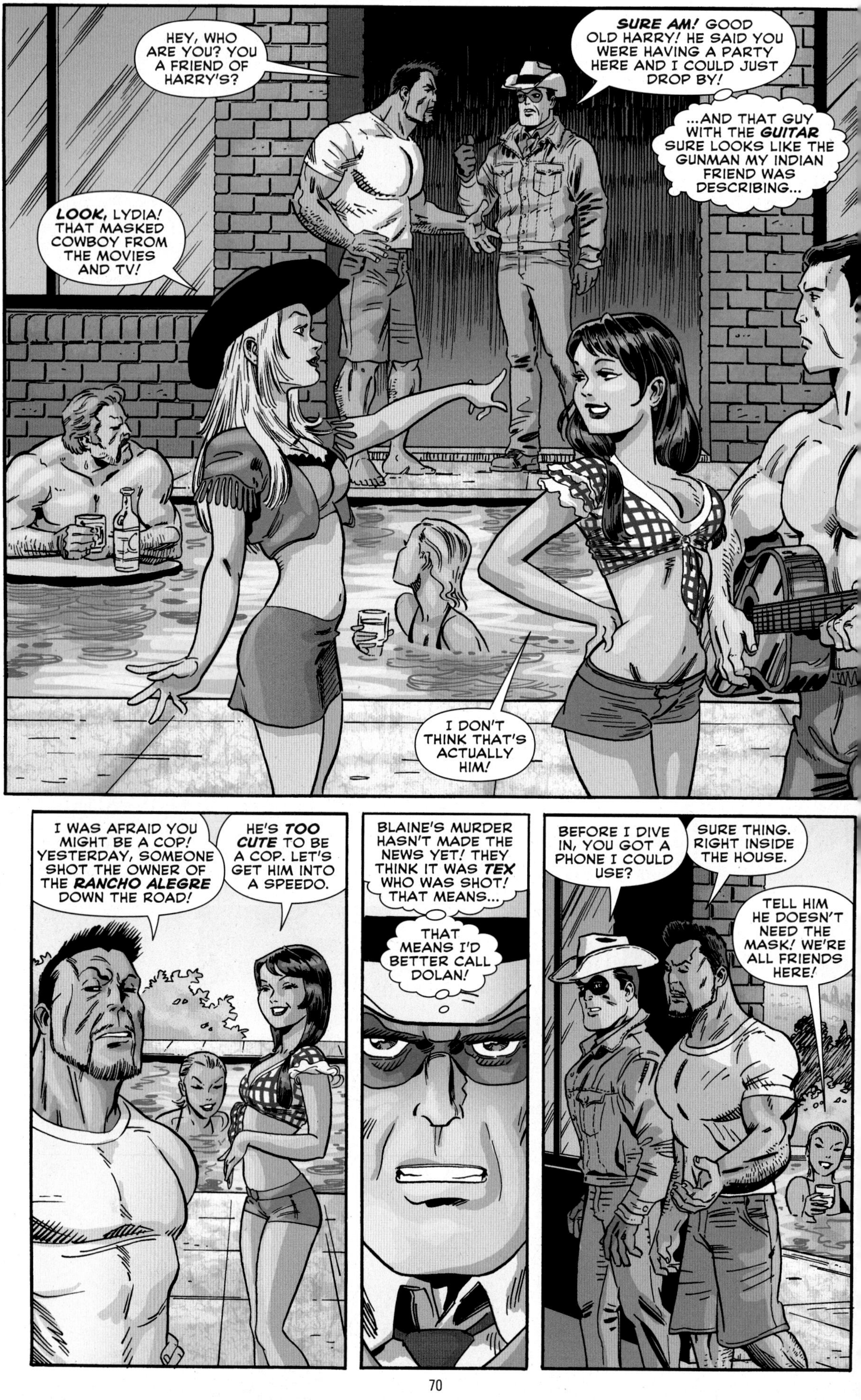

HEY, WHO ARE YOU? YOU A FRIEND OF HARRY'S?
SURE AM! GOOD OLD HARRY! HE SAID YOU WERE HAVING A PARTY HERE AND I COULD JUST DROP BY!
...AND THAT GUY WITH THE GUITAR SURE LOOKS LIKE THE GUNMAN MY INDIAN FRIEND WAS DESCRIBING...
LOOK, LYDIA! THAT MASKED COWBOY FROM THE MOVIES AND TV!
I DON'T THINK THAT'S ACTUALLY HIM!
I WAS AFRAID YOU MIGHT BE A COP! YESTERDAY, SOMEONE SHOT THE OWNER OF THE RANCHO ALEGRE DOWN THE ROAD!
HE'S TOO CUTE TO BE A COP. LET'S GET HIM INTO A SPEEDO.
BLAINE'S MURDER HASN'T MADE THE NEWS YET! THEY THINK IT WAS TEX WHO WAS SHOT! THAT MEANS...
THAT MEANS I'D BETTER CALL DOLAN!
BEFORE I DIVE IN, YOU GOT A PHONE I COULD USE?
SURE THING. RIGHT INSIDE THE HOUSE.
TELL HIM HE DOESN'T NEED THE MASK! WE'RE ALL FRIENDS HERE!

DOLAN? DOLAN, IT'S ME. LISTEN... THEY SHOT THE WRONG GUY! IT WAS TEX THEY WERE TRYING TO KILL! THEY--

"WRONG GUY"? THAT IDIOT!

CAN'T TRUST *ANYONE* ANYMORE!

YOU JERK! YOU SHOT THE *WRONG MAN!*

YOU SAID TO SHOOT THE GUY RIDING THE PINTO! I SHOT THE GUY RIDING THE PINTO!

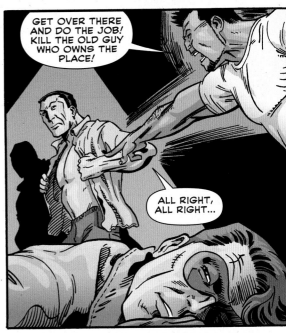

GET OVER THERE AND DO THE JOB! KILL THE OLD GUY WHO OWNS THE PLACE!

ALL RIGHT, ALL RIGHT...

COME ON! WE'LL THROW THIS GUY OFF THE CLIFF SO IT LOOKS LIKE AN ACCIDENT!

HE'S REALLY *OUT COLD!*

NO, HE ISN'T...

...BUT *YOU* WILL BE!

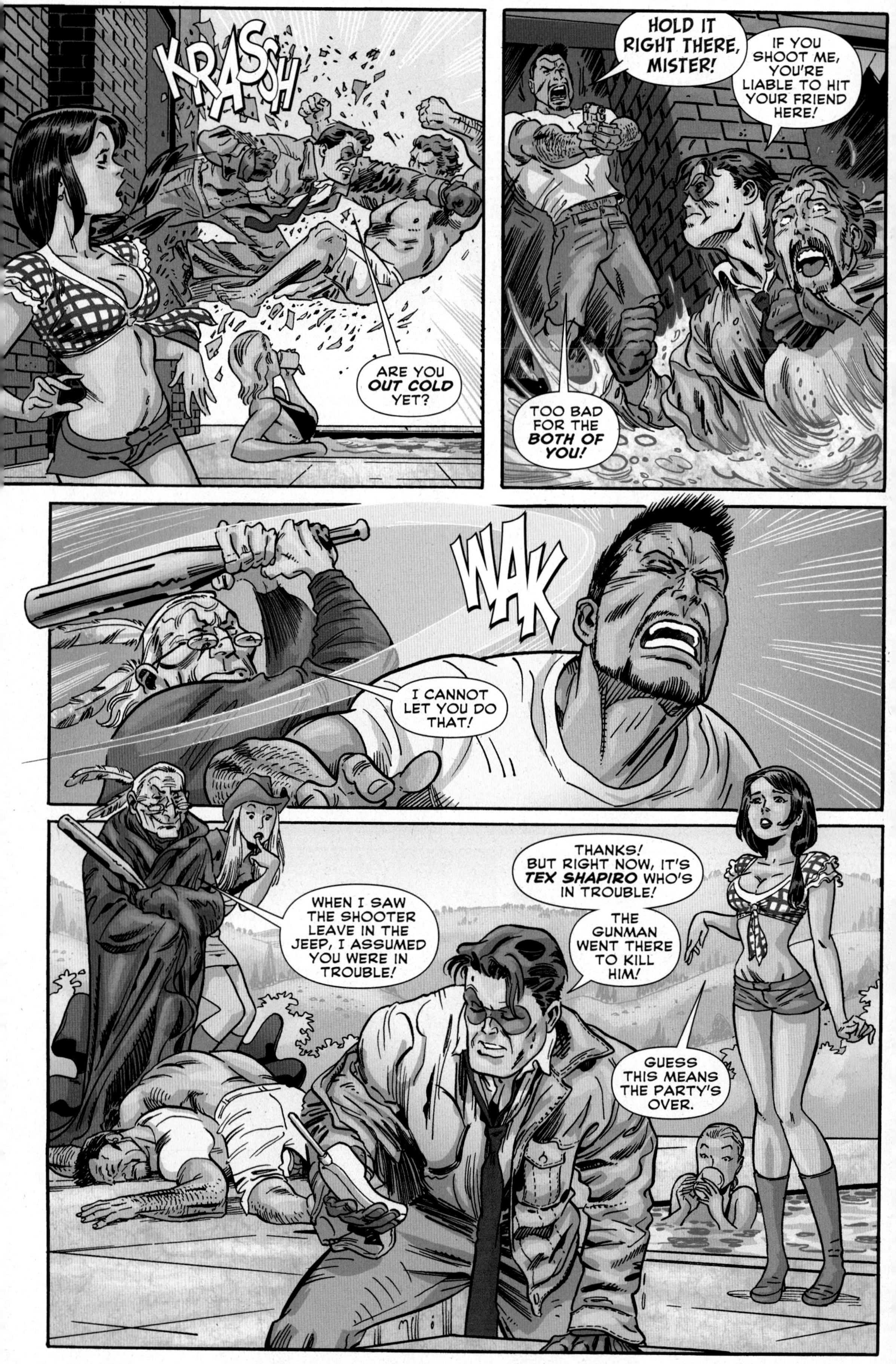
KRASSH
ARE YOU OUT COLD YET?
HOLD IT RIGHT THERE, MISTER!
IF YOU SHOOT ME, YOU'RE LIABLE TO HIT YOUR FRIEND HERE!
TOO BAD FOR THE BOTH OF YOU!
WAK
I CANNOT LET YOU DO THAT!
WHEN I SAW THE SHOOTER LEAVE IN THE JEEP, I ASSUMED YOU WERE IN TROUBLE!
THANKS! BUT RIGHT NOW, IT'S TEX SHAPIRO WHO'S IN TROUBLE!
THE GUNMAN WENT THERE TO KILL HIM!
GUESS THIS MEANS THE PARTY'S OVER.

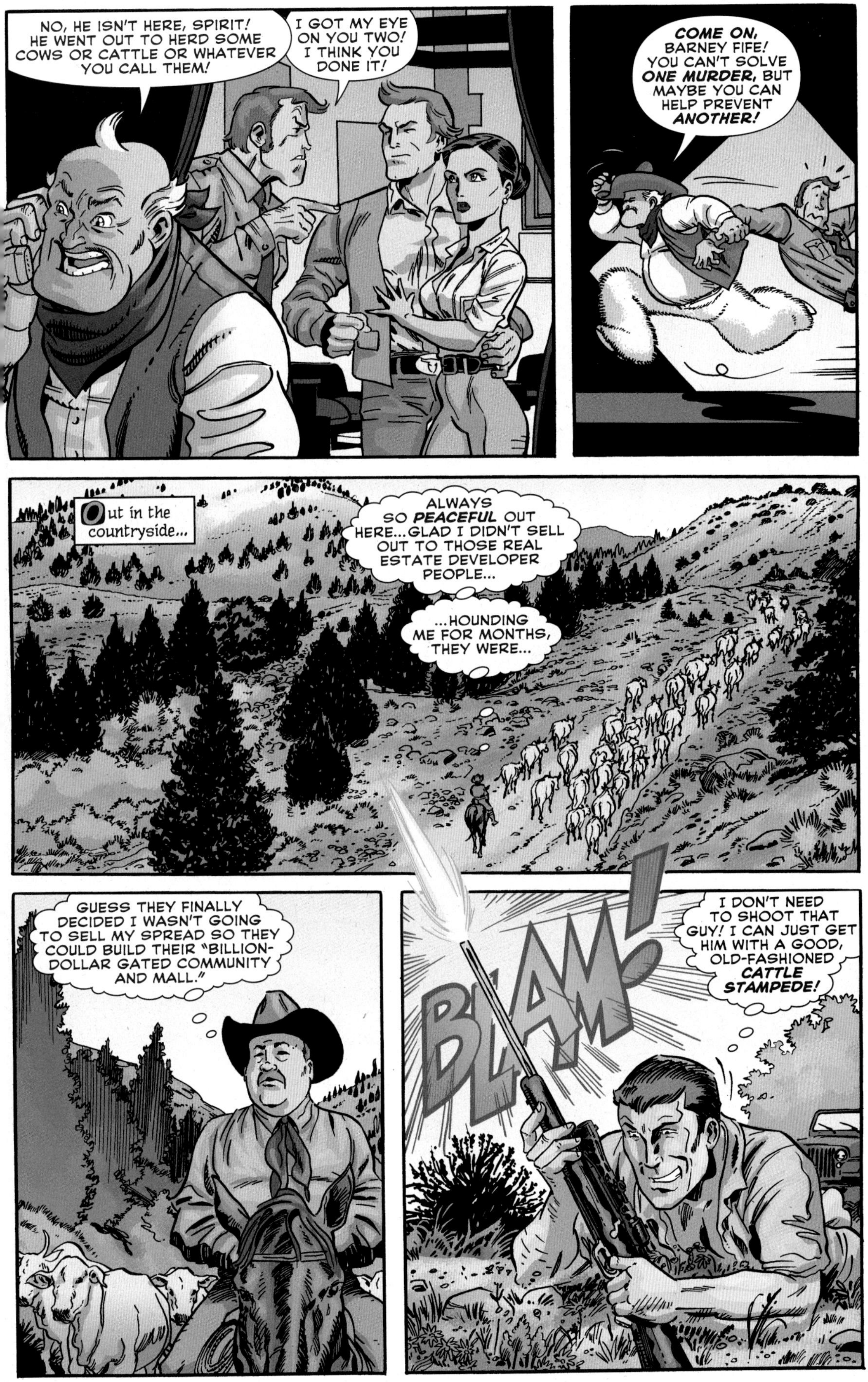
NO, HE ISN'T HERE, SPIRIT! HE WENT OUT TO HERD SOME COWS OR CATTLE OR WHATEVER YOU CALL THEM!
I GOT MY EYE ON YOU TWO! I THINK YOU DONE IT!
COME ON, BARNEY FIFE! YOU CAN'T SOLVE ONE MURDER, BUT MAYBE YOU CAN HELP PREVENT ANOTHER!
Out in the countryside...
ALWAYS SO PEACEFUL OUT HERE...GLAD I DIDN'T SELL OUT TO THOSE REAL ESTATE DEVELOPER PEOPLE...
...HOUNDING ME FOR MONTHS, THEY WERE...
GUESS THEY FINALLY DECIDED I WASN'T GOING TO SELL MY SPREAD SO THEY COULD BUILD THEIR "BILLION-DOLLAR GATED COMMUNITY AND MALL."
BLAM!
I DON'T NEED TO SHOOT THAT GUY! I CAN JUST GET HIM WITH A GOOD, OLD-FASHIONED CATTLE STAMPEDE!

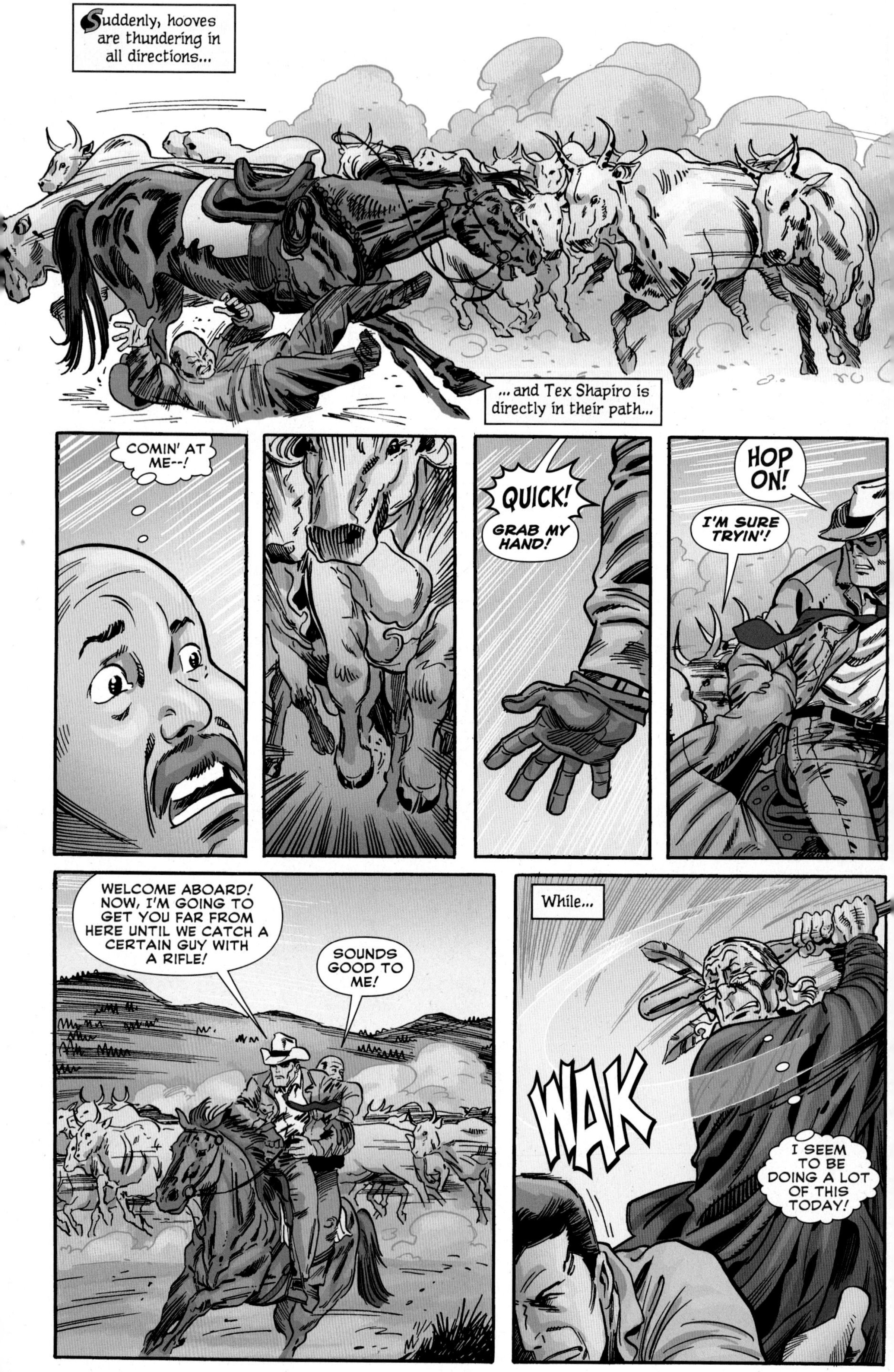
Suddenly, hooves are thundering in all directions...
...and Tex Shapiro is directly in their path...
COMIN' AT ME--!
QUICK!
GRAB MY HAND!
HOP ON!
I'M SURE TRYIN'!
WELCOME ABOARD! NOW, I'M GOING TO GET YOU FAR FROM HERE UNTIL WE CATCH A CERTAIN GUY WITH A RIFLE!
SOUNDS GOOD TO ME!
While...
WAK
I SEEM TO BE DOING A LOT OF THIS TODAY!

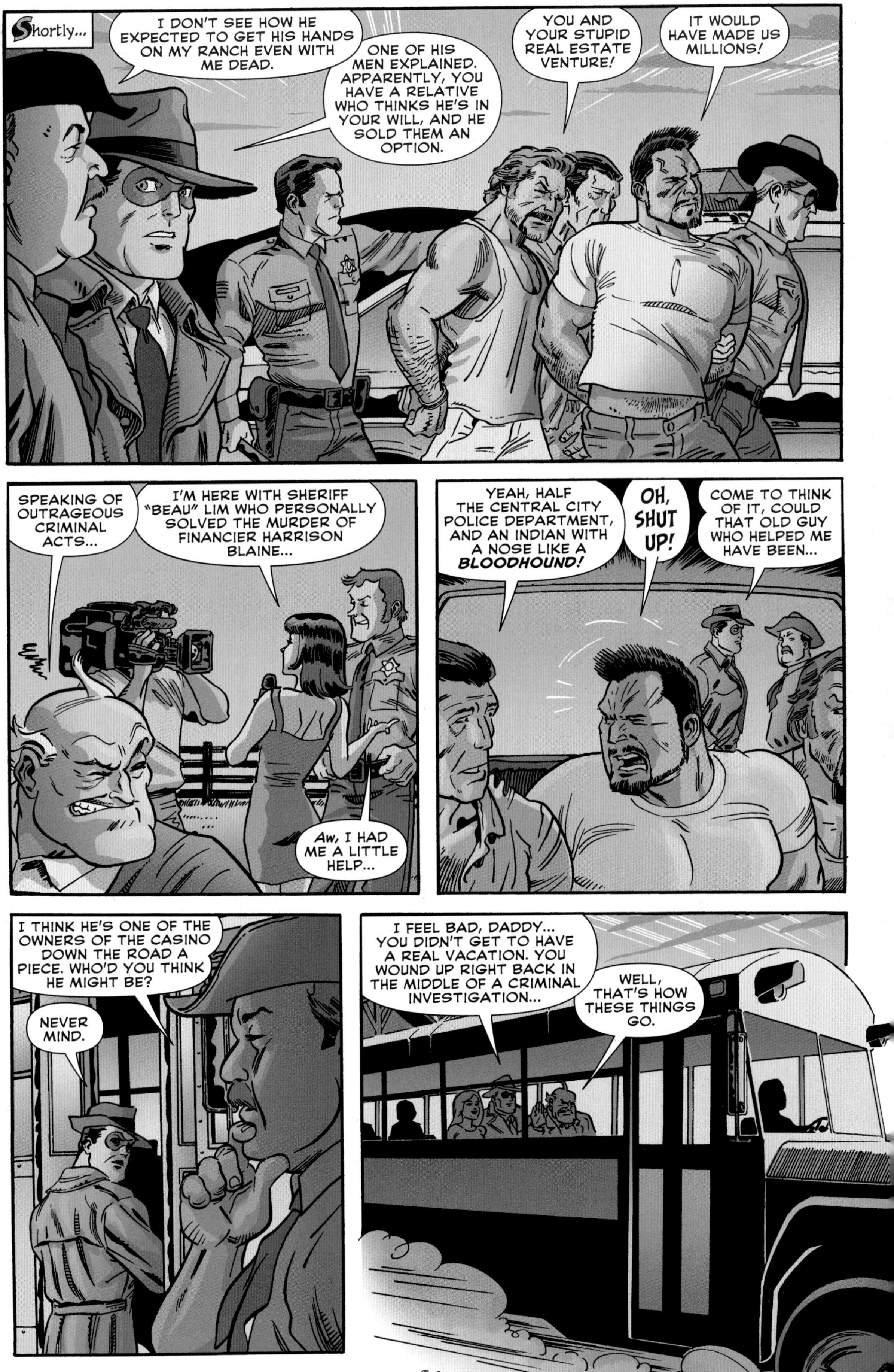
Shortly...
I DON'T SEE HOW HE EXPECTED TO GET HIS HANDS ON MY RANCH EVEN WITH ME DEAD.
ONE OF HIS MEN EXPLAINED. APPARENTLY, YOU HAVE A RELATIVE WHO THINKS HE'S IN YOUR WILL, AND HE SOLD THEM AN OPTION.
YOU AND YOUR STUPID REAL ESTATE VENTURE!
IT WOULD HAVE MADE US MILLIONS!
SPEAKING OF OUTRAGEOUS CRIMINAL ACTS...
I'M HERE WITH SHERIFF "BEAU" LIM WHO PERSONALLY SOLVED THE MURDER OF FINANCIER HARRISON BLAINE...
AW, I HAD ME A LITTLE HELP...
YEAH, HALF THE CENTRAL CITY POLICE DEPARTMENT, AND AN INDIAN WITH A NOSE LIKE A BLOODHOUND!
OH, SHUT UP!
COME TO THINK OF IT, COULD THAT OLD GUY WHO HELPED ME HAVE BEEN...
I THINK HE'S ONE OF THE OWNERS OF THE CASINO DOWN THE ROAD A PIECE. WHO'D YOU THINK HE MIGHT BE?
NEVER MIND.
I FEEL BAD, DADDY... YOU DIDN'T GET TO HAVE A REAL VACATION. YOU WOUND UP RIGHT BACK IN THE MIDDLE OF A CRIMINAL INVESTIGATION...
WELL, THAT'S HOW THESE THINGS GO.

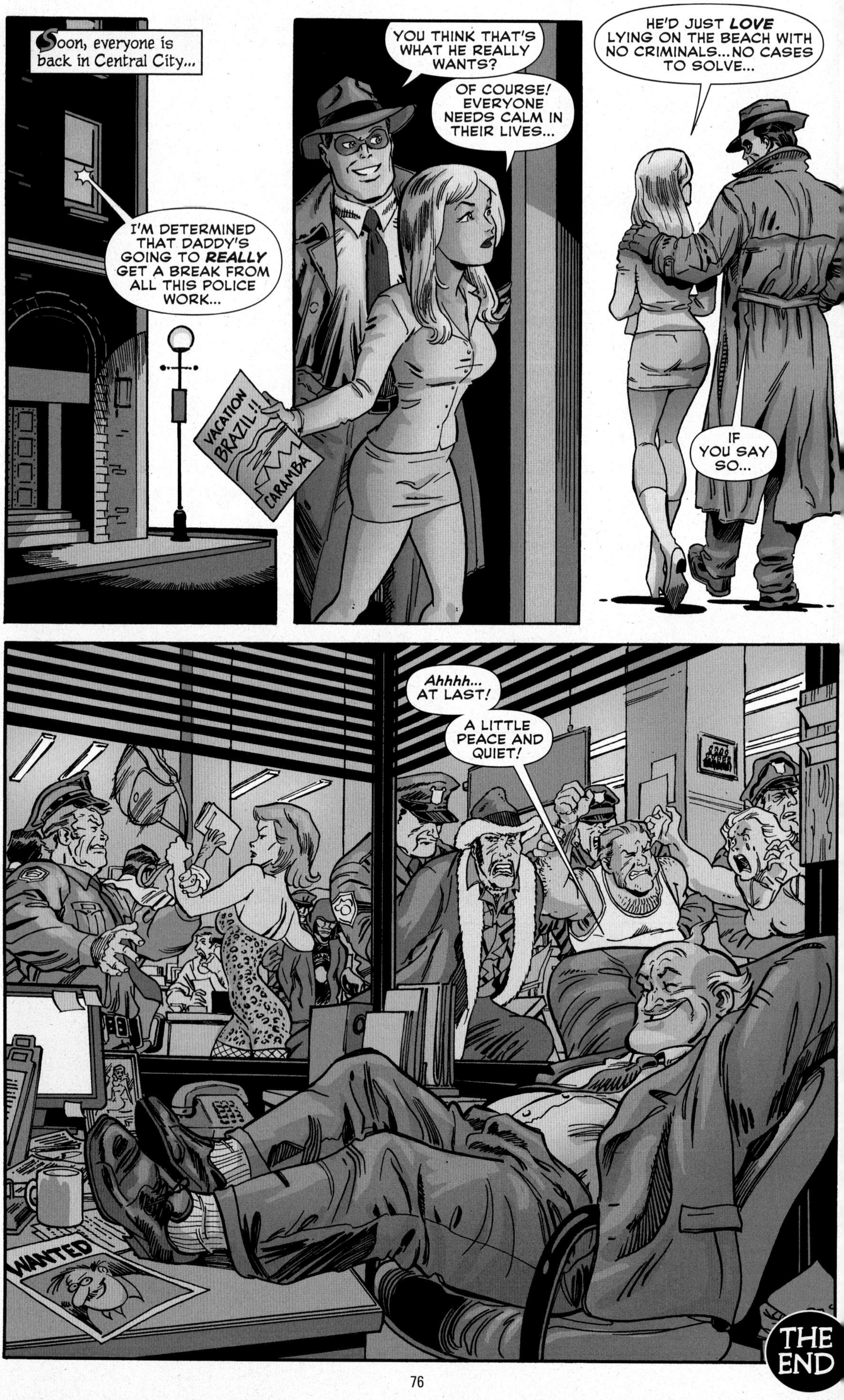

Soon, everyone is back in Central City...
I'M DETERMINED THAT DADDY'S GOING TO **REALLY** GET A BREAK FROM ALL THIS POLICE WORK...
VACATION BRAZIL!! CARAMBA
YOU THINK THAT'S WHAT HE REALLY WANTS?
OF COURSE! EVERYONE NEEDS CALM IN THEIR LIVES...
HE'D JUST **LOVE** LYING ON THE BEACH WITH NO CRIMINALS...NO CASES TO SOLVE...
IF YOU SAY SO...
Ahhhh... AT LAST!
A LITTLE PEACE AND QUIET!
WANTED
THE END

4

ACTION · Mystery · ADVENTURE

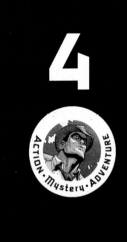

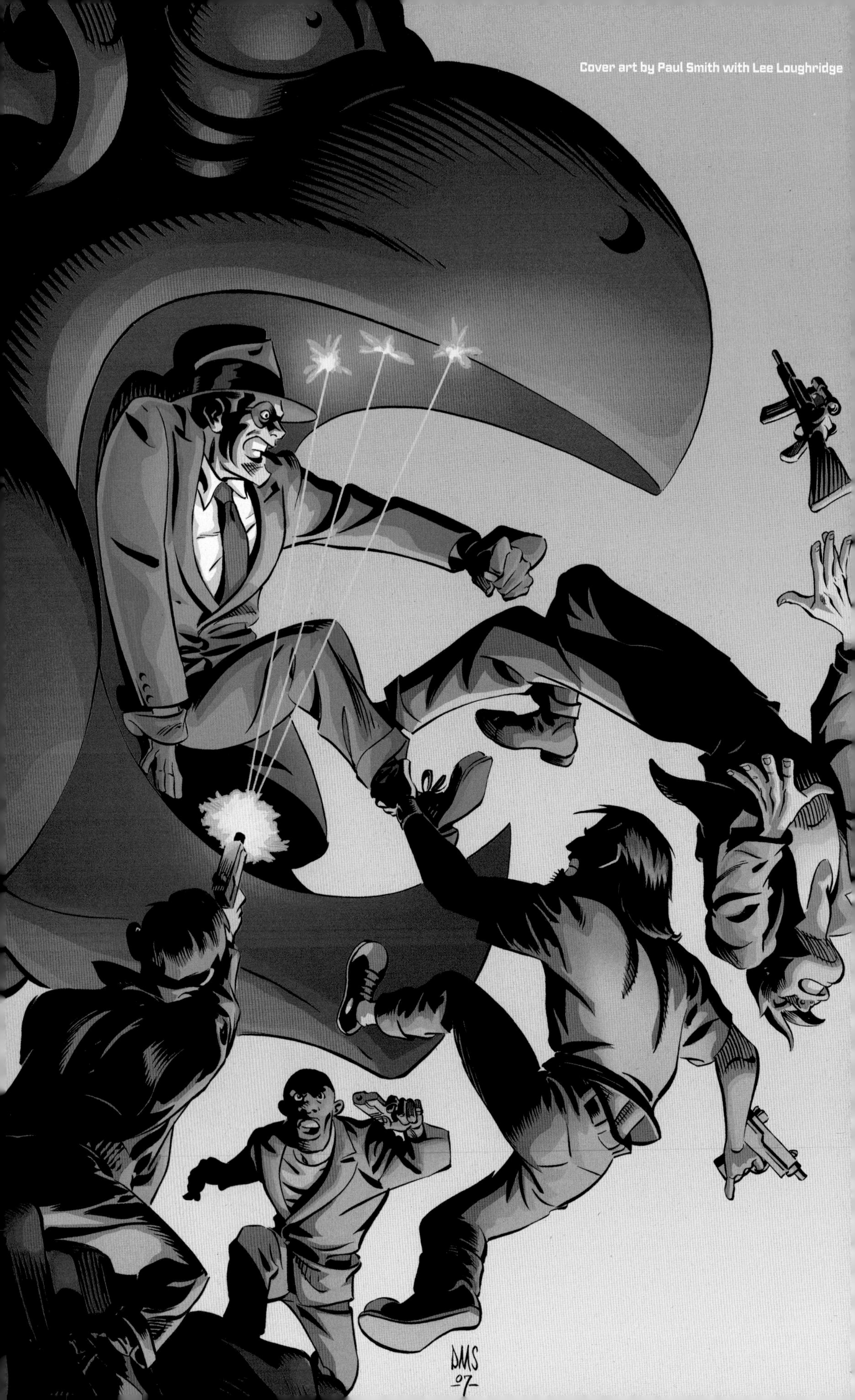

Cover art by Paul Smith with Lee Loughridge

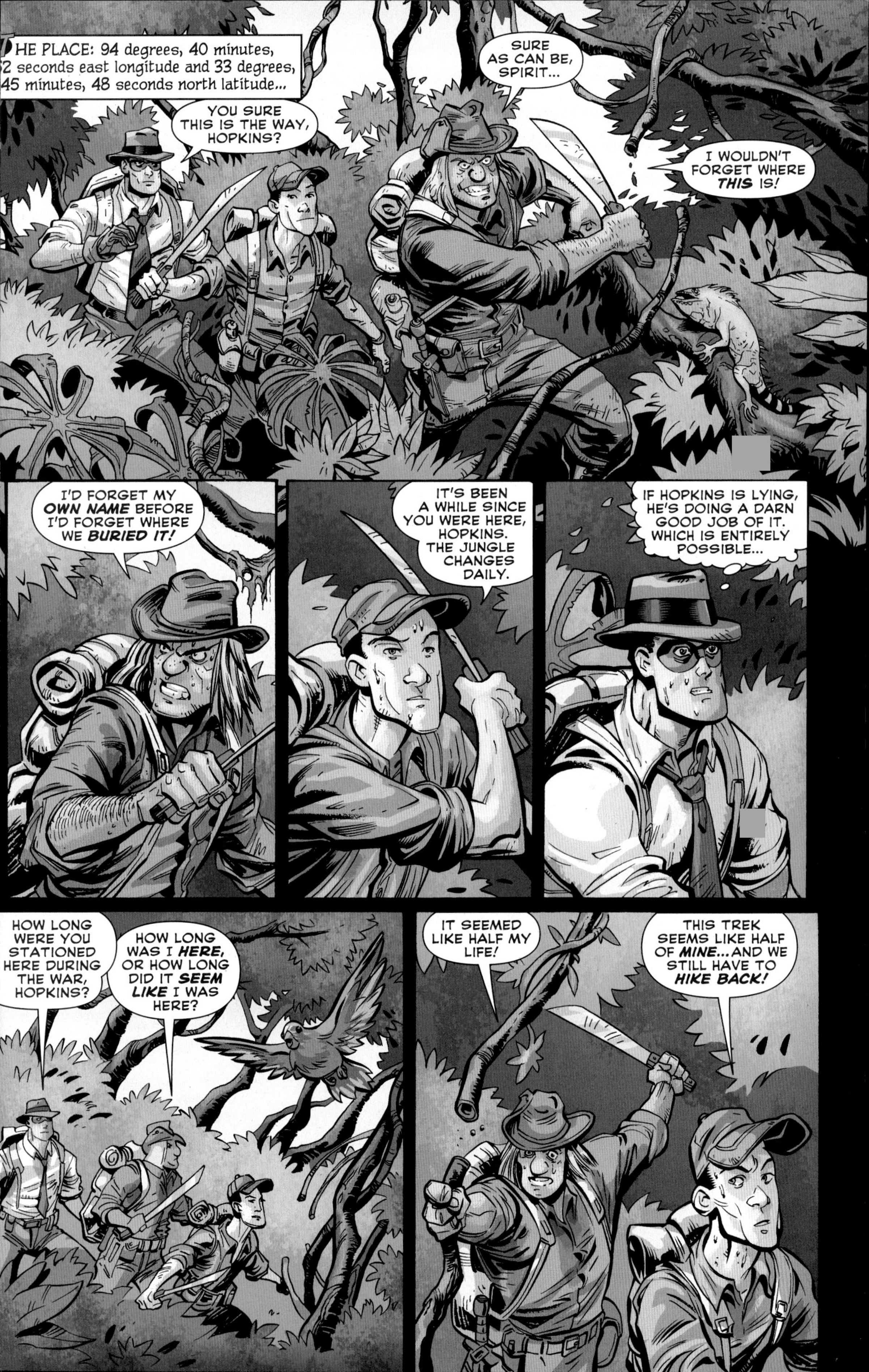

HE PLACE: 94 degrees, 40 minutes, 2 seconds east longitude and 33 degrees, 45 minutes, 48 seconds north latitude...
YOU SURE THIS IS THE WAY, HOPKINS?
SURE AS CAN BE, SPIRIT...
I WOULDN'T FORGET WHERE THIS IS!
I'D FORGET MY OWN NAME BEFORE I'D FORGET WHERE WE BURIED IT!
IT'S BEEN A WHILE SINCE YOU WERE HERE, HOPKINS. THE JUNGLE CHANGES DAILY.
IF HOPKINS IS LYING, HE'S DOING A DARN GOOD JOB OF IT. WHICH IS ENTIRELY POSSIBLE...
HOW LONG WERE YOU STATIONED HERE DURING THE WAR, HOPKINS?
HOW LONG WAS I HERE, OR HOW LONG DID IT SEEM LIKE I WAS HERE?
IT SEEMED LIKE HALF MY LIFE!
THIS TREK SEEMS LIKE HALF OF MINE...AND WE STILL HAVE TO HIKE BACK!

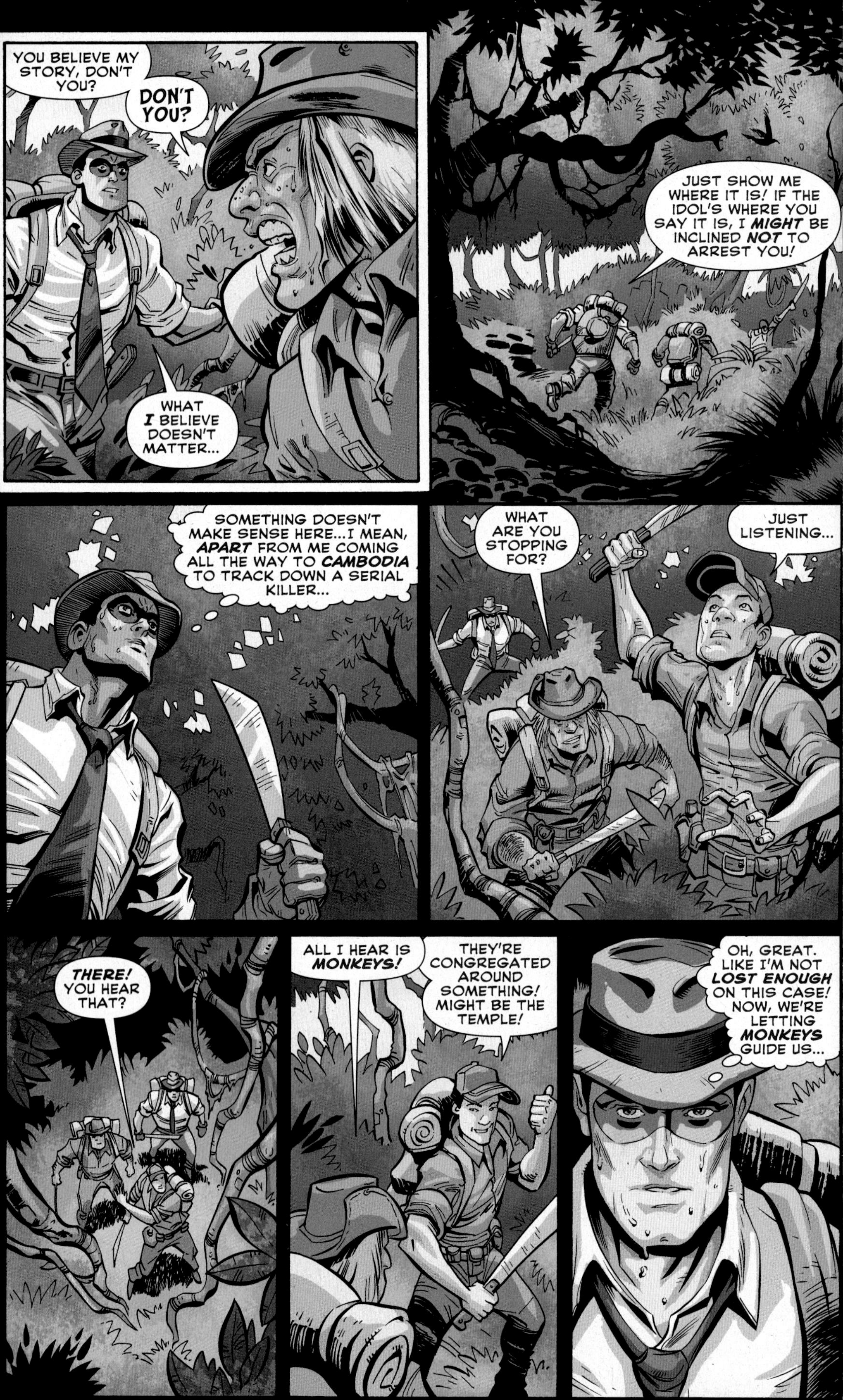

YOU BELIEVE MY STORY, DON'T YOU?
DON'T YOU?
WHAT *I* BELIEVE DOESN'T MATTER...
JUST SHOW ME WHERE IT IS! IF THE IDOL'S WHERE YOU SAY IT IS, I ***MIGHT*** BE INCLINED ***NOT*** TO ARREST YOU!
SOMETHING DOESN'T MAKE SENSE HERE...I MEAN, ***APART*** FROM ME COMING ALL THE WAY TO ***CAMBODIA*** TO TRACK DOWN A SERIAL KILLER...
WHAT ARE YOU STOPPING FOR?
JUST LISTENING...
THERE! YOU HEAR THAT?
ALL I HEAR IS ***MONKEYS!***
THEY'RE CONGREGATED AROUND SOMETHING! MIGHT BE THE TEMPLE!
OH, GREAT. LIKE I'M NOT ***LOST ENOUGH*** ON THIS CASE! NOW, WE'RE LETTING ***MONKEYS*** GUIDE US...

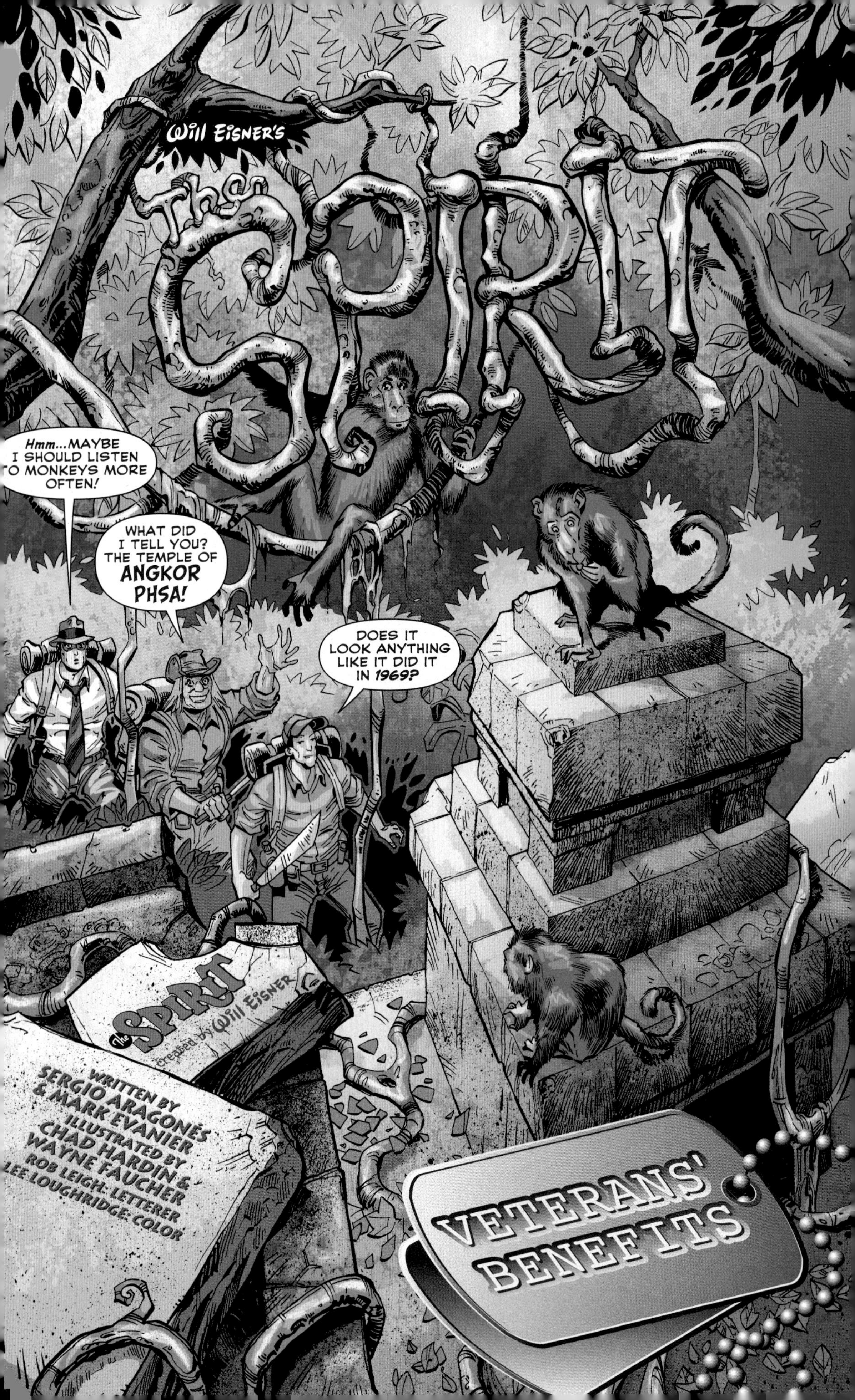
Will Eisner's
The Spirit
Hmm...MAYBE I SHOULD LISTEN TO MONKEYS MORE OFTEN!
WHAT DID I TELL YOU? THE TEMPLE OF ANGKOR PHSA!
DOES IT LOOK ANYTHING LIKE IT DID IT IN 1969?
The Spirit created by Will Eisner
WRITTEN BY SERGIO ARAGONÉS & MARK EVANIER
ILLUSTRATED BY CHAD HARDIN & WAYNE FAUCHER
ROB LEIGH: LETTERER
LEE LOUGHRIDGE: COLOR
VETERANS' BENEFITS

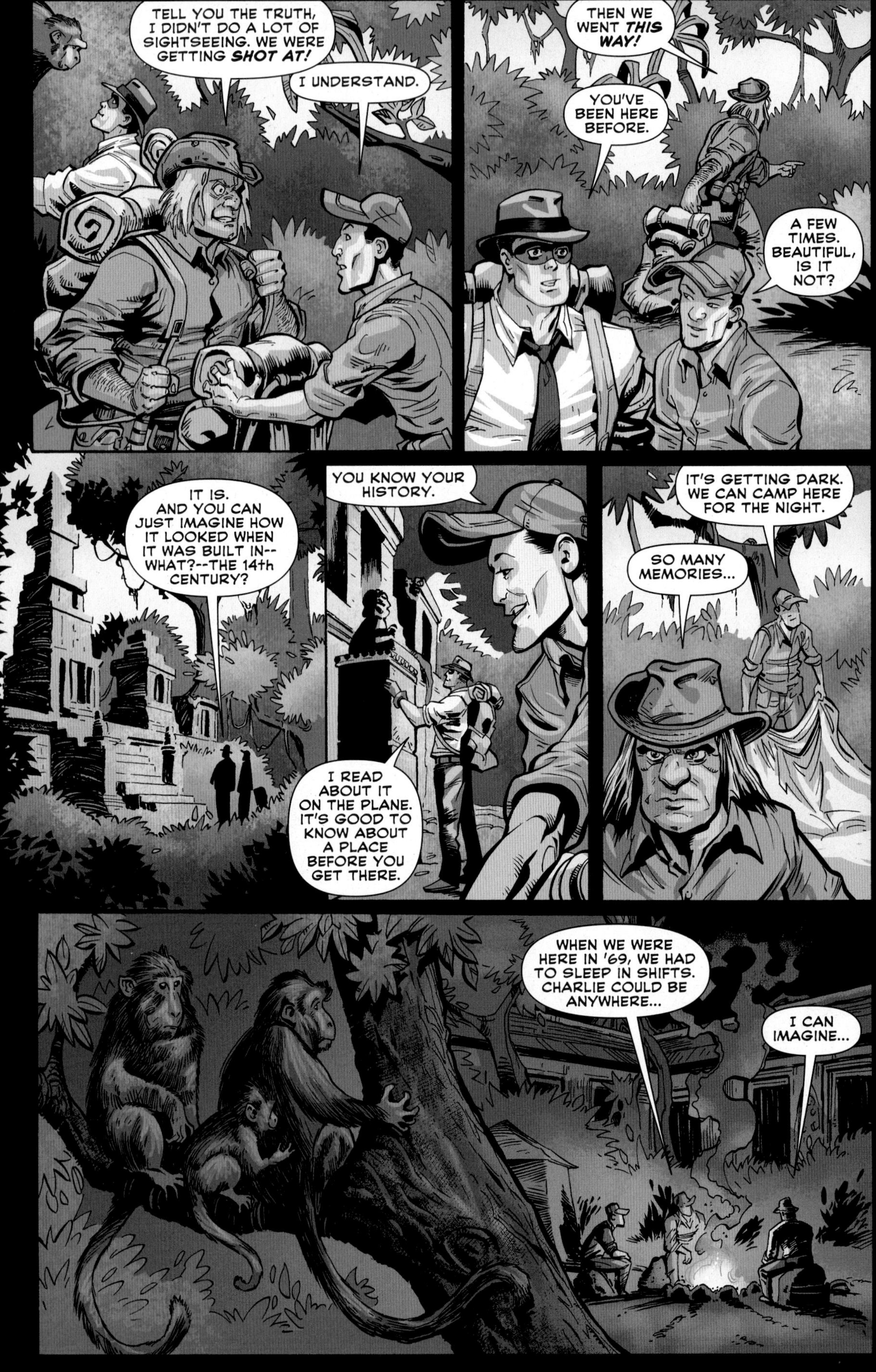
TELL YOU THE TRUTH, I DIDN'T DO A LOT OF SIGHTSEEING. WE WERE GETTING SHOT AT!
I UNDERSTAND.
THEN WE WENT THIS WAY!
YOU'VE BEEN HERE BEFORE.
A FEW TIMES. BEAUTIFUL, IS IT NOT?
IT IS. AND YOU CAN JUST IMAGINE HOW IT LOOKED WHEN IT WAS BUILT IN--WHAT?--THE 14th CENTURY?
YOU KNOW YOUR HISTORY.
I READ ABOUT IT ON THE PLANE. IT'S GOOD TO KNOW ABOUT A PLACE BEFORE YOU GET THERE.
IT'S GETTING DARK. WE CAN CAMP HERE FOR THE NIGHT.
SO MANY MEMORIES...
WHEN WE WERE HERE IN '69, WE HAD TO SLEEP IN SHIFTS. CHARLIE COULD BE ANYWHERE...
I CAN IMAGINE...

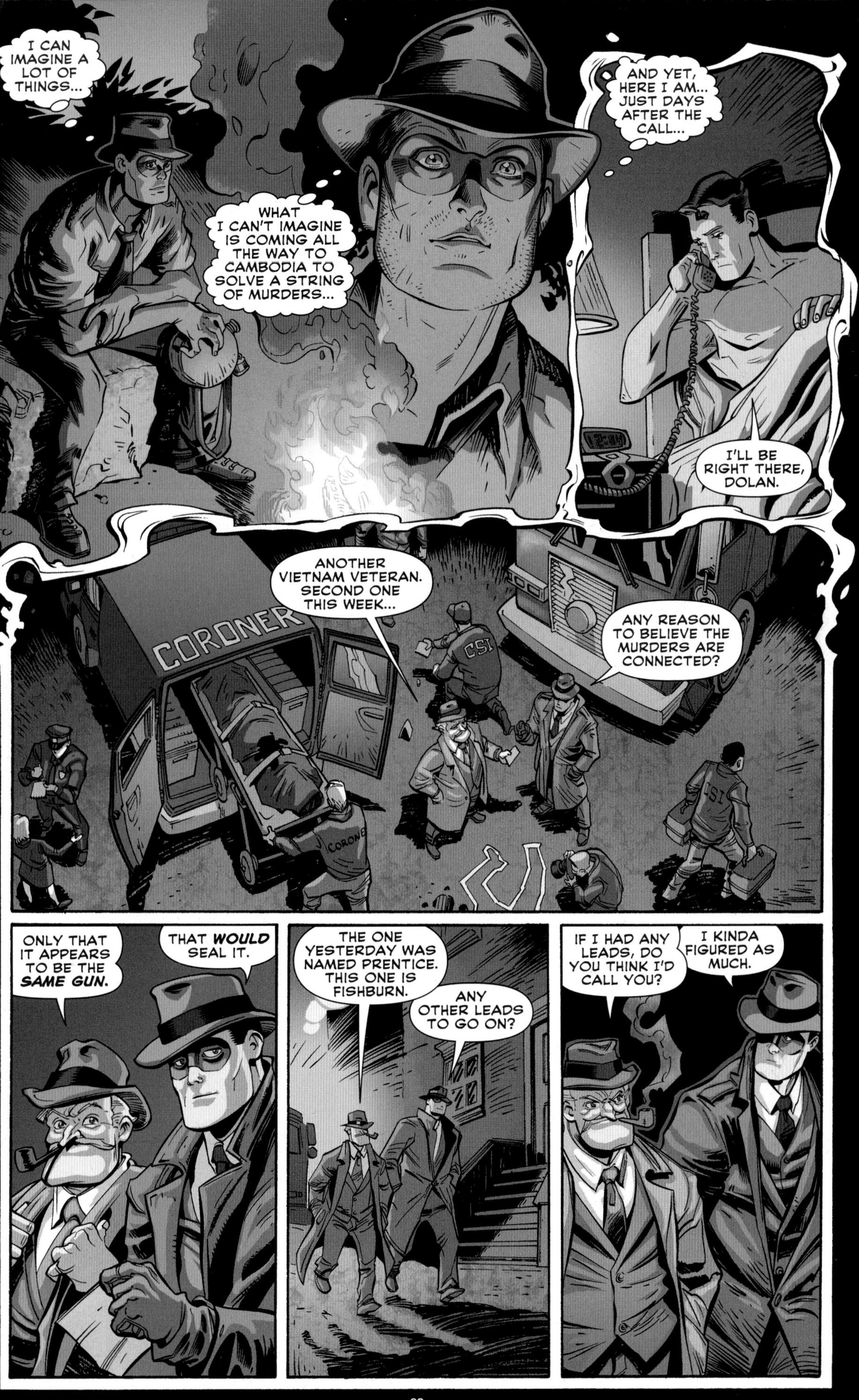

I CAN IMAGINE A LOT OF THINGS...
WHAT I CAN'T IMAGINE IS COMING ALL THE WAY TO CAMBODIA TO SOLVE A STRING OF MURDERS...
AND YET, HERE I AM... JUST DAYS AFTER THE CALL...
I'LL BE RIGHT THERE, DOLAN.
CORONER
ANOTHER VIETNAM VETERAN. SECOND ONE THIS WEEK...
ANY REASON TO BELIEVE THE MURDERS ARE CONNECTED?
CSI
ONLY THAT IT APPEARS TO BE THE SAME GUN.
THAT WOULD SEAL IT.
THE ONE YESTERDAY WAS NAMED PRENTICE. THIS ONE IS FISHBURN.
ANY OTHER LEADS TO GO ON?
IF I HAD ANY LEADS, DO YOU THINK I'D CALL YOU?
I KINDA FIGURED AS MUCH.

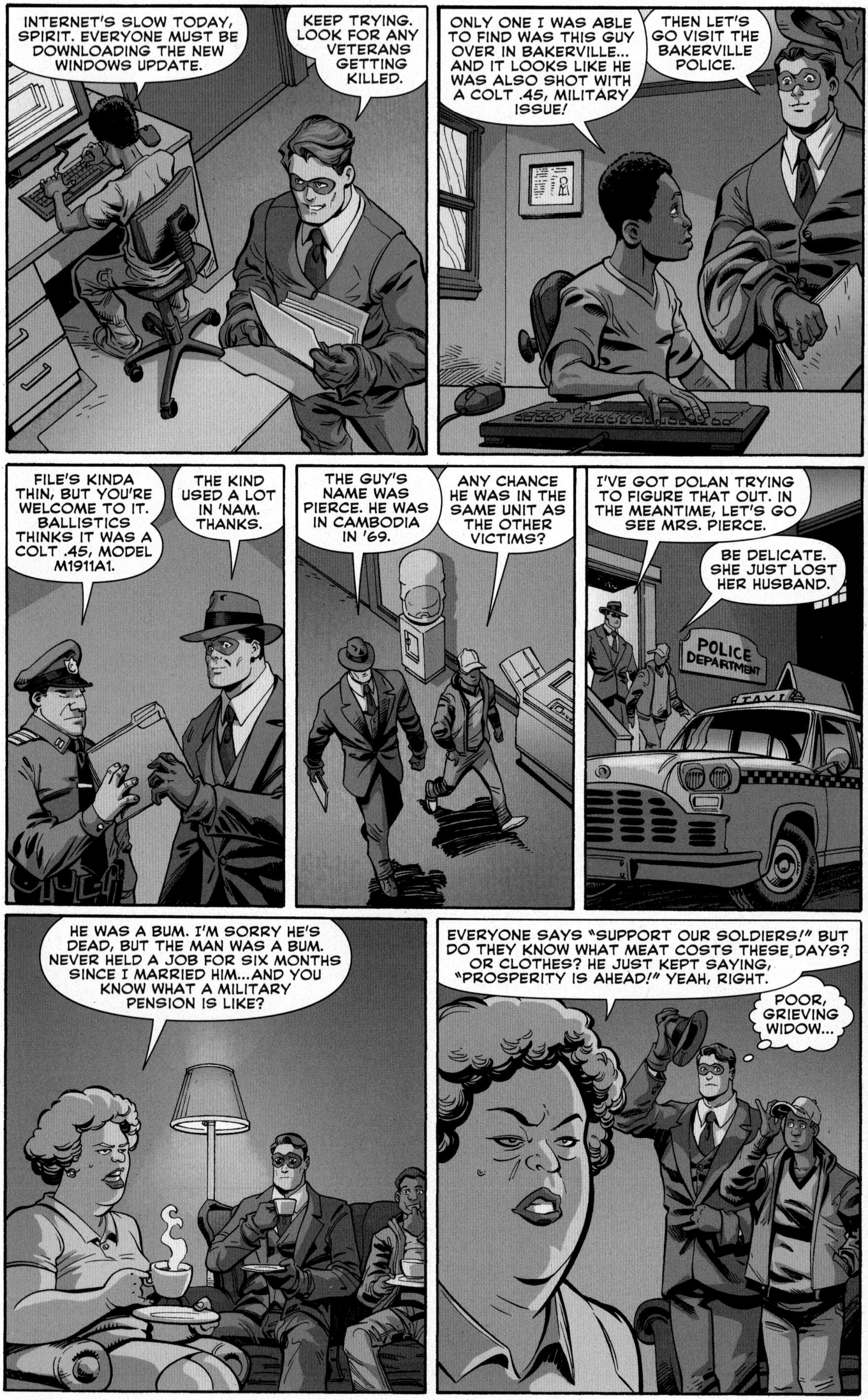
INTERNET'S SLOW TODAY, SPIRIT. EVERYONE MUST BE DOWNLOADING THE NEW WINDOWS UPDATE.
KEEP TRYING. LOOK FOR ANY VETERANS GETTING KILLED.
ONLY ONE I WAS ABLE TO FIND WAS THIS GUY OVER IN BAKERVILLE... AND IT LOOKS LIKE HE WAS ALSO SHOT WITH A COLT .45, MILITARY ISSUE!
THEN LET'S GO VISIT THE BAKERVILLE POLICE.
FILE'S KINDA THIN, BUT YOU'RE WELCOME TO IT. BALLISTICS THINKS IT WAS A COLT .45, MODEL M1911A1.
THE KIND USED A LOT IN 'NAM. THANKS.
THE GUY'S NAME WAS PIERCE. HE WAS IN CAMBODIA IN '69.
ANY CHANCE HE WAS IN THE SAME UNIT AS THE OTHER VICTIMS?
I'VE GOT DOLAN TRYING TO FIGURE THAT OUT. IN THE MEANTIME, LET'S GO SEE MRS. PIERCE.
BE DELICATE. SHE JUST LOST HER HUSBAND.
POLICE DEPARTMENT
TAXI
HE WAS A BUM. I'M SORRY HE'S DEAD, BUT THE MAN WAS A BUM. NEVER HELD A JOB FOR SIX MONTHS SINCE I MARRIED HIM...AND YOU KNOW WHAT A MILITARY PENSION IS LIKE?
EVERYONE SAYS "SUPPORT OUR SOLDIERS!" BUT DO THEY KNOW WHAT MEAT COSTS THESE DAYS? OR CLOTHES? HE JUST KEPT SAYING, "PROSPERITY IS AHEAD!" YEAH, RIGHT.
POOR, GRIEVING WIDOW...

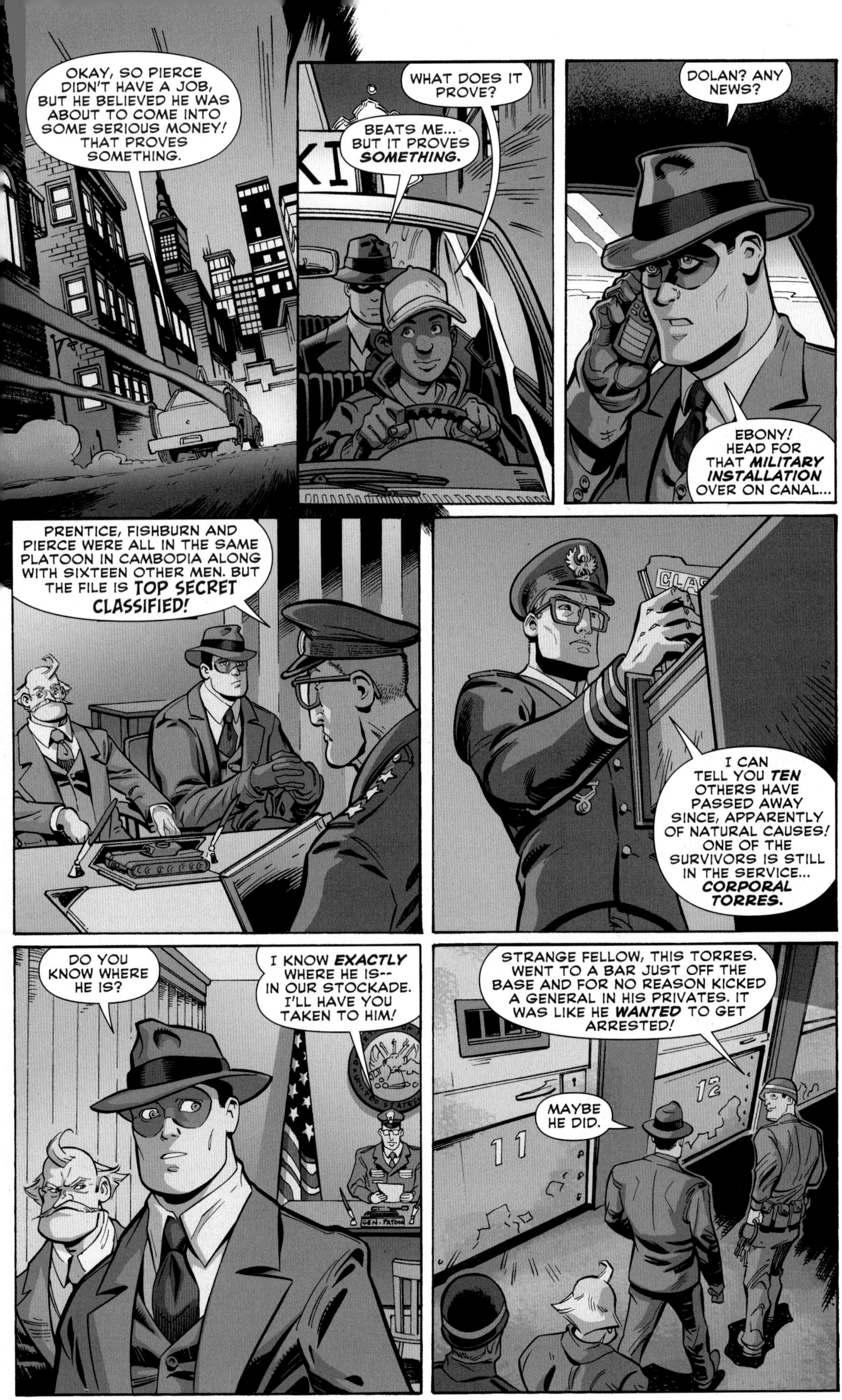
OKAY, SO PIERCE DIDN'T HAVE A JOB, BUT HE BELIEVED HE WAS ABOUT TO COME INTO SOME SERIOUS MONEY! THAT PROVES SOMETHING.
WHAT DOES IT PROVE?
BEATS ME... BUT IT PROVES SOMETHING.
DOLAN? ANY NEWS?
EBONY! HEAD FOR THAT MILITARY INSTALLATION OVER ON CANAL...
PRENTICE, FISHBURN AND PIERCE WERE ALL IN THE SAME PLATOON IN CAMBODIA ALONG WITH SIXTEEN OTHER MEN. BUT THE FILE IS TOP SECRET CLASSIFIED!
I CAN TELL YOU TEN OTHERS HAVE PASSED AWAY SINCE, APPARENTLY OF NATURAL CAUSES! ONE OF THE SURVIVORS IS STILL IN THE SERVICE... CORPORAL TORRES.
DO YOU KNOW WHERE HE IS?
I KNOW EXACTLY WHERE HE IS-- IN OUR STOCKADE. I'LL HAVE YOU TAKEN TO HIM!
GEN. PATON
STRANGE FELLOW, THIS TORRES. WENT TO A BAR JUST OFF THE BASE AND FOR NO REASON KICKED A GENERAL IN HIS PRIVATES. IT WAS LIKE HE WANTED TO GET ARRESTED!
MAYBE HE DID.

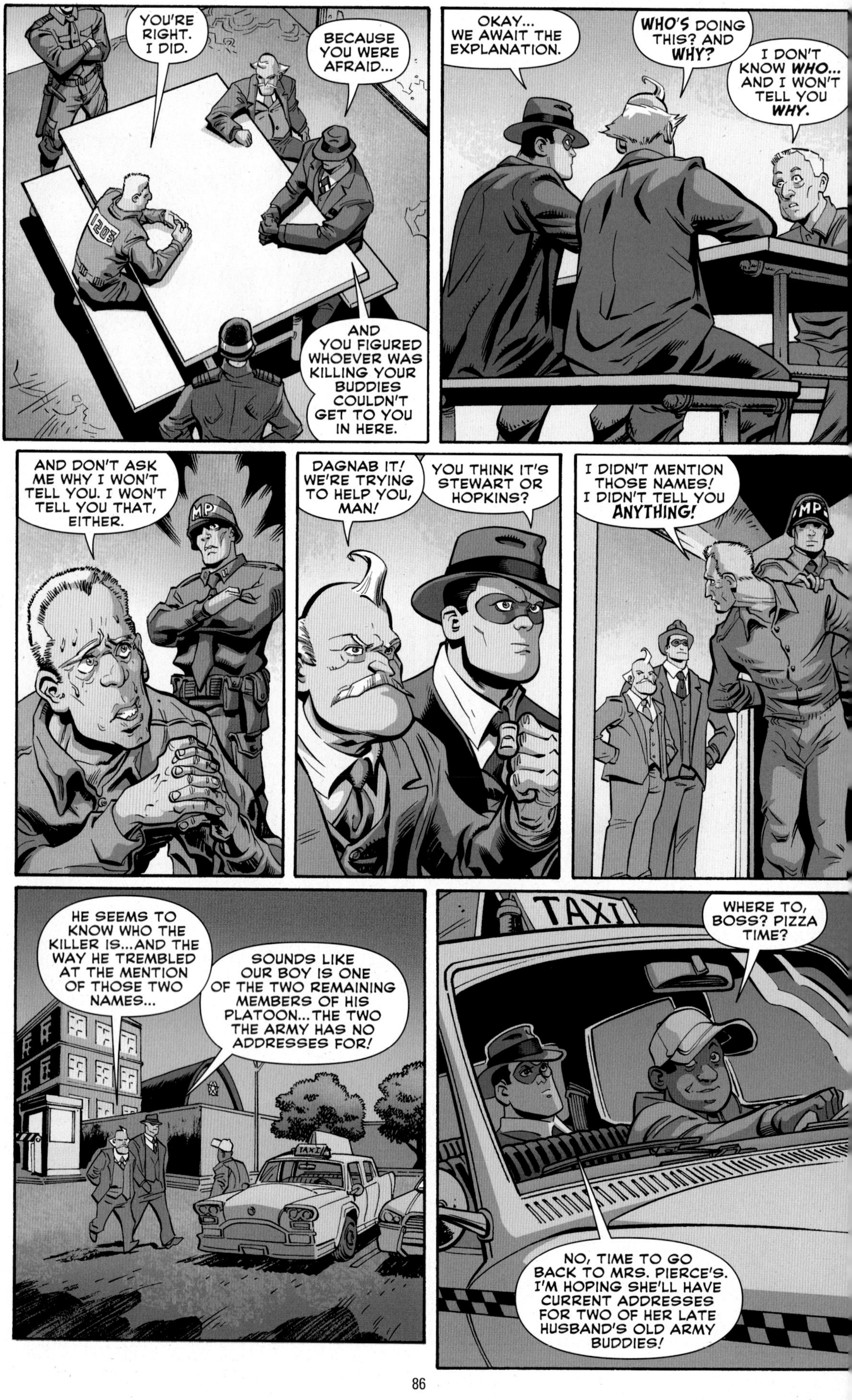
YOU'RE RIGHT. I DID.
BECAUSE YOU WERE AFRAID...
AND YOU FIGURED WHOEVER WAS KILLING YOUR BUDDIES COULDN'T GET TO YOU IN HERE.
OKAY... WE AWAIT THE EXPLANATION.
WHO'S DOING THIS? AND WHY?
I DON'T KNOW WHO... AND I WON'T TELL YOU WHY.
AND DON'T ASK ME WHY I WON'T TELL YOU. I WON'T TELL YOU THAT, EITHER.
MP
DAGNAB IT! WE'RE TRYING TO HELP YOU, MAN!
YOU THINK IT'S STEWART OR HOPKINS?
I DIDN'T MENTION THOSE NAMES! I DIDN'T TELL YOU ANYTHING!
MP
HE SEEMS TO KNOW WHO THE KILLER IS...AND THE WAY HE TREMBLED AT THE MENTION OF THOSE TWO NAMES...
SOUNDS LIKE OUR BOY IS ONE OF THE TWO REMAINING MEMBERS OF HIS PLATOON...THE TWO THE ARMY HAS NO ADDRESSES FOR!
TAXI
TAXI
WHERE TO, BOSS? PIZZA TIME?
NO, TIME TO GO BACK TO MRS. PIERCE'S. I'M HOPING SHE'LL HAVE CURRENT ADDRESSES FOR TWO OF HER LATE HUSBAND'S OLD ARMY BUDDIES!

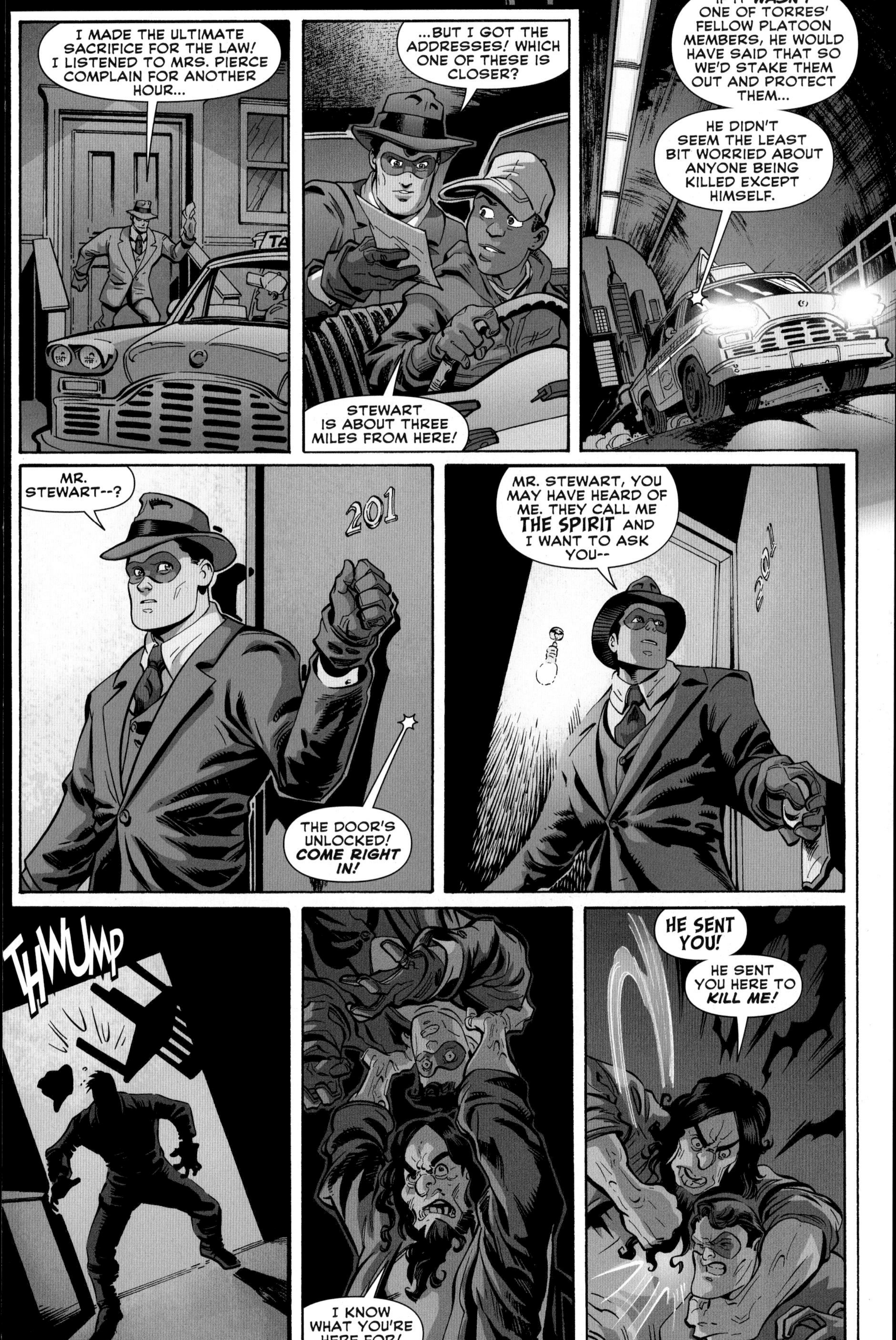
I MADE THE ULTIMATE SACRIFICE FOR THE LAW! I LISTENED TO MRS. PIERCE COMPLAIN FOR ANOTHER HOUR...
...BUT I GOT THE ADDRESSES! WHICH ONE OF THESE IS CLOSER?
STEWART IS ABOUT THREE MILES FROM HERE!
IF IT WASN'T ONE OF TORRES' FELLOW PLATOON MEMBERS, HE WOULD HAVE SAID THAT SO WE'D STAKE THEM OUT AND PROTECT THEM...
HE DIDN'T SEEM THE LEAST BIT WORRIED ABOUT ANYONE BEING KILLED EXCEPT HIMSELF.
MR. STEWART--?
201
THE DOOR'S UNLOCKED! COME RIGHT IN!
MR. STEWART, YOU MAY HAVE HEARD OF ME. THEY CALL ME THE SPIRIT AND I WANT TO ASK YOU--
THWUMP
I KNOW WHAT YOU'RE HERE FOR!
HE SENT YOU!
HE SENT YOU HERE TO KILL ME!

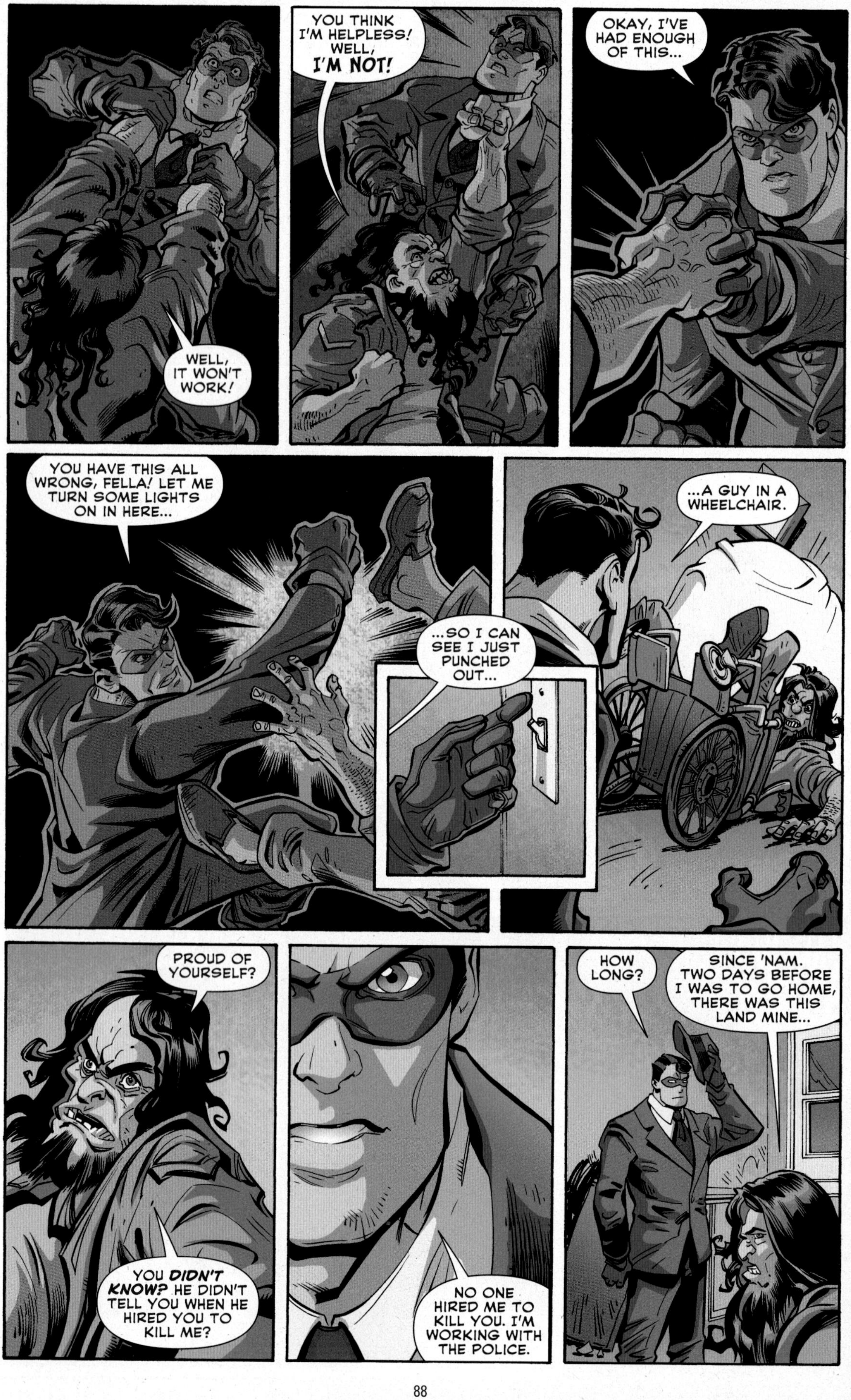
WELL, IT WON'T WORK!
YOU THINK I'M HELPLESS! WELL, I'M NOT!
OKAY, I'VE HAD ENOUGH OF THIS...
YOU HAVE THIS ALL WRONG, FELLA! LET ME TURN SOME LIGHTS ON IN HERE...
...SO I CAN SEE I JUST PUNCHED OUT...
...A GUY IN A WHEELCHAIR.
PROUD OF YOURSELF?
YOU DIDN'T KNOW? HE DIDN'T TELL YOU WHEN HE HIRED YOU TO KILL ME?
NO ONE HIRED ME TO KILL YOU. I'M WORKING WITH THE POLICE.
HOW LONG?
SINCE 'NAM. TWO DAYS BEFORE I WAS TO GO HOME, THERE WAS THIS LAND MINE...

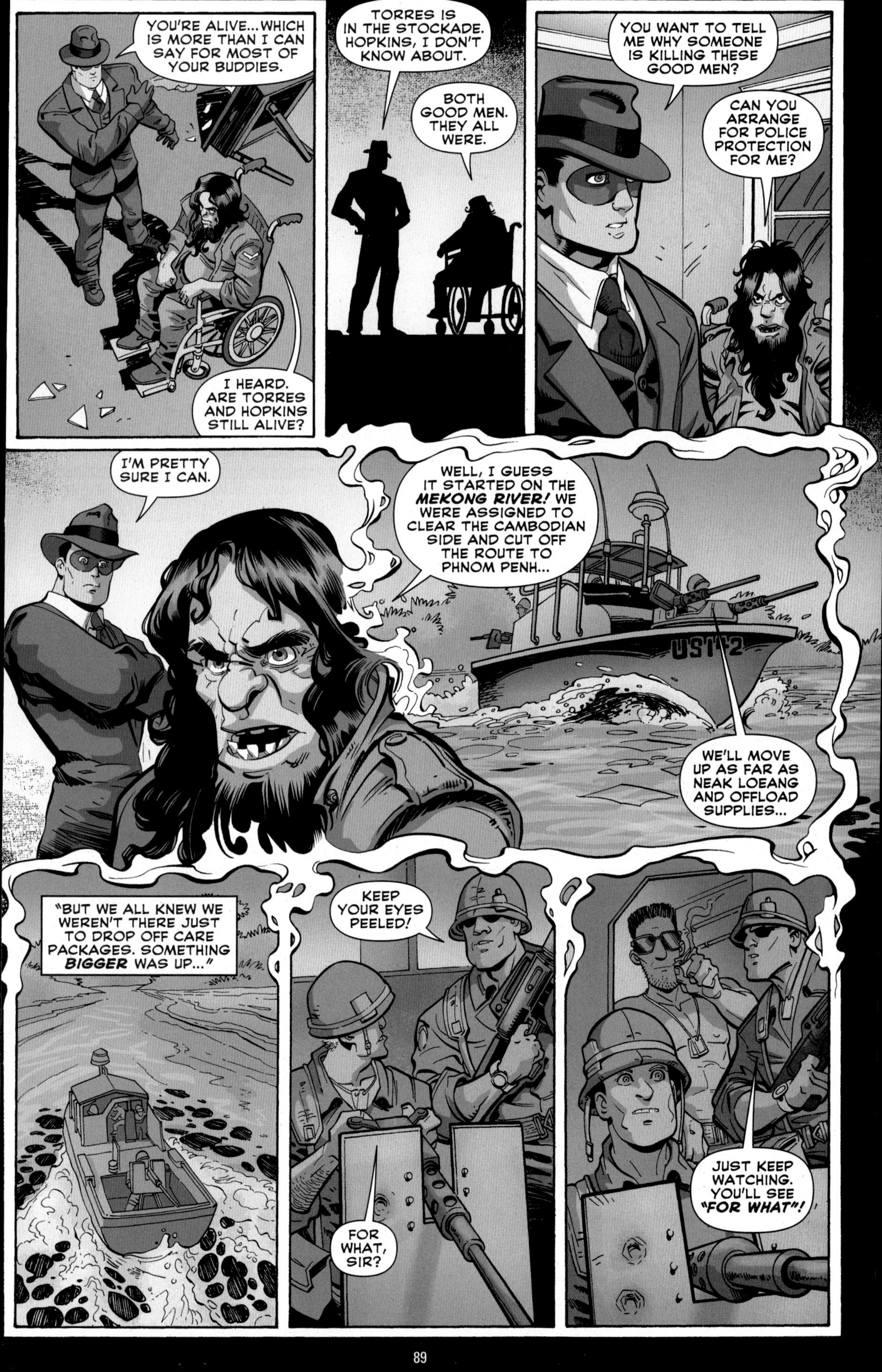
YOU'RE ALIVE...WHICH IS MORE THAN I CAN SAY FOR MOST OF YOUR BUDDIES.
I HEARD. ARE TORRES AND HOPKINS STILL ALIVE?
TORRES IS IN THE STOCKADE. HOPKINS, I DON'T KNOW ABOUT.
BOTH GOOD MEN. THEY ALL WERE.
YOU WANT TO TELL ME WHY SOMEONE IS KILLING THESE GOOD MEN?
CAN YOU ARRANGE FOR POLICE PROTECTION FOR ME?
I'M PRETTY SURE I CAN.
WELL, I GUESS IT STARTED ON THE *MEKONG RIVER!* WE WERE ASSIGNED TO CLEAR THE CAMBODIAN SIDE AND CUT OFF THE ROUTE TO PHNOM PENH...
WE'LL MOVE UP AS FAR AS NEAK LOEANG AND OFFLOAD SUPPLIES...
"BUT WE ALL KNEW WE WEREN'T THERE JUST TO DROP OFF CARE PACKAGES. SOMETHING *BIGGER* WAS UP..."
KEEP YOUR EYES PEELED!
FOR WHAT, SIR?
JUST KEEP WATCHING. YOU'LL SEE *"FOR WHAT"!*

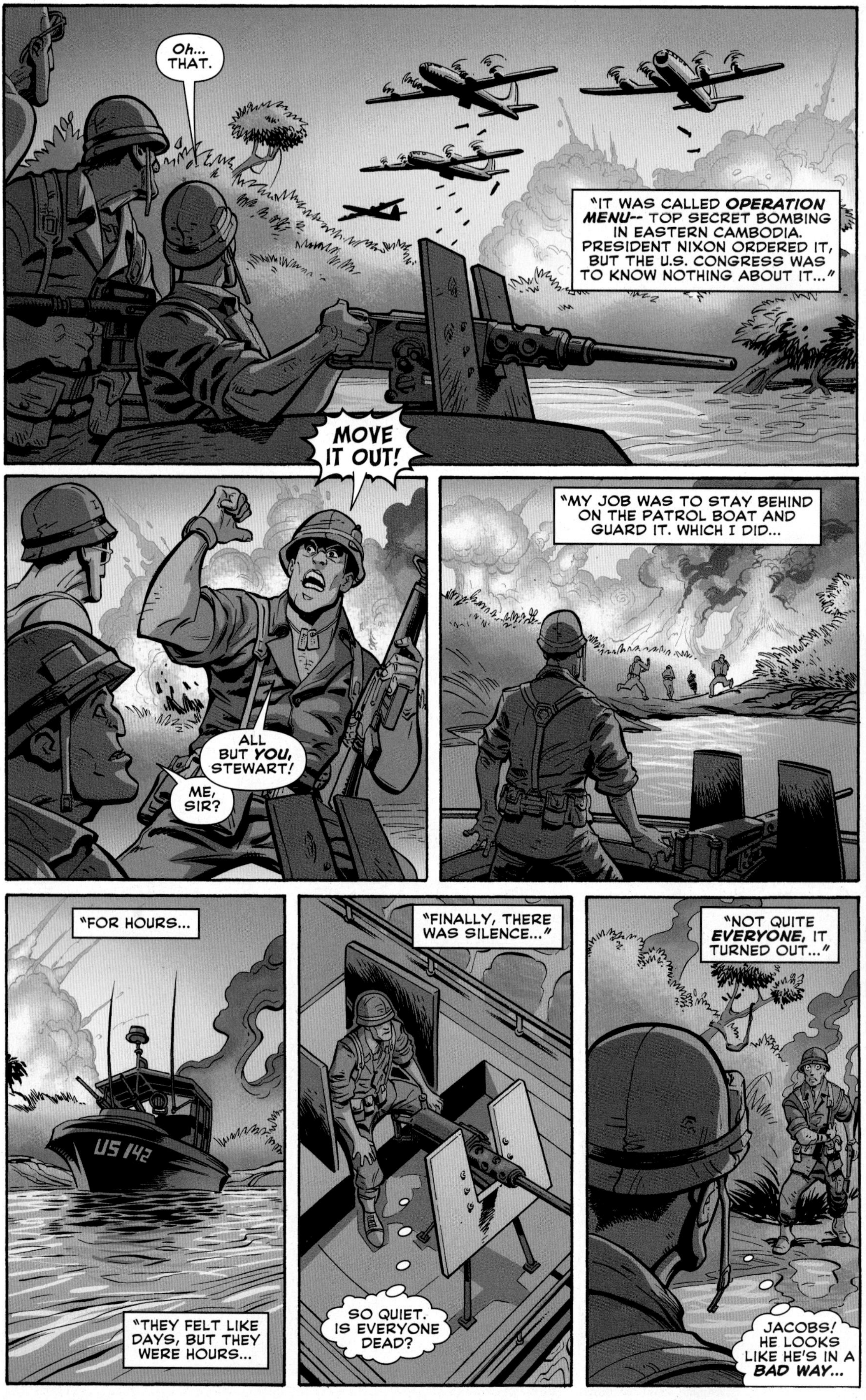
Oh...
THAT.
"IT WAS CALLED OPERATION MENU-- TOP SECRET BOMBING IN EASTERN CAMBODIA. PRESIDENT NIXON ORDERED IT, BUT THE U.S. CONGRESS WAS TO KNOW NOTHING ABOUT IT..."
MOVE IT OUT!
ALL BUT YOU, STEWART!
ME, SIR?
"MY JOB WAS TO STAY BEHIND ON THE PATROL BOAT AND GUARD IT. WHICH I DID...
"FOR HOURS...
US 142
"THEY FELT LIKE DAYS, BUT THEY WERE HOURS...
"FINALLY, THERE WAS SILENCE..."
SO QUIET. IS EVERYONE DEAD?
"NOT QUITE EVERYONE, IT TURNED OUT..."
JACOBS! HE LOOKS LIKE HE'S IN A BAD WAY...

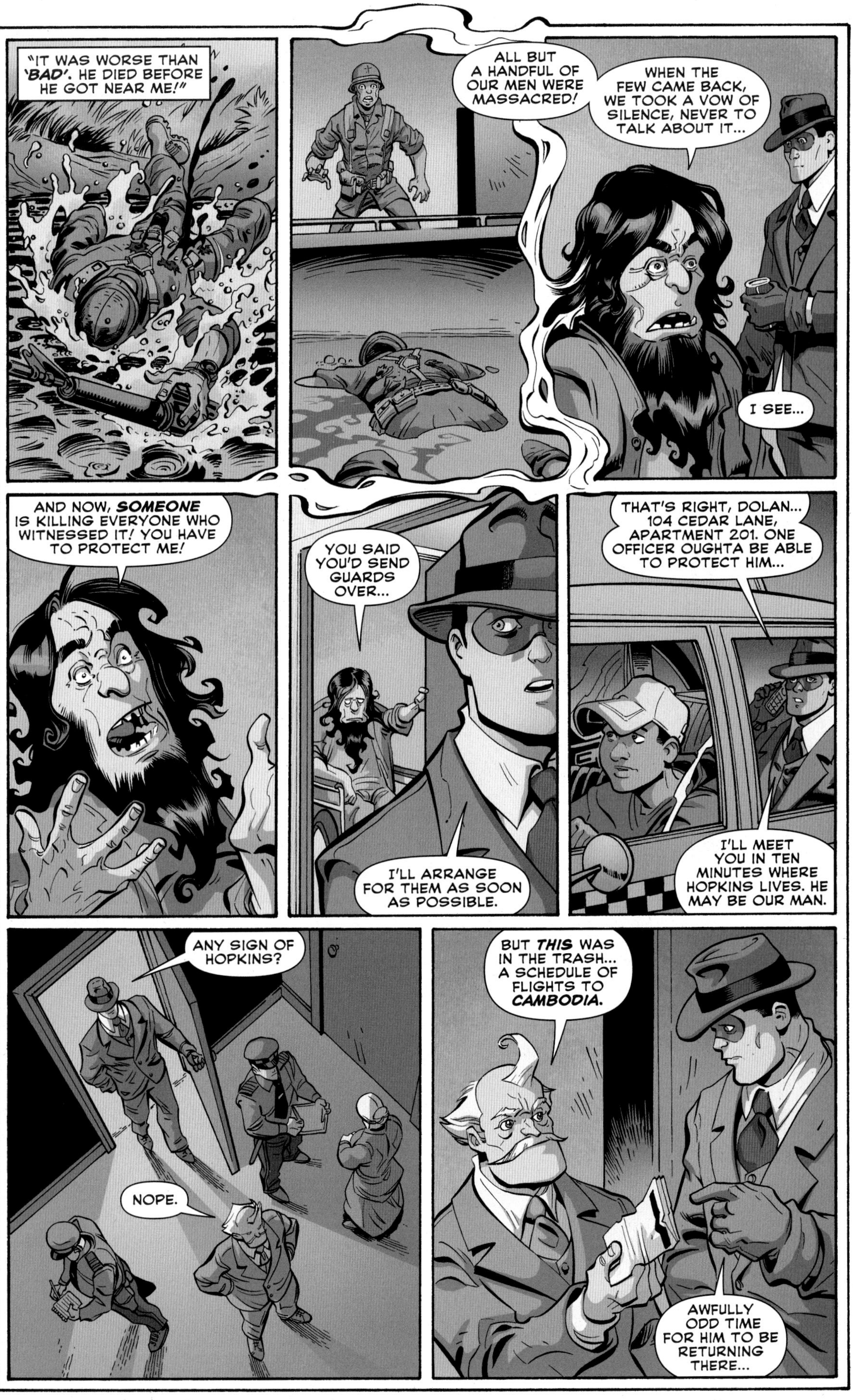
"IT WAS WORSE THAN 'BAD'. HE DIED BEFORE HE GOT NEAR ME!"
ALL BUT A HANDFUL OF OUR MEN WERE MASSACRED!
WHEN THE FEW CAME BACK, WE TOOK A VOW OF SILENCE, NEVER TO TALK ABOUT IT...
I SEE...
AND NOW, SOMEONE IS KILLING EVERYONE WHO WITNESSED IT! YOU HAVE TO PROTECT ME!
YOU SAID YOU'D SEND GUARDS OVER...
I'LL ARRANGE FOR THEM AS SOON AS POSSIBLE.
THAT'S RIGHT, DOLAN... 104 CEDAR LANE, APARTMENT 201. ONE OFFICER OUGHTA BE ABLE TO PROTECT HIM...
I'LL MEET YOU IN TEN MINUTES WHERE HOPKINS LIVES. HE MAY BE OUR MAN.
ANY SIGN OF HOPKINS?
NOPE.
BUT THIS WAS IN THE TRASH... A SCHEDULE OF FLIGHTS TO CAMBODIA.
AWFULLY ODD TIME FOR HIM TO BE RETURNING THERE...

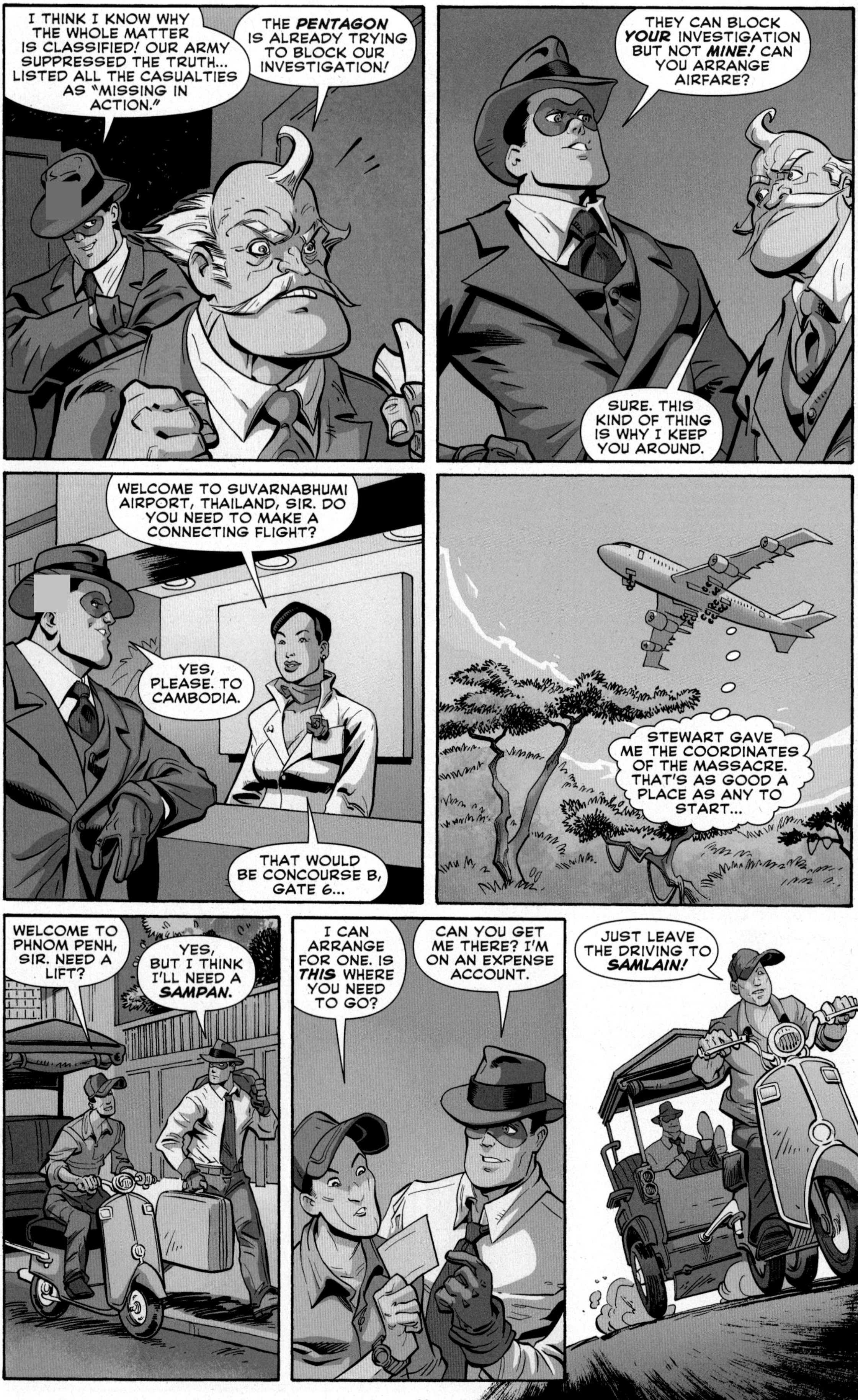
I THINK I KNOW WHY THE WHOLE MATTER IS CLASSIFIED! OUR ARMY SUPPRESSED THE TRUTH... LISTED ALL THE CASUALTIES AS "MISSING IN ACTION."
THE PENTAGON IS ALREADY TRYING TO BLOCK OUR INVESTIGATION!
THEY CAN BLOCK YOUR INVESTIGATION BUT NOT MINE! CAN YOU ARRANGE AIRFARE?
SURE. THIS KIND OF THING IS WHY I KEEP YOU AROUND.
WELCOME TO SUVARNABHUMI AIRPORT, THAILAND, SIR. DO YOU NEED TO MAKE A CONNECTING FLIGHT?
YES, PLEASE. TO CAMBODIA.
THAT WOULD BE CONCOURSE B, GATE 6...
STEWART GAVE ME THE COORDINATES OF THE MASSACRE. THAT'S AS GOOD A PLACE AS ANY TO START...
WELCOME TO PHNOM PENH, SIR. NEED A LIFT?
YES, BUT I THINK I'LL NEED A SAMPAN.
I CAN ARRANGE FOR ONE. IS THIS WHERE YOU NEED TO GO?
CAN YOU GET ME THERE? I'M ON AN EXPENSE ACCOUNT.
JUST LEAVE THE DRIVING TO SAMLAIN!

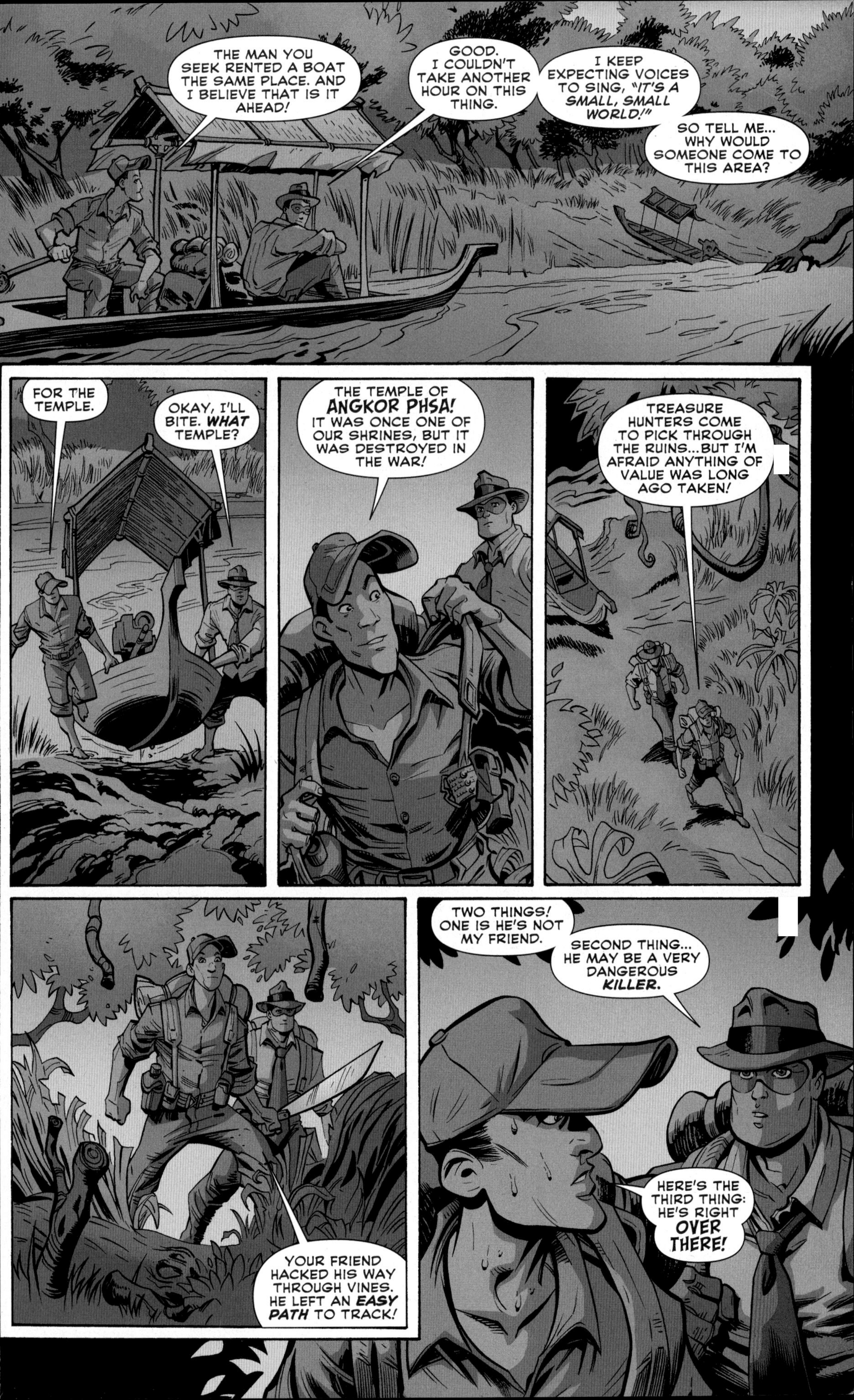
THE MAN YOU SEEK RENTED A BOAT THE SAME PLACE. AND I BELIEVE THAT IS IT AHEAD!
GOOD. I COULDN'T TAKE ANOTHER HOUR ON THIS THING.
I KEEP EXPECTING VOICES TO SING, "IT'S A SMALL, SMALL WORLD!"
SO TELL ME... WHY WOULD SOMEONE COME TO THIS AREA?
FOR THE TEMPLE.
OKAY, I'LL BITE. WHAT TEMPLE?
THE TEMPLE OF ANGKOR PHSA! IT WAS ONCE ONE OF OUR SHRINES, BUT IT WAS DESTROYED IN THE WAR!
TREASURE HUNTERS COME TO PICK THROUGH THE RUINS...BUT I'M AFRAID ANYTHING OF VALUE WAS LONG AGO TAKEN!
YOUR FRIEND HACKED HIS WAY THROUGH VINES. HE LEFT AN EASY PATH TO TRACK!
TWO THINGS! ONE IS HE'S NOT MY FRIEND.
SECOND THING... HE MAY BE A VERY DANGEROUS KILLER.
HERE'S THE THIRD THING: HE'S RIGHT OVER THERE!

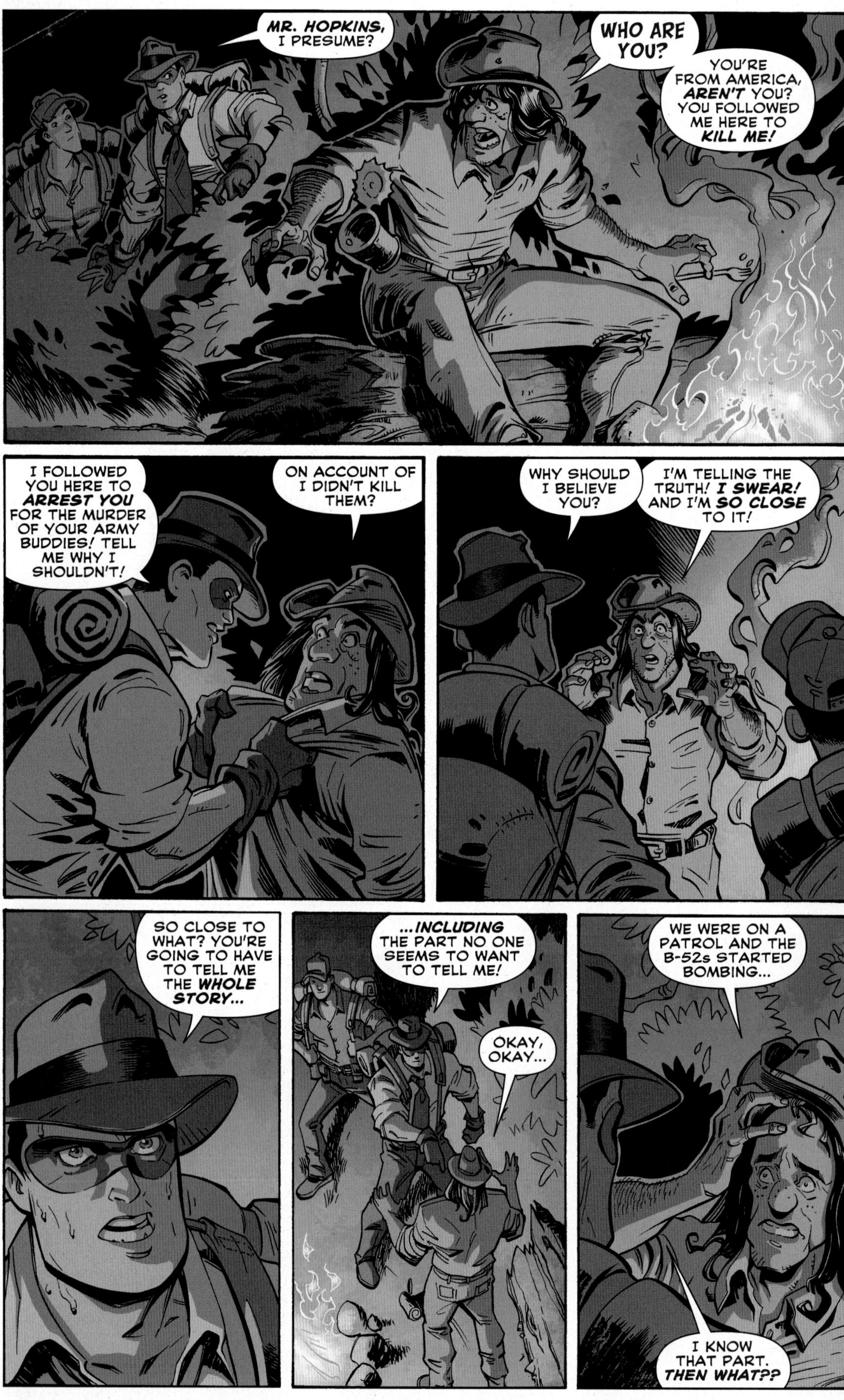
MR. HOPKINS, I PRESUME?
WHO ARE YOU?
YOU'RE FROM AMERICA, AREN'T YOU? YOU FOLLOWED ME HERE TO KILL ME!
I FOLLOWED YOU HERE TO ARREST YOU FOR THE MURDER OF YOUR ARMY BUDDIES! TELL ME WHY I SHOULDN'T!
ON ACCOUNT OF I DIDN'T KILL THEM?
WHY SHOULD I BELIEVE YOU?
I'M TELLING THE TRUTH! I SWEAR! AND I'M SO CLOSE TO IT!
SO CLOSE TO WHAT? YOU'RE GOING TO HAVE TO TELL ME THE WHOLE STORY...
...INCLUDING THE PART NO ONE SEEMS TO WANT TO TELL ME!
OKAY, OKAY...
WE WERE ON A PATROL AND THE B-52s STARTED BOMBING...
I KNOW THAT PART. THEN WHAT??

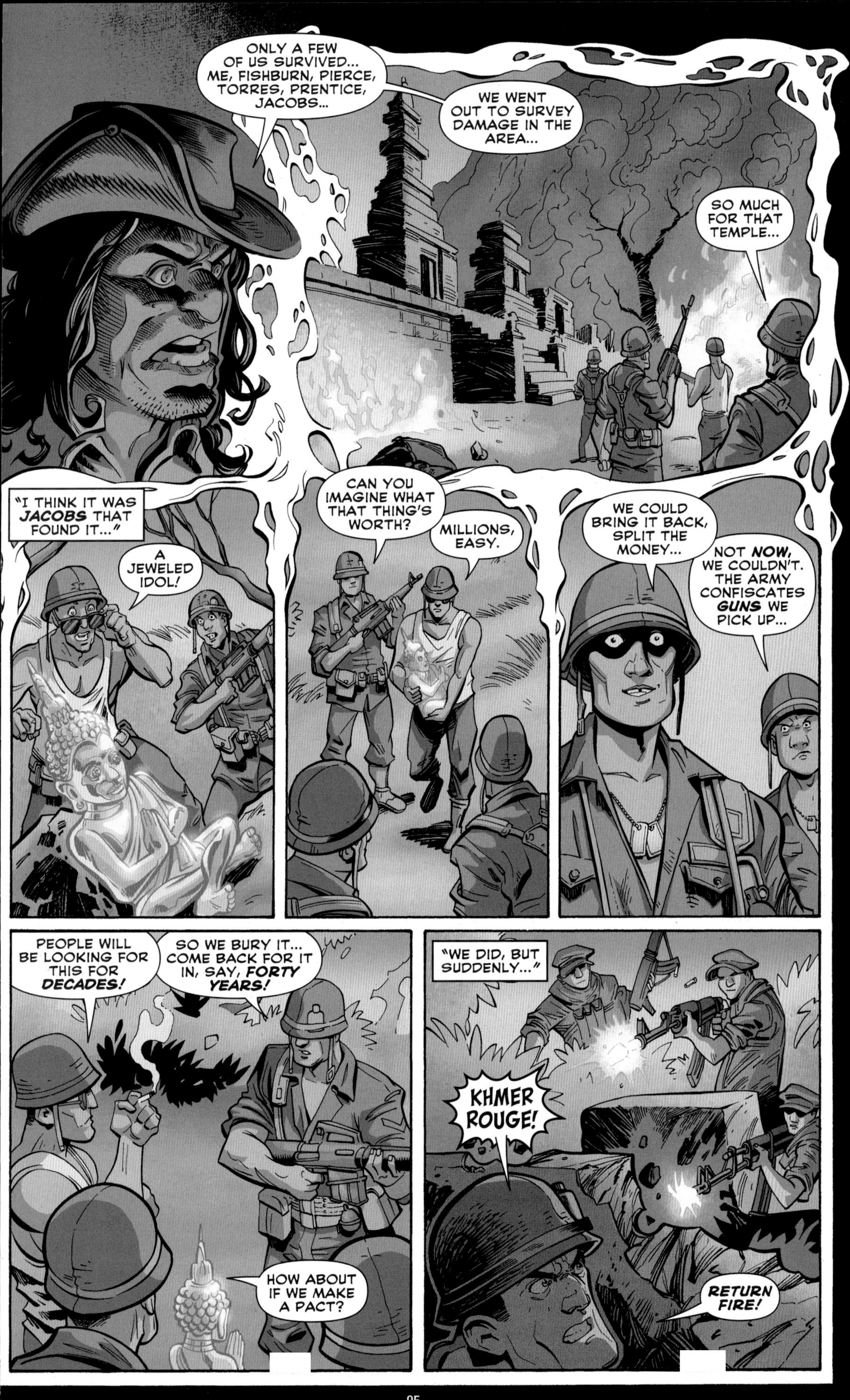

ONLY A FEW OF US SURVIVED... ME, FISHBURN, PIERCE, TORRES, PRENTICE, JACOBS...
WE WENT OUT TO SURVEY DAMAGE IN THE AREA...
SO MUCH FOR THAT TEMPLE...
"I THINK IT WAS JACOBS THAT FOUND IT..."
A JEWELED IDOL!
CAN YOU IMAGINE WHAT THAT THING'S WORTH?
MILLIONS, EASY.
WE COULD BRING IT BACK, SPLIT THE MONEY...
NOT NOW, WE COULDN'T. THE ARMY CONFISCATES GUNS WE PICK UP...
PEOPLE WILL BE LOOKING FOR THIS FOR DECADES!
SO WE BURY IT... COME BACK FOR IT IN, SAY, FORTY YEARS!
HOW ABOUT IF WE MAKE A PACT?
"WE DID, BUT SUDDENLY..."
KHMER ROUGE!
RETURN FIRE!

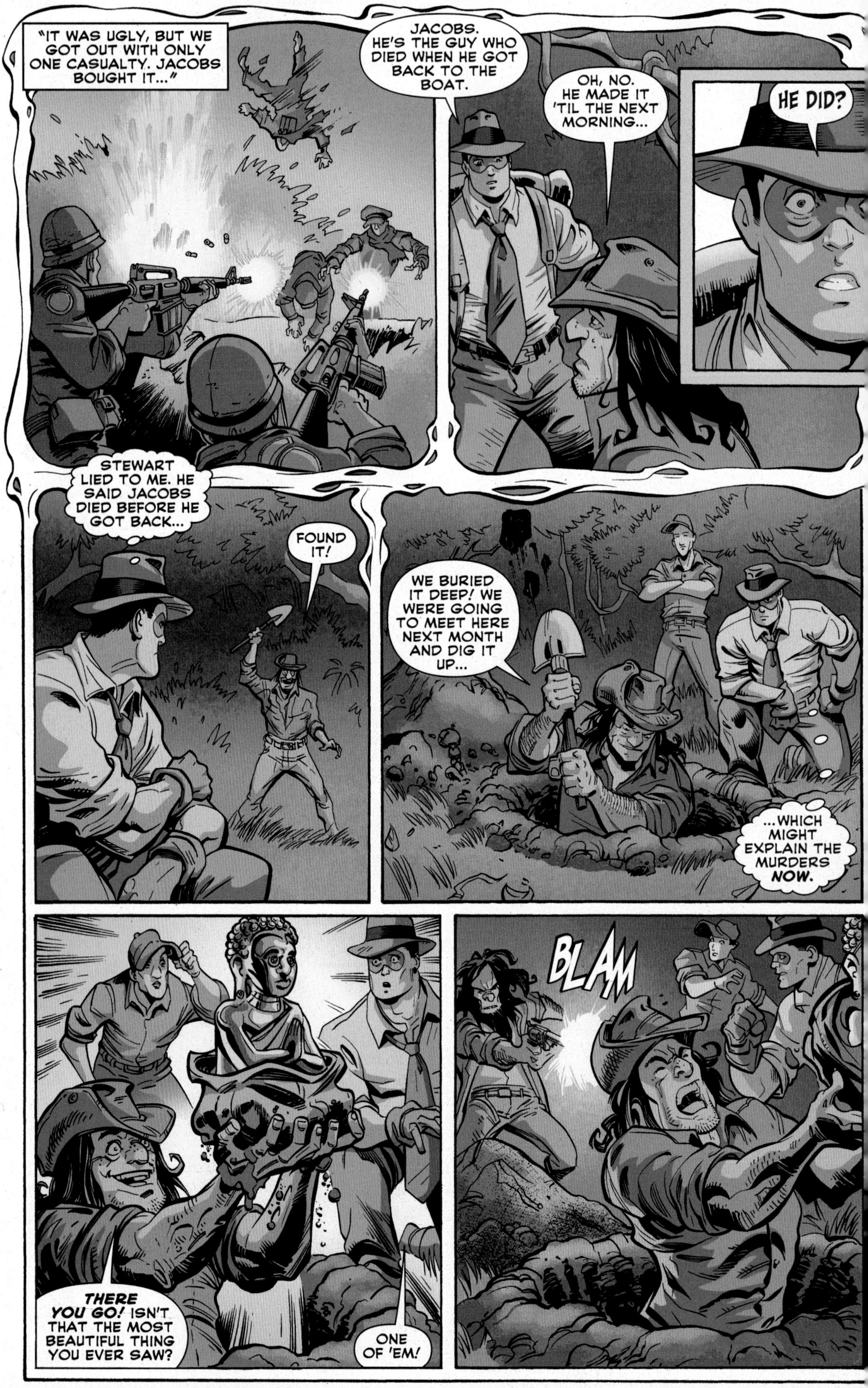
"IT WAS UGLY, BUT WE GOT OUT WITH ONLY ONE CASUALTY. JACOBS BOUGHT IT..."
JACOBS. HE'S THE GUY WHO DIED WHEN HE GOT BACK TO THE BOAT.
OH, NO. HE MADE IT 'TIL THE NEXT MORNING...
HE DID?
STEWART LIED TO ME. HE SAID JACOBS DIED BEFORE HE GOT BACK...
FOUND IT!
WE BURIED IT DEEP! WE WERE GOING TO MEET HERE NEXT MONTH AND DIG IT UP...
...WHICH MIGHT EXPLAIN THE MURDERS NOW.
THERE YOU GO! ISN'T THAT THE MOST BEAUTIFUL THING YOU EVER SAW?
ONE OF 'EM!
BLAM

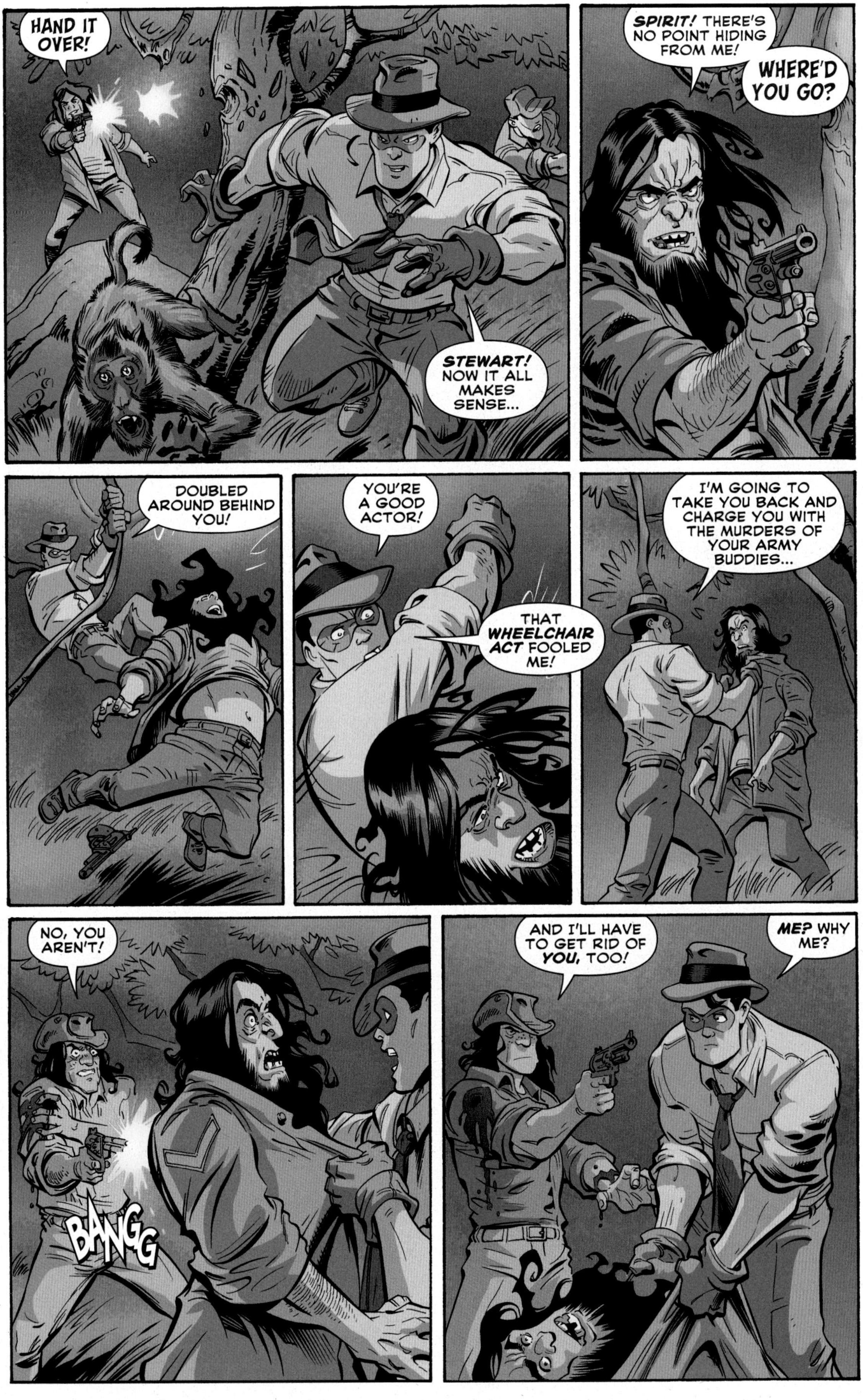
HAND IT OVER!
STEWART! NOW IT ALL MAKES SENSE...
SPIRIT! THERE'S NO POINT HIDING FROM ME!
WHERE'D YOU GO?
DOUBLED AROUND BEHIND YOU!
YOU'RE A GOOD ACTOR!
THAT WHEELCHAIR ACT FOOLED ME!
I'M GOING TO TAKE YOU BACK AND CHARGE YOU WITH THE MURDERS OF YOUR ARMY BUDDIES...
NO, YOU AREN'T!
BANGG
AND I'LL HAVE TO GET RID OF YOU, TOO!
ME? WHY ME?

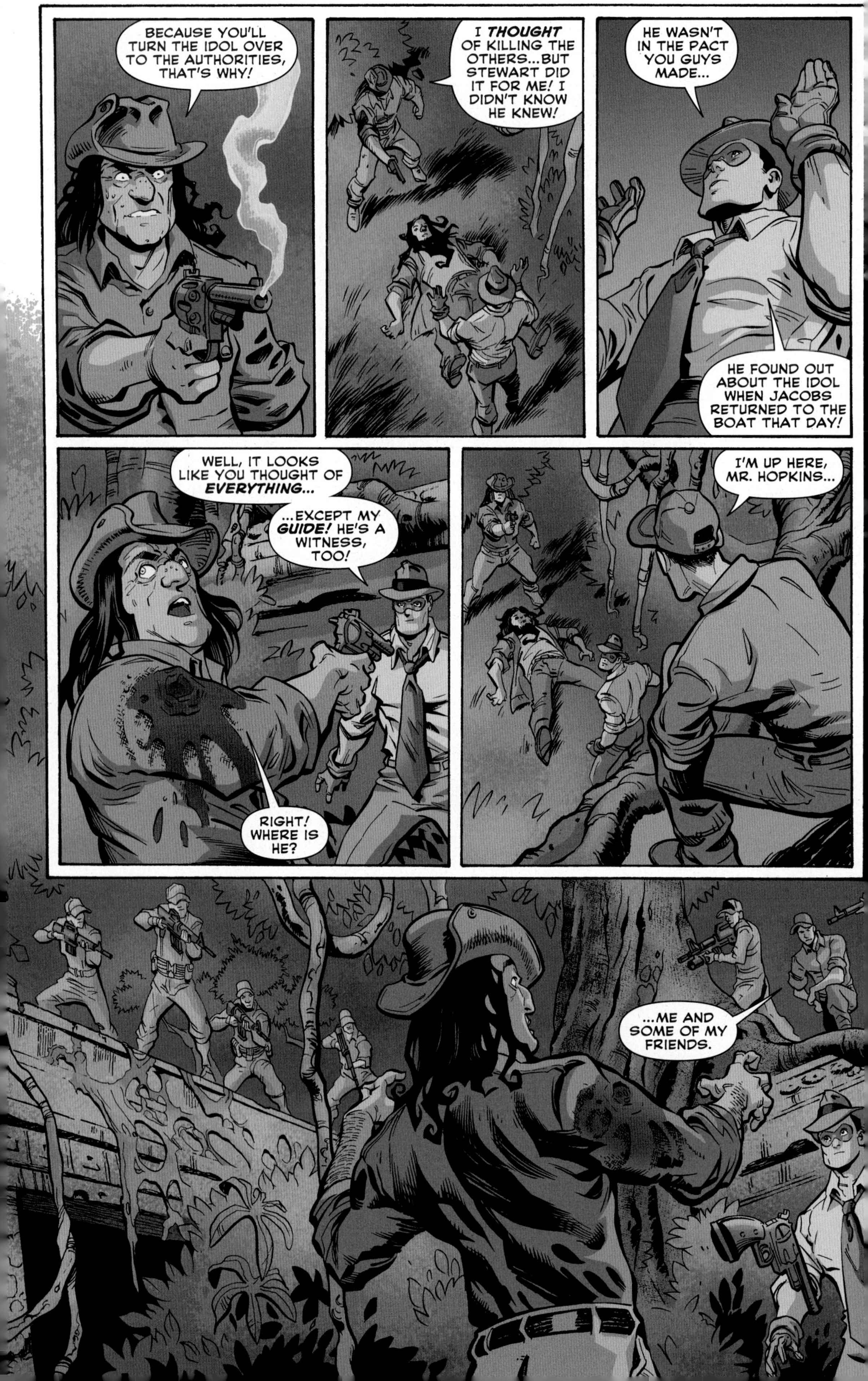
BECAUSE YOU'LL TURN THE IDOL OVER TO THE AUTHORITIES, THAT'S WHY!
I THOUGHT OF KILLING THE OTHERS...BUT STEWART DID IT FOR ME! I DIDN'T KNOW HE KNEW!
HE WASN'T IN THE PACT YOU GUYS MADE...
HE FOUND OUT ABOUT THE IDOL WHEN JACOBS RETURNED TO THE BOAT THAT DAY!
WELL, IT LOOKS LIKE YOU THOUGHT OF EVERYTHING...
...EXCEPT MY GUIDE! HE'S A WITNESS, TOO!
RIGHT! WHERE IS HE?
I'M UP HERE, MR. HOPKINS...
...ME AND SOME OF MY FRIENDS.

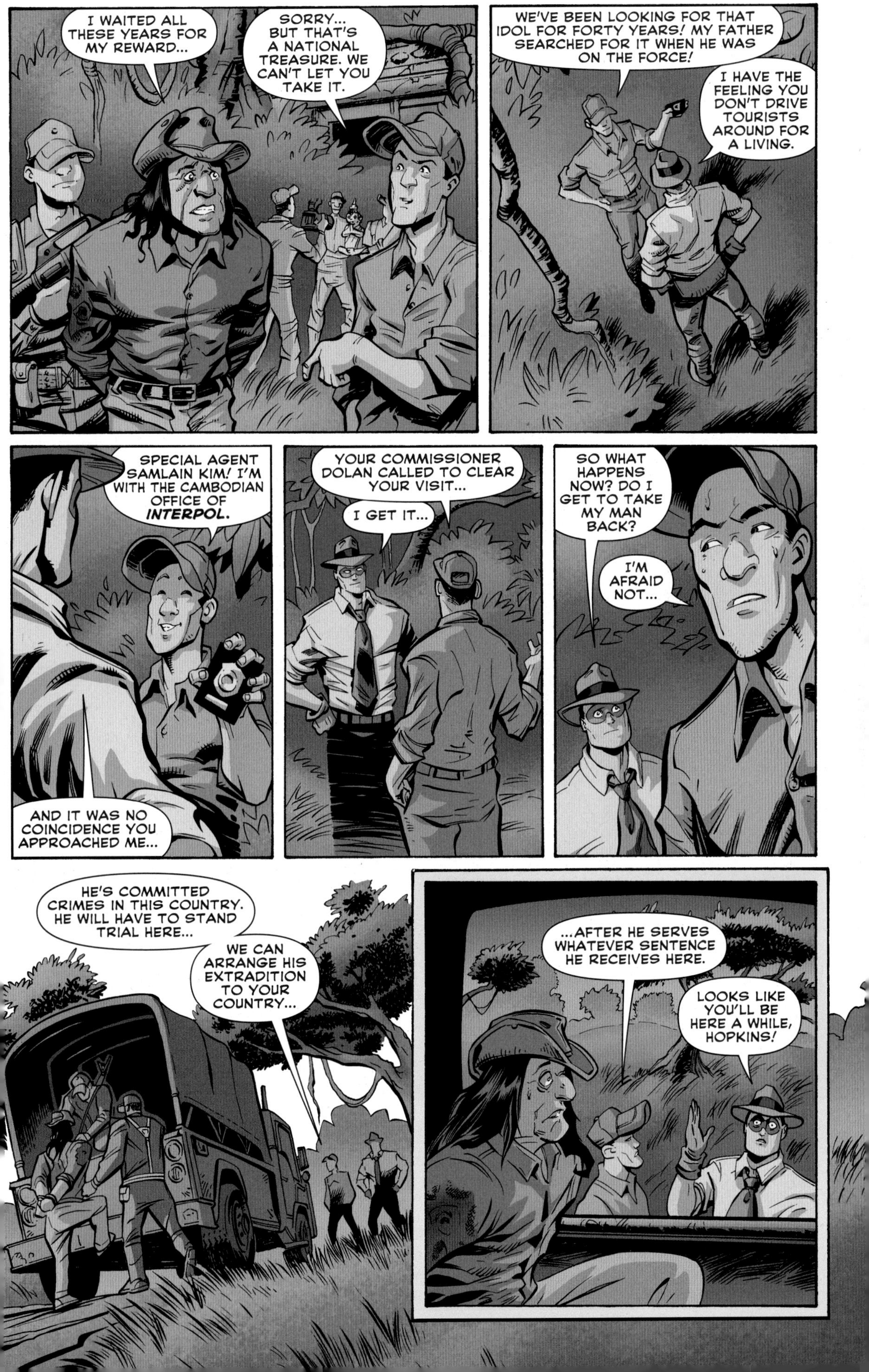
I WAITED ALL THESE YEARS FOR MY REWARD...
SORRY... BUT THAT'S A NATIONAL TREASURE. WE CAN'T LET YOU TAKE IT.
WE'VE BEEN LOOKING FOR THAT IDOL FOR FORTY YEARS! MY FATHER SEARCHED FOR IT WHEN HE WAS ON THE FORCE!
I HAVE THE FEELING YOU DON'T DRIVE TOURISTS AROUND FOR A LIVING.
SPECIAL AGENT SAMLAIN KIM! I'M WITH THE CAMBODIAN OFFICE OF ***INTERPOL***.
AND IT WAS NO COINCIDENCE YOU APPROACHED ME...
YOUR COMMISSIONER DOLAN CALLED TO CLEAR YOUR VISIT...
I GET IT...
SO WHAT HAPPENS NOW? DO I GET TO TAKE MY MAN BACK?
I'M AFRAID NOT...
HE'S COMMITTED CRIMES IN THIS COUNTRY. HE WILL HAVE TO STAND TRIAL HERE...
WE CAN ARRANGE HIS EXTRADITION TO YOUR COUNTRY...
...AFTER HE SERVES WHATEVER SENTENCE HE RECEIVES HERE.
LOOKS LIKE YOU'LL BE HERE A WHILE, HOPKINS!

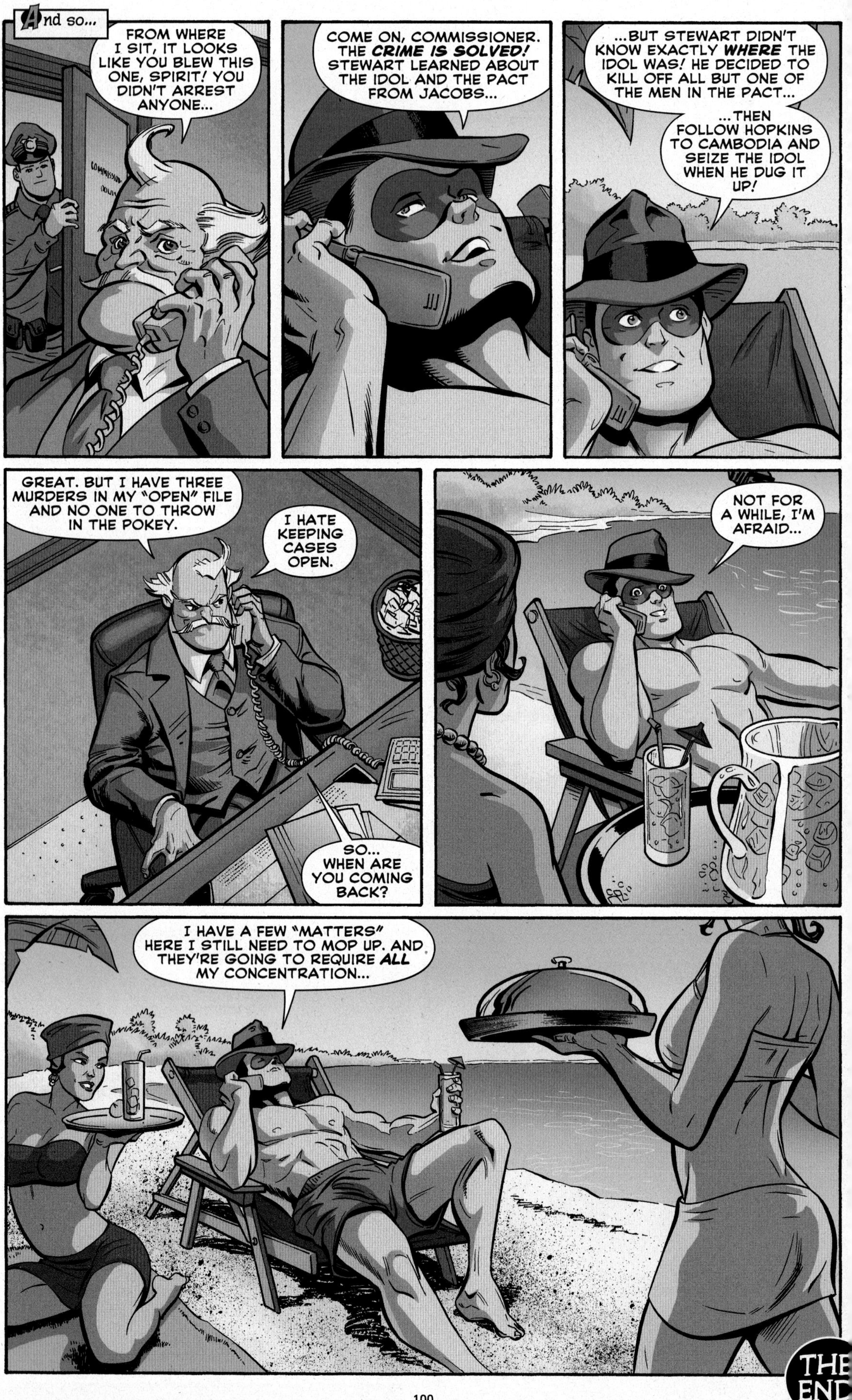
And so...
FROM WHERE I SIT, IT LOOKS LIKE YOU BLEW THIS ONE, SPIRIT! YOU DIDN'T ARREST ANYONE...
COME ON, COMMISSIONER. THE CRIME IS SOLVED! STEWART LEARNED ABOUT THE IDOL AND THE PACT FROM JACOBS...
...BUT STEWART DIDN'T KNOW EXACTLY WHERE THE IDOL WAS! HE DECIDED TO KILL OFF ALL BUT ONE OF THE MEN IN THE PACT...
...THEN FOLLOW HOPKINS TO CAMBODIA AND SEIZE THE IDOL WHEN HE DUG IT UP!
GREAT. BUT I HAVE THREE MURDERS IN MY "OPEN" FILE AND NO ONE TO THROW IN THE POKEY.
I HATE KEEPING CASES OPEN.
SO... WHEN ARE YOU COMING BACK?
NOT FOR A WHILE, I'M AFRAID...
I HAVE A FEW "MATTERS" HERE I STILL NEED TO MOP UP. AND THEY'RE GOING TO REQUIRE ALL MY CONCENTRATION...
THE END

5

ACTION • Mystery • ADVENTURE

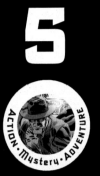

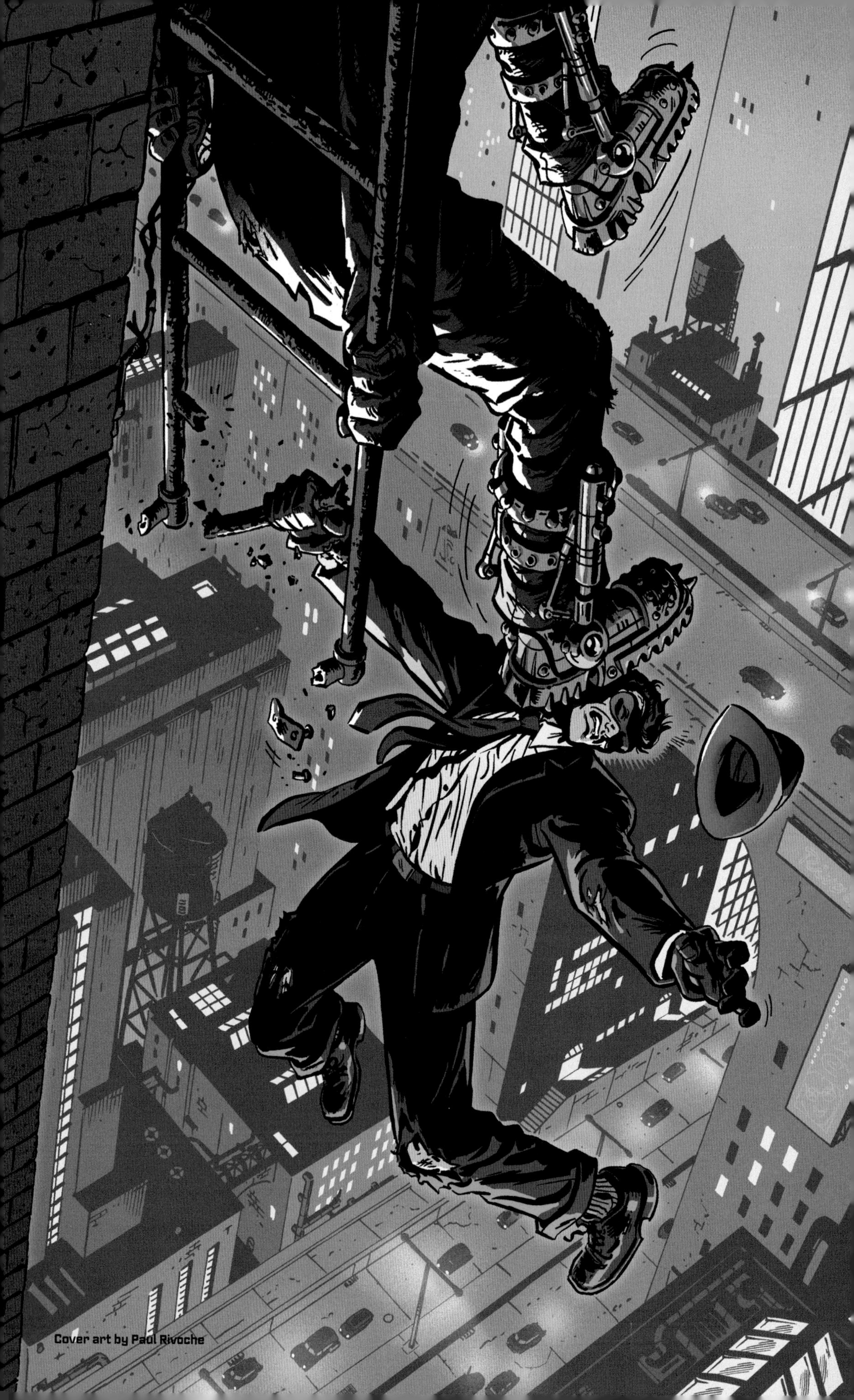

Cover art by Paul Rivoche

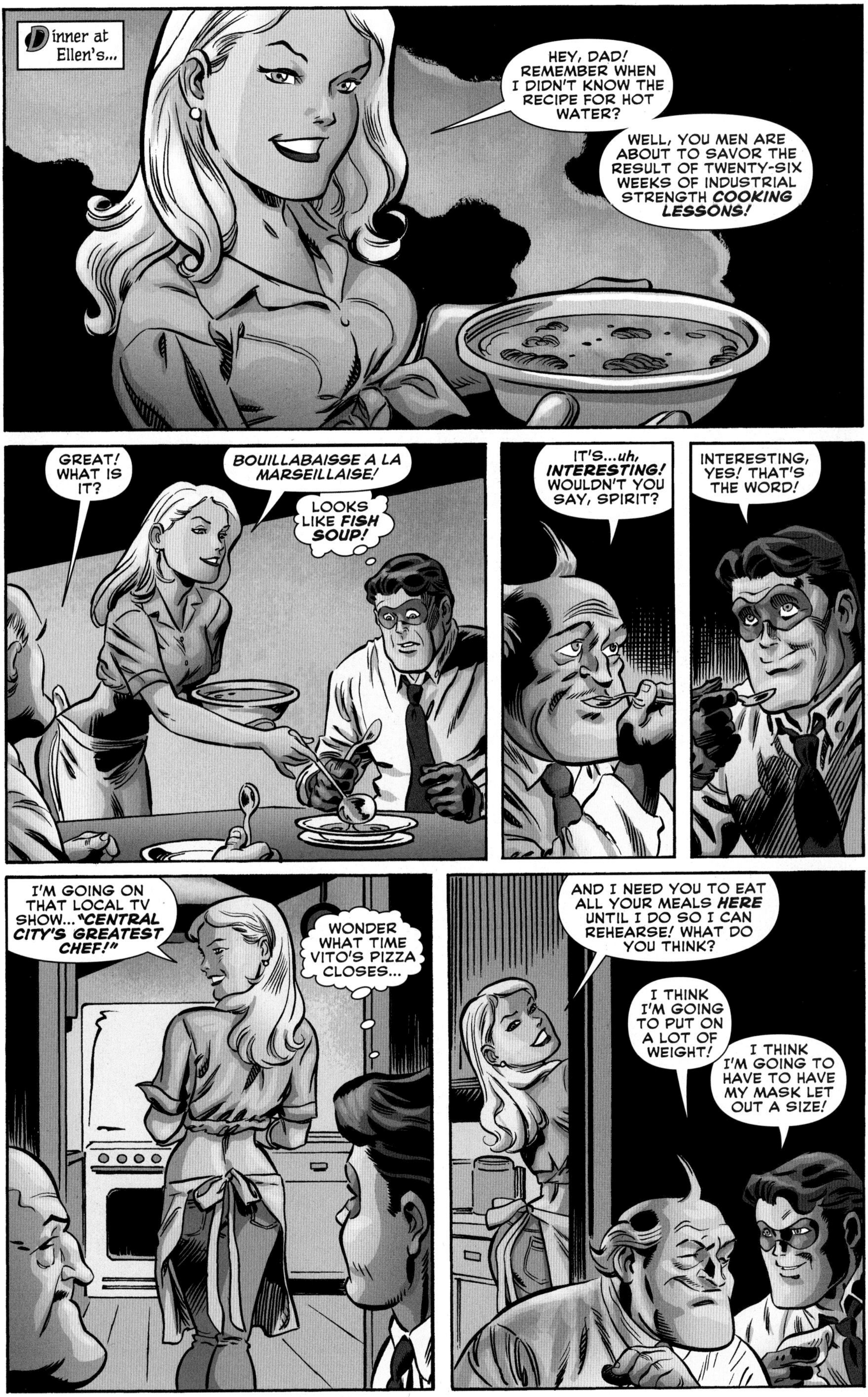
Dinner at Ellen's...
HEY, DAD! REMEMBER WHEN I DIDN'T KNOW THE RECIPE FOR HOT WATER?
WELL, YOU MEN ARE ABOUT TO SAVOR THE RESULT OF TWENTY-SIX WEEKS OF INDUSTRIAL STRENGTH COOKING LESSONS!
GREAT! WHAT IS IT?
BOUILLABAISSE A LA MARSEILLAISE!
LOOKS LIKE FISH SOUP!
IT'S...uh, INTERESTING! WOULDN'T YOU SAY, SPIRIT?
INTERESTING, YES! THAT'S THE WORD!
I'M GOING ON THAT LOCAL TV SHOW... "CENTRAL CITY'S GREATEST CHEF!"
WONDER WHAT TIME VITO'S PIZZA CLOSES...
AND I NEED YOU TO EAT ALL YOUR MEALS HERE UNTIL I DO SO I CAN REHEARSE! WHAT DO YOU THINK?
I THINK I'M GOING TO PUT ON A LOT OF WEIGHT!
I THINK I'M GOING TO HAVE TO HAVE MY MASK LET OUT A SIZE!

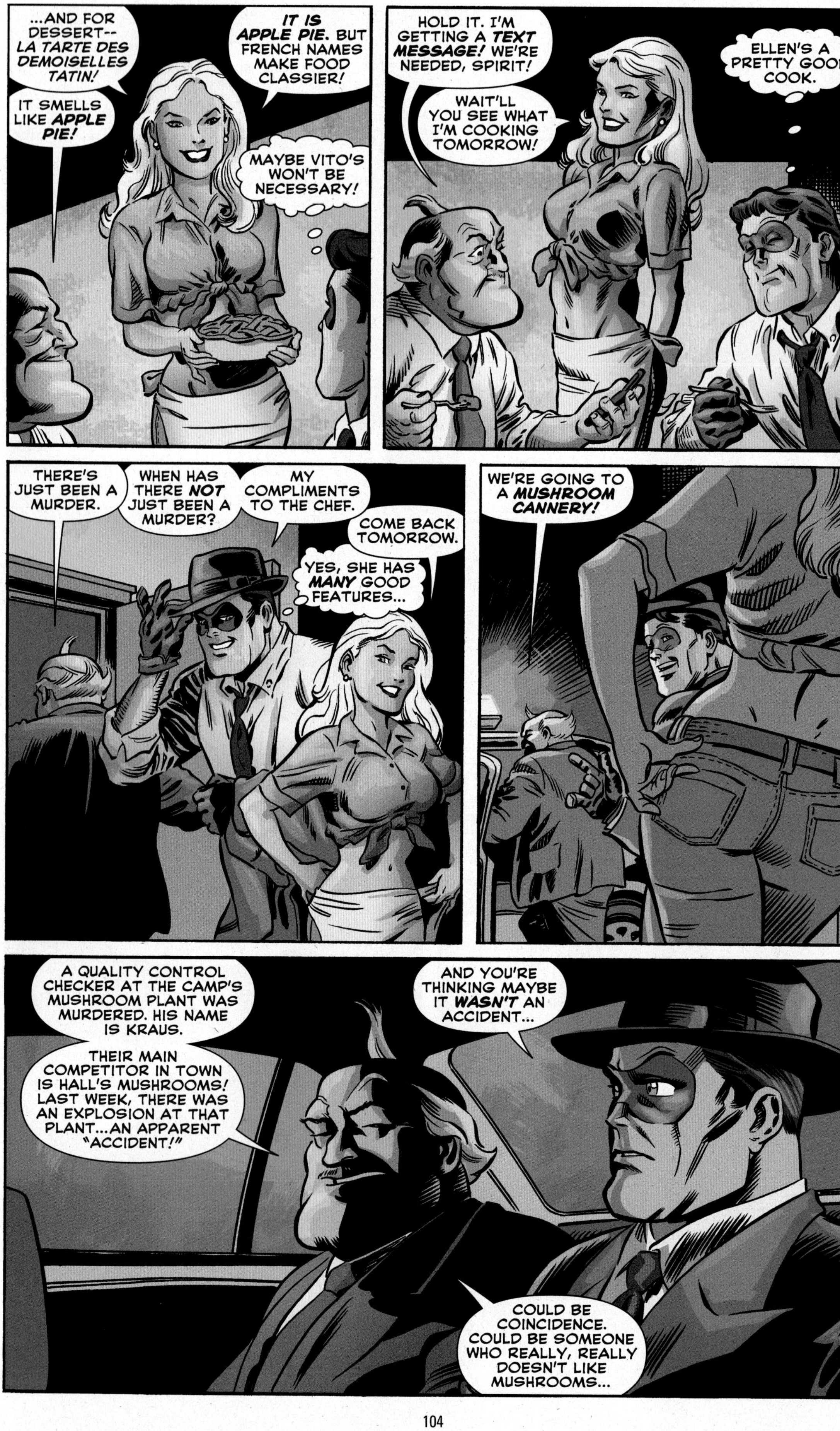
...AND FOR DESSERT-- LA TARTE DES DEMOISELLES TATIN!
IT SMELLS LIKE APPLE PIE!
IT IS APPLE PIE. BUT FRENCH NAMES MAKE FOOD CLASSIER!
MAYBE VITO'S WON'T BE NECESSARY!
HOLD IT. I'M GETTING A TEXT MESSAGE! WE'RE NEEDED, SPIRIT!
WAIT'LL YOU SEE WHAT I'M COOKING TOMORROW!
ELLEN'S A PRETTY GOOD COOK.
THERE'S JUST BEEN A MURDER.
WHEN HAS THERE NOT JUST BEEN A MURDER?
MY COMPLIMENTS TO THE CHEF.
COME BACK TOMORROW.
YES, SHE HAS MANY GOOD FEATURES...
WE'RE GOING TO A MUSHROOM CANNERY!
A QUALITY CONTROL CHECKER AT THE CAMP'S MUSHROOM PLANT WAS MURDERED. HIS NAME IS KRAUS.
THEIR MAIN COMPETITOR IN TOWN IS HALL'S MUSHROOMS! LAST WEEK, THERE WAS AN EXPLOSION AT THAT PLANT...AN APPARENT "ACCIDENT!"
AND YOU'RE THINKING MAYBE IT WASN'T AN ACCIDENT...
COULD BE COINCIDENCE. COULD BE SOMEONE WHO REALLY, REALLY DOESN'T LIKE MUSHROOMS...

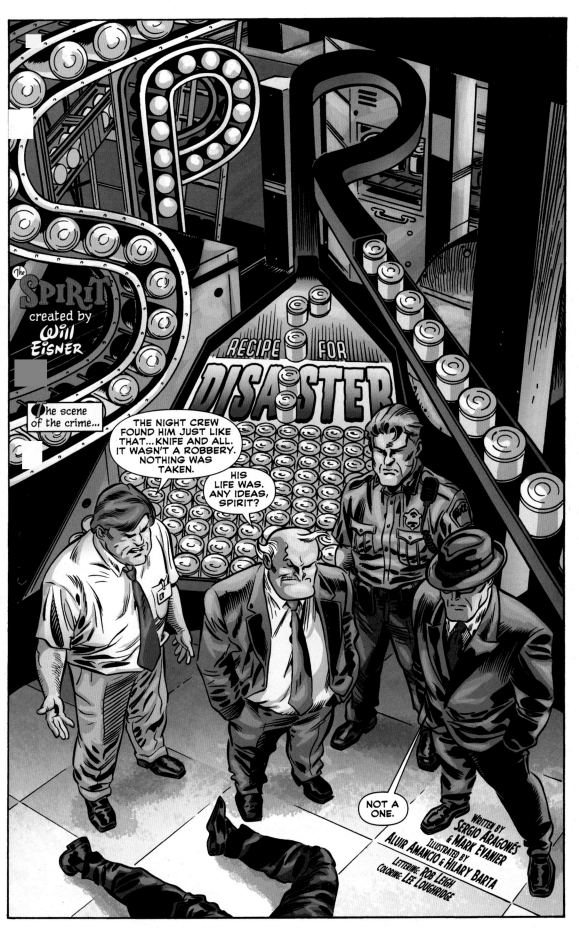

The SPIRIT created by Will Eisner

RECIPE FOR DISASTER

The scene of the crime...

THE NIGHT CREW FOUND HIM JUST LIKE THAT...KNIFE AND ALL. IT WASN'T A ROBBERY. NOTHING WAS TAKEN.

HIS LIFE WAS. ANY IDEAS, SPIRIT?

NOT A ONE.

WRITTEN BY SERGIO ARAGONÉS & MARK EVANIER
ILLUSTRATED BY ALUIR AMANCIO & HILARY BARTA
LETTERING: ROB LEIGH
COLORING: LEE LOUGHRIDGE

WHAT GIVES, COMMISSIONER? YOU HEARD ABOUT WHAT HAPPENED AT HALL'S MUSHROOMS LAST WEEK.

IMPORTING AND CANNING MUSHROOMS ISN'T SUPPOSED TO BE *DANGEROUS!*

ALL YOU DO HERE IS CAN THEM, *huh?*

FIRST THING I WANT TO DO IS CLOSE THE PLANT DOWN. HALT ALL PRODUCTION. NOTHING GOES IN OR OUT.

I'LL GET ON IT RIGHT AWAY, COMMISSIONER.

WE HAVE EMPLOYEES WHO NEED TO MAKE A LIVING! *WHY CLOSE US DOWN?*

BECAUSE SOMEONE KILLED THE GUY IN CHARGE OF MAKING SURE YOUR PRODUCT IS SAFE! YOU DON'T SHIP ANYTHING OUT UNTIL *I SAY SO!*

BUT THERE'S NOTHING WRONG WITH OUR MUSHROOMS! SEE, I'LL EAT A WHOLE CAN OF THEM!

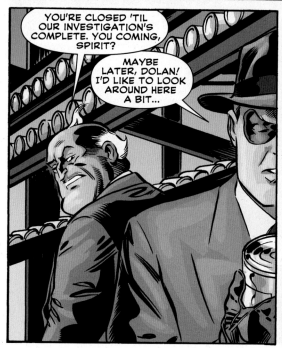

YOU'RE CLOSED 'TIL OUR INVESTIGATION'S COMPLETE. YOU COMING, SPIRIT?

MAYBE LATER, DOLAN! I'D LIKE TO LOOK AROUND HERE A BIT...

BETWEEN THE HALL COMPANY AND OURS, WE HAD 96.2% OF THE LOCAL MARKET! WHERE WILL PEOPLE GET CANNED MUSHROOMS?

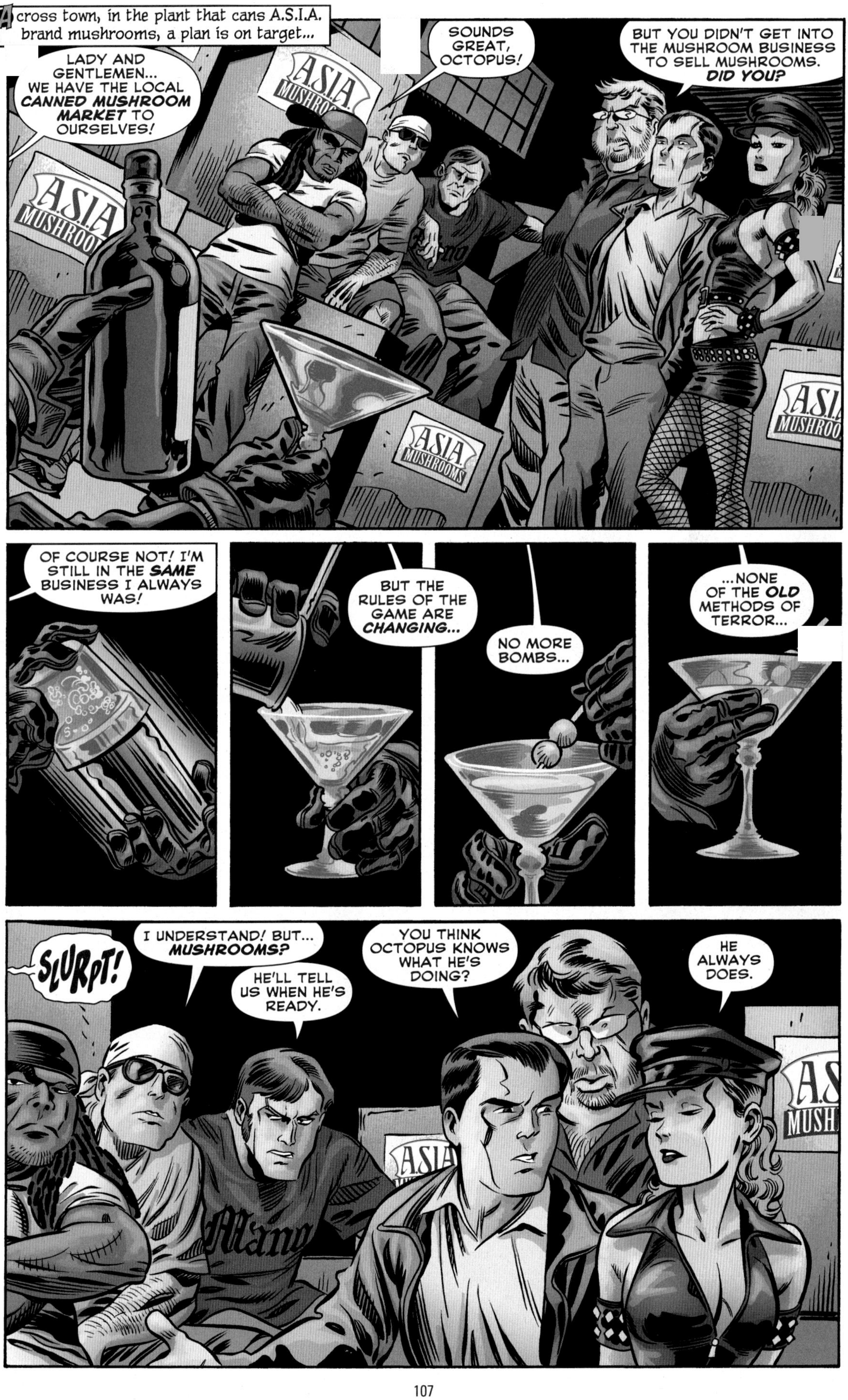
Across town, in the plant that cans A.S.I.A. brand mushrooms, a plan is on target...
LADY AND GENTLEMEN... WE HAVE THE LOCAL CANNED MUSHROOM MARKET TO OURSELVES!
SOUNDS GREAT, OCTOPUS!
BUT YOU DIDN'T GET INTO THE MUSHROOM BUSINESS TO SELL MUSHROOMS. DID YOU?
A.S.I.A. MUSHROOMS
OF COURSE NOT! I'M STILL IN THE SAME BUSINESS I ALWAYS WAS!
BUT THE RULES OF THE GAME ARE CHANGING...
NO MORE BOMBS...
...NONE OF THE OLD METHODS OF TERROR...
SLURPT!
I UNDERSTAND! BUT... MUSHROOMS?
HE'LL TELL US WHEN HE'S READY.
YOU THINK OCTOPUS KNOWS WHAT HE'S DOING?
HE ALWAYS DOES.

ALREADY, SUPPLIERS ARE CALLING FOR OUR MUSHROOMS...BUT IT'S NOT ENOUGH! I NEED TO GET OUR PRODUCT OUT THERE *QUICKLY!*

YOU GUYS GET ON THE PHONES AND *SELL HARD!* TELL BUYERS THAT NOT ONLY CAN WE DELIVER MUSHROOMS IMMEDIATELY, BUT I'VE *LOWERED* PRICES!

"LOWERED"? AREN'T YOU SUPPOSED TO *RAISE* PRICES WHEN YOU HAVE A MONOPOLY?

A.S.I.A. MUSHROOMS

I MEAN, WE *DO* HAVE TRUCKLOADS, BUT...

STILL THINK HE KNOWS WHAT'S DOING?

I THINK THE IDEA IS TO GET OUR PRODUCT INTO AS MANY STORES AS WE CAN, IMMEDIATELY.

SO LET US IN ON IT, BOSS. WHAT'S THE ANGLE?

THE LESS YOU KNOW, THE BETTER! BUT STORES ARE GETTING DESPERATE FOR CANNED MUSHROOMS...EVER SINCE WE "ARRANGED" THE LITTLE ACCIDENT THAT CLOSED THE HALL'S CANNERY...

WE'RE GOING TO CREATE THE GREATEST DISASTER IN HISTORY...

...SO GREAT THAT THEY'LL PAY ME *BILLIONS* NOT TO DO ANYTHING LIKE IT AGAIN!

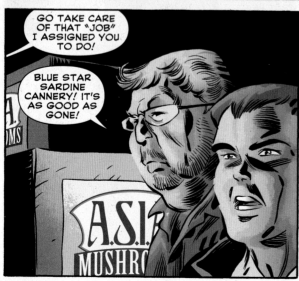

GO TAKE CARE OF THAT "JOB" I ASSIGNED YOU TO DO!

BLUE STAR SARDINE CANNERY! IT'S AS GOOD AS GONE!

SO DO YOU UNDERSTAND WHAT HE'S UP TO, BRUNO?

JUST THAT HE'S GONNA DO SOMETHING THAT'S GONNA GET A LOT OF PEOPLE KILLED... AND IT HAS SOMETHING TO DO WITH CANNED MUSHROOMS...

OTHER THAN THAT, NO.

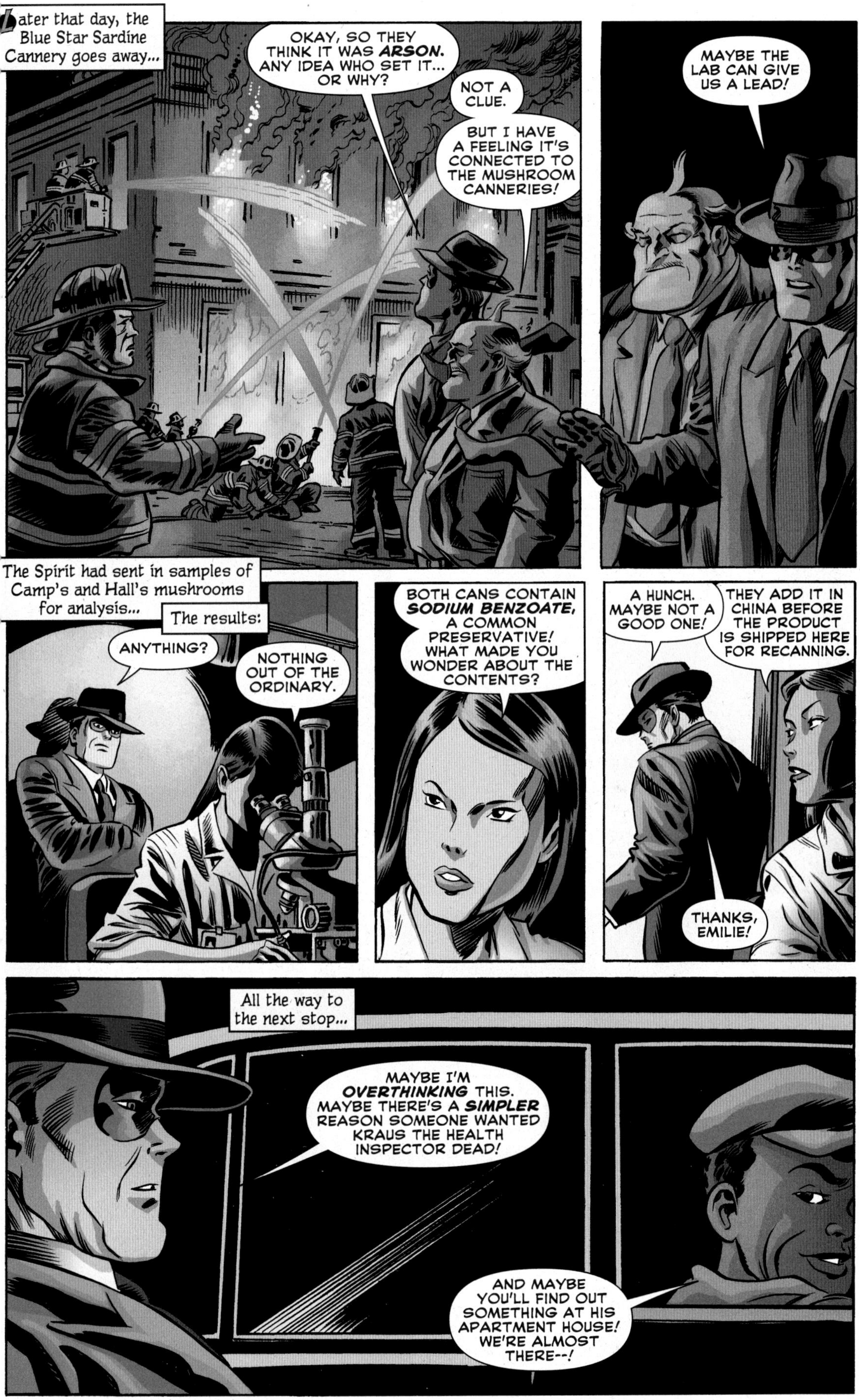
Later that day, the Blue Star Sardine Cannery goes away...
OKAY, SO THEY THINK IT WAS ARSON. ANY IDEA WHO SET IT... OR WHY?
NOT A CLUE.
BUT I HAVE A FEELING IT'S CONNECTED TO THE MUSHROOM CANNERIES!
MAYBE THE LAB CAN GIVE US A LEAD!
The Spirit had sent in samples of Camp's and Hall's mushrooms for analysis...
The results:
ANYTHING?
NOTHING OUT OF THE ORDINARY.
BOTH CANS CONTAIN SODIUM BENZOATE, A COMMON PRESERVATIVE! WHAT MADE YOU WONDER ABOUT THE CONTENTS?
A HUNCH. MAYBE NOT A GOOD ONE!
THEY ADD IT IN CHINA BEFORE THE PRODUCT IS SHIPPED HERE FOR RECANNING.
THANKS, EMILIE!
All the way to the next stop...
MAYBE I'M OVERTHINKING THIS. MAYBE THERE'S A SIMPLER REASON SOMEONE WANTED KRAUS THE HEALTH INSPECTOR DEAD!
AND MAYBE YOU'LL FIND OUT SOMETHING AT HIS APARTMENT HOUSE! WE'RE ALMOST THERE--!

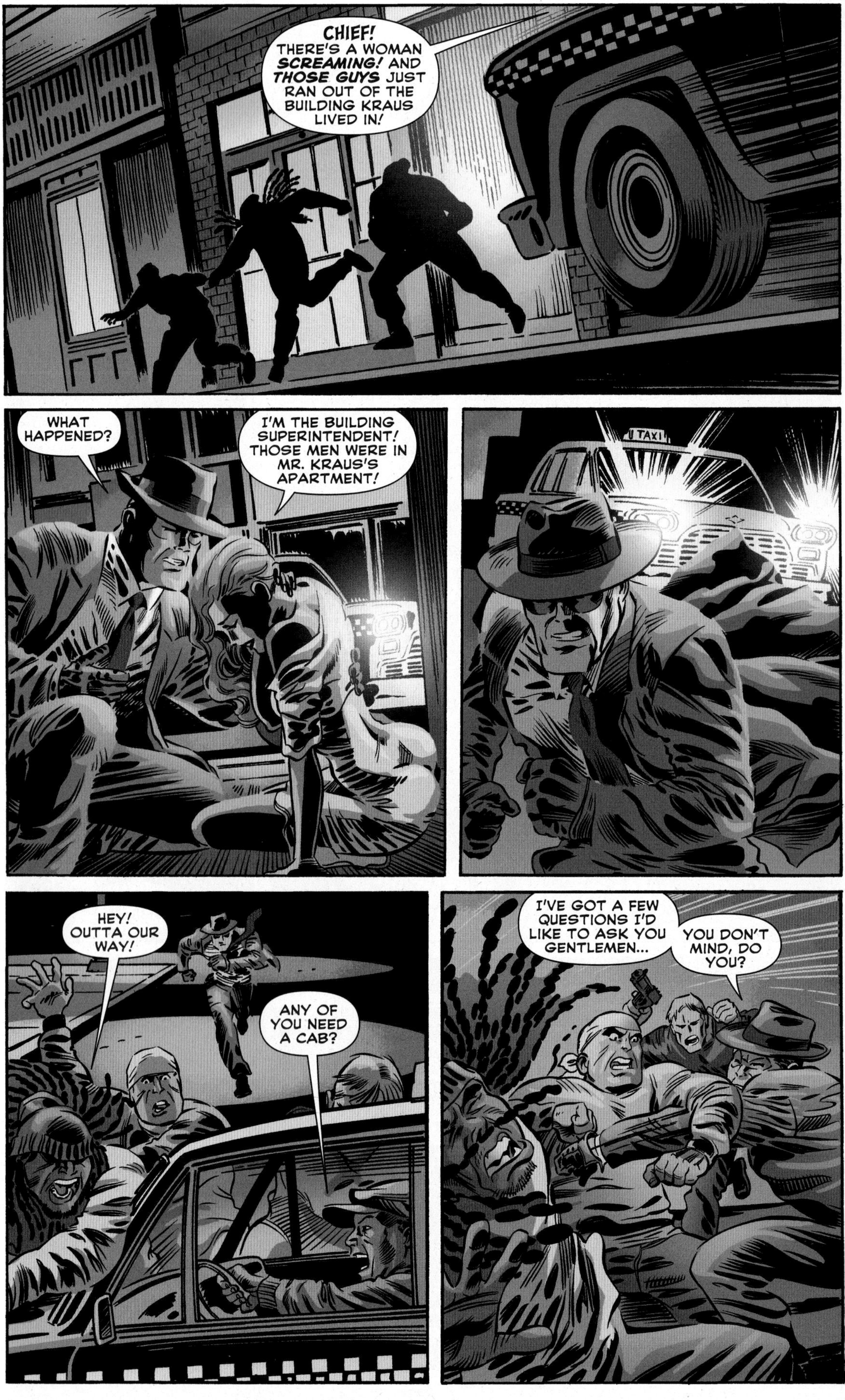
CHIEF! THERE'S A WOMAN SCREAMING! AND THOSE GUYS JUST RAN OUT OF THE BUILDING KRAUS LIVED IN!
WHAT HAPPENED?
I'M THE BUILDING SUPERINTENDENT! THOSE MEN WERE IN MR. KRAUS'S APARTMENT!
TAXI
HEY! OUTTA OUR WAY!
ANY OF YOU NEED A CAB?
I'VE GOT A FEW QUESTIONS I'D LIKE TO ASK YOU GENTLEMEN...
YOU DON'T MIND, DO YOU?

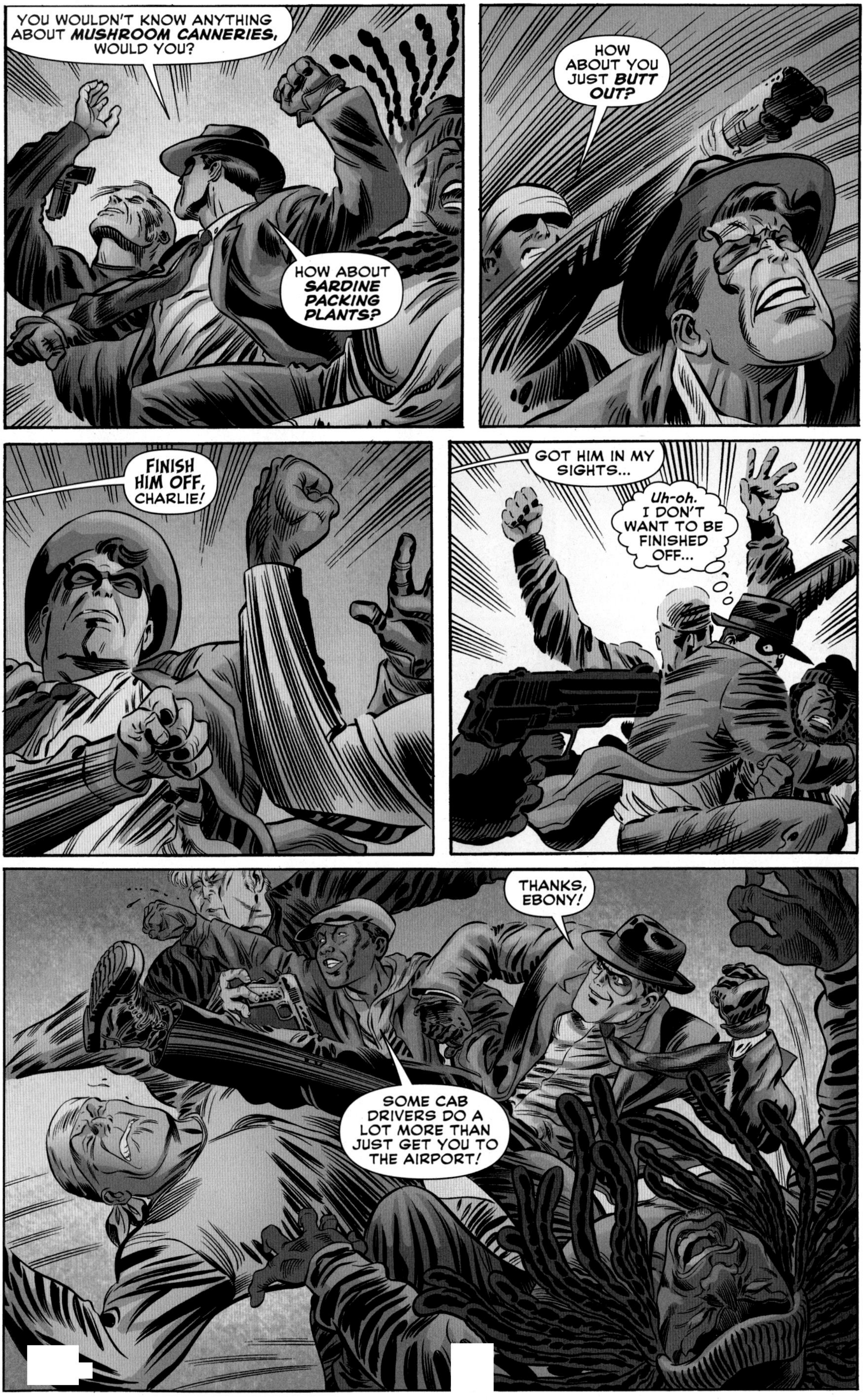

YOU WOULDN'T KNOW ANYTHING ABOUT MUSHROOM CANNERIES, WOULD YOU?
HOW ABOUT SARDINE PACKING PLANTS?
HOW ABOUT YOU JUST BUTT OUT?
FINISH HIM OFF, CHARLIE!
GOT HIM IN MY SIGHTS...
Uh-oh. I DON'T WANT TO BE FINISHED OFF...
THANKS, EBONY!
SOME CAB DRIVERS DO A LOT MORE THAN JUST GET YOU TO THE AIRPORT!

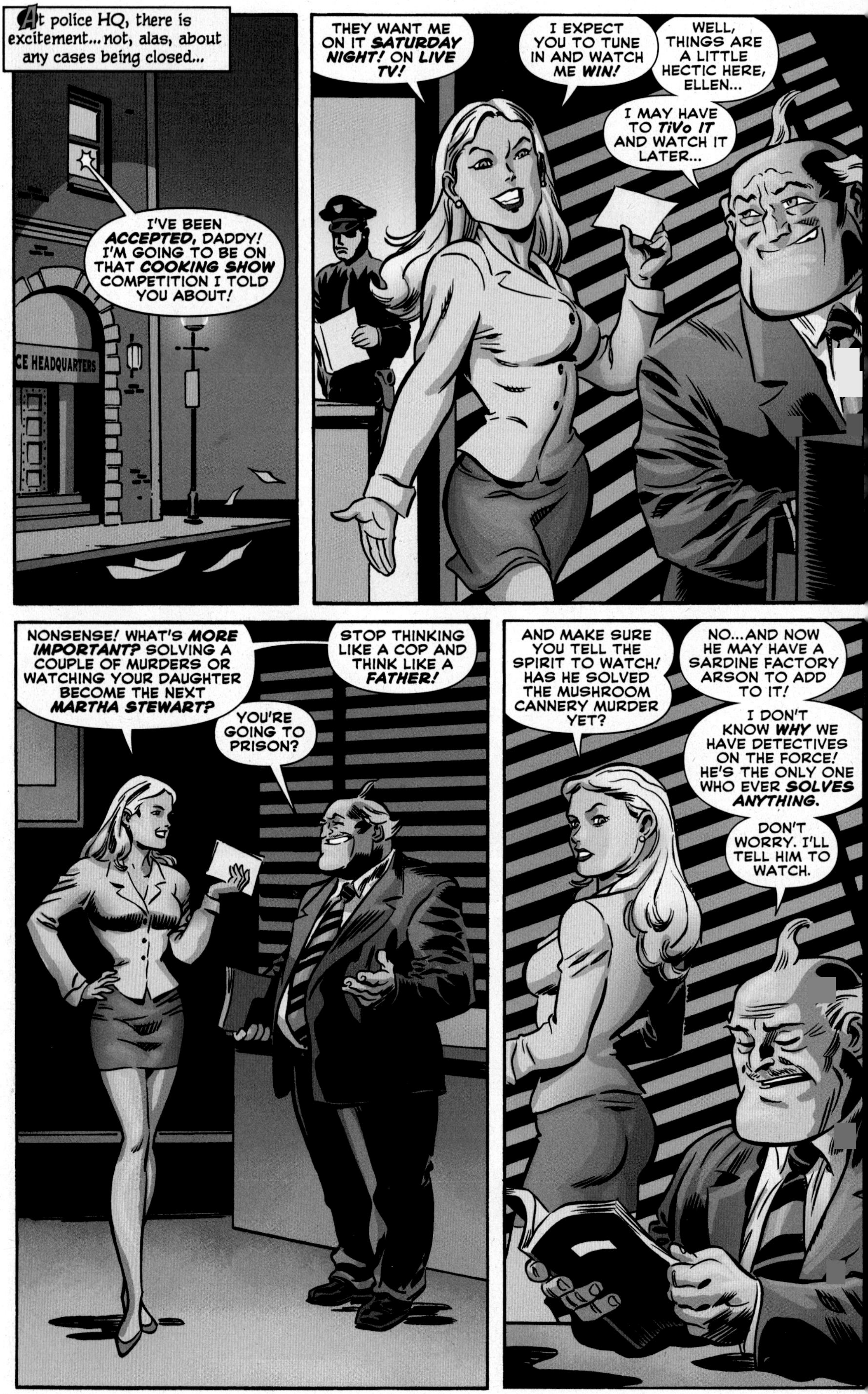
At police HQ, there is excitement... not, alas, about any cases being closed...
I'VE BEEN ACCEPTED, DADDY! I'M GOING TO BE ON THAT COOKING SHOW COMPETITION I TOLD YOU ABOUT!
CE HEADQUARTERS
THEY WANT ME ON IT SATURDAY NIGHT! ON LIVE TV!
I EXPECT YOU TO TUNE IN AND WATCH ME WIN!
WELL, THINGS ARE A LITTLE HECTIC HERE, ELLEN...
I MAY HAVE TO TiVo IT AND WATCH IT LATER...
NONSENSE! WHAT'S MORE IMPORTANT? SOLVING A COUPLE OF MURDERS OR WATCHING YOUR DAUGHTER BECOME THE NEXT MARTHA STEWART?
STOP THINKING LIKE A COP AND THINK LIKE A FATHER!
YOU'RE GOING TO PRISON?
AND MAKE SURE YOU TELL THE SPIRIT TO WATCH! HAS HE SOLVED THE MUSHROOM CANNERY MURDER YET?
NO... AND NOW HE MAY HAVE A SARDINE FACTORY ARSON TO ADD TO IT!
I DON'T KNOW WHY WE HAVE DETECTIVES ON THE FORCE! HE'S THE ONLY ONE WHO EVER SOLVES ANYTHING.
DON'T WORRY. I'LL TELL HIM TO WATCH.

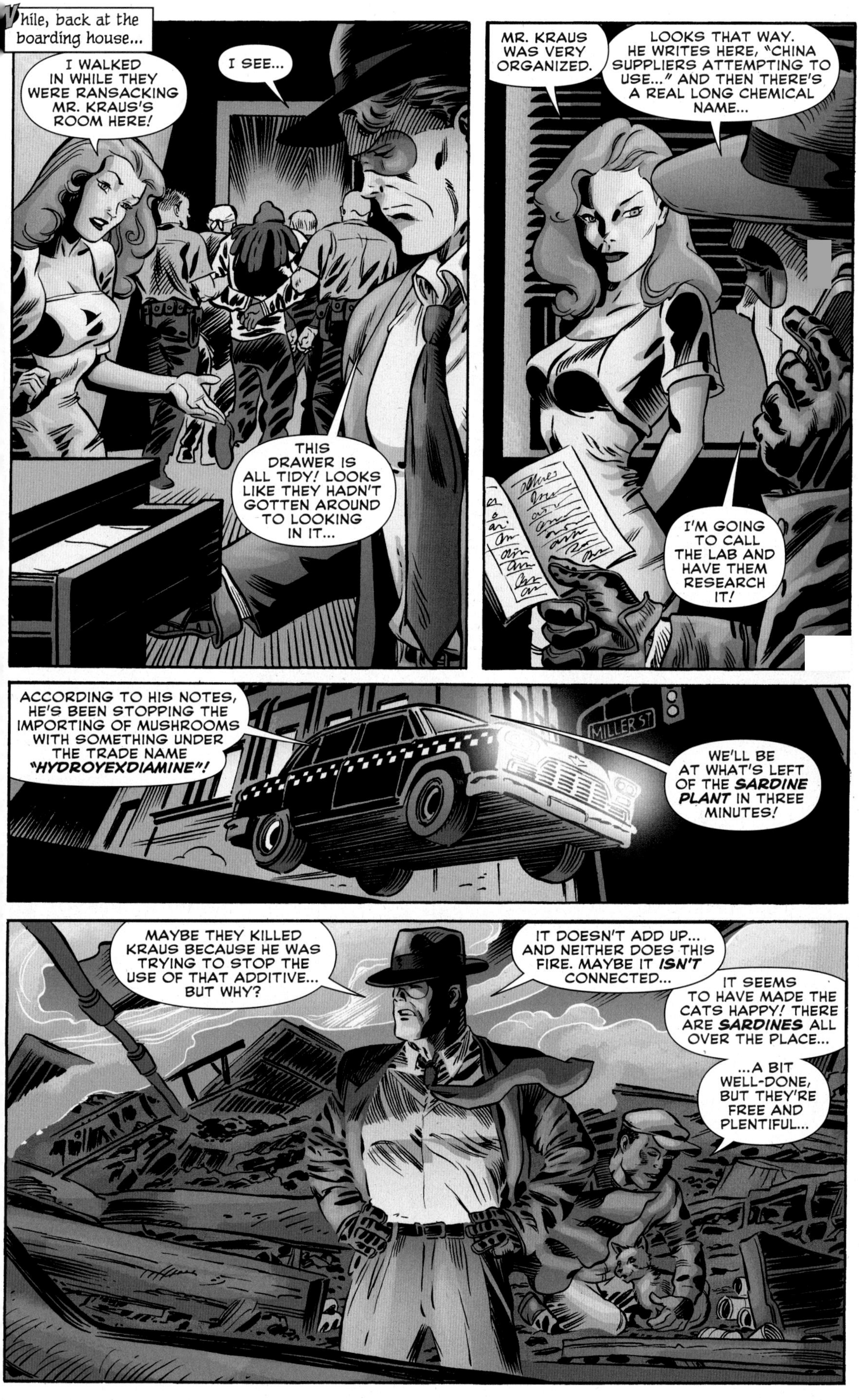

While, back at the boarding house...
I WALKED IN WHILE THEY WERE RANSACKING MR. KRAUS'S ROOM HERE!
I SEE...
THIS DRAWER IS ALL TIDY! LOOKS LIKE THEY HADN'T GOTTEN AROUND TO LOOKING IN IT...
MR. KRAUS WAS VERY ORGANIZED.
LOOKS THAT WAY. HE WRITES HERE, "CHINA SUPPLIERS ATTEMPTING TO USE..." AND THEN THERE'S A REAL LONG CHEMICAL NAME...
I'M GOING TO CALL THE LAB AND HAVE THEM RESEARCH IT!
ACCORDING TO HIS NOTES, HE'S BEEN STOPPING THE IMPORTING OF MUSHROOMS WITH SOMETHING UNDER THE TRADE NAME ***"HYDROYEXDIAMINE"!***
MILLER ST
WE'LL BE AT WHAT'S LEFT OF THE ***SARDINE PLANT*** IN THREE MINUTES!
MAYBE THEY KILLED KRAUS BECAUSE HE WAS TRYING TO STOP THE USE OF THAT ADDITIVE... BUT WHY?
IT DOESN'T ADD UP... AND NEITHER DOES THIS FIRE. MAYBE IT ***ISN'T*** CONNECTED...
IT SEEMS TO HAVE MADE THE CATS HAPPY! THERE ARE ***SARDINES*** ALL OVER THE PLACE...
...A BIT WELL-DONE, BUT THEY'RE FREE AND PLENTIFUL...

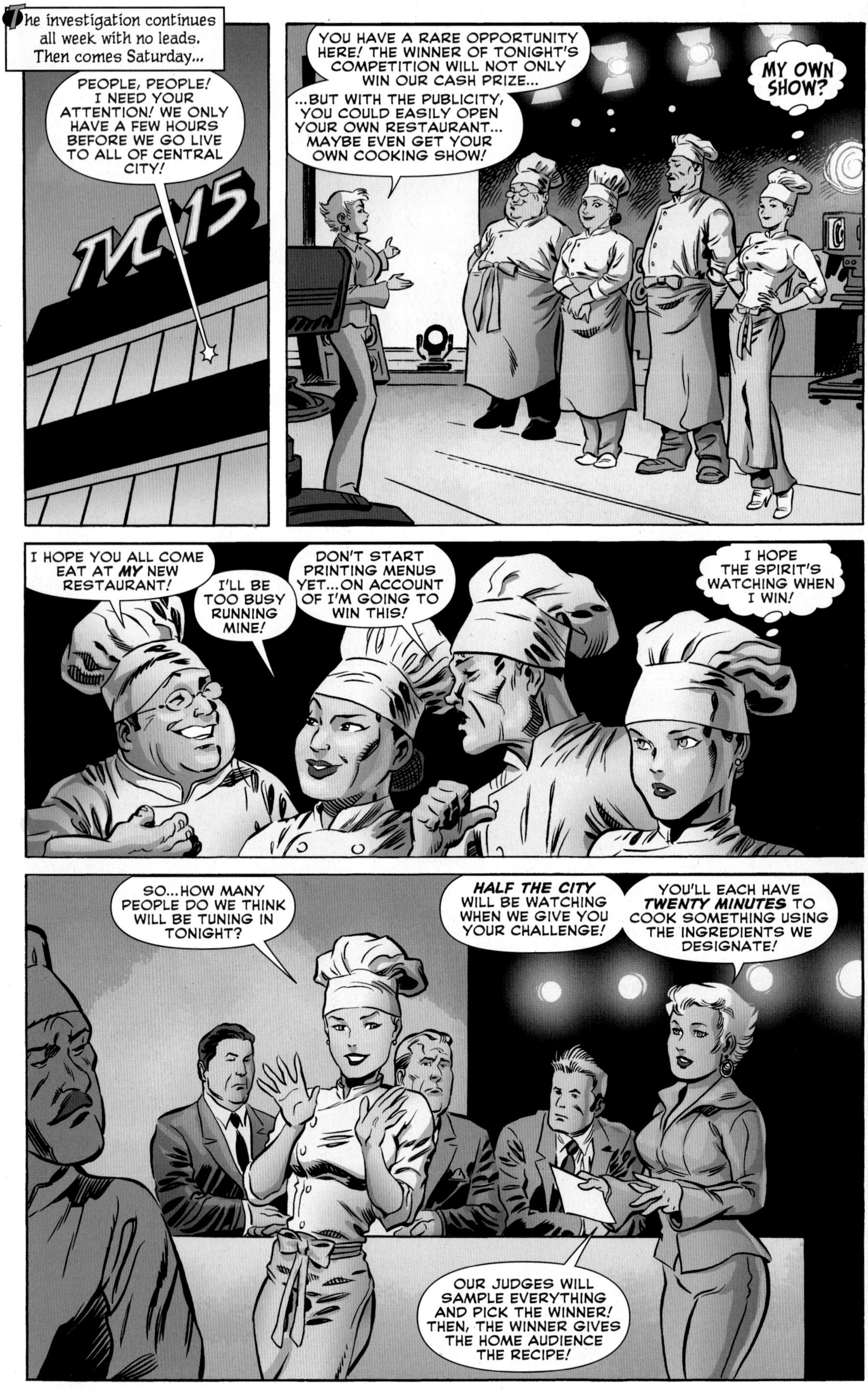
The investigation continues all week with no leads. Then comes Saturday...
PEOPLE, PEOPLE! I NEED YOUR ATTENTION! WE ONLY HAVE A FEW HOURS BEFORE WE GO LIVE TO ALL OF CENTRAL CITY!
TVC 15
YOU HAVE A RARE OPPORTUNITY HERE! THE WINNER OF TONIGHT'S COMPETITION WILL NOT ONLY WIN OUR CASH PRIZE...
...BUT WITH THE PUBLICITY, YOU COULD EASILY OPEN YOUR OWN RESTAURANT... MAYBE EVEN GET YOUR OWN COOKING SHOW!
MY OWN SHOW?
I HOPE YOU ALL COME EAT AT MY NEW RESTAURANT!
I'LL BE TOO BUSY RUNNING MINE!
DON'T START PRINTING MENUS YET...ON ACCOUNT OF I'M GOING TO WIN THIS!
I HOPE THE SPIRIT'S WATCHING WHEN I WIN!
SO...HOW MANY PEOPLE DO WE THINK WILL BE TUNING IN TONIGHT?
HALF THE CITY WILL BE WATCHING WHEN WE GIVE YOU YOUR CHALLENGE!
YOU'LL EACH HAVE TWENTY MINUTES TO COOK SOMETHING USING THE INGREDIENTS WE DESIGNATE!
OUR JUDGES WILL SAMPLE EVERYTHING AND PICK THE WINNER! THEN, THE WINNER GIVES THE HOME AUDIENCE THE RECIPE!

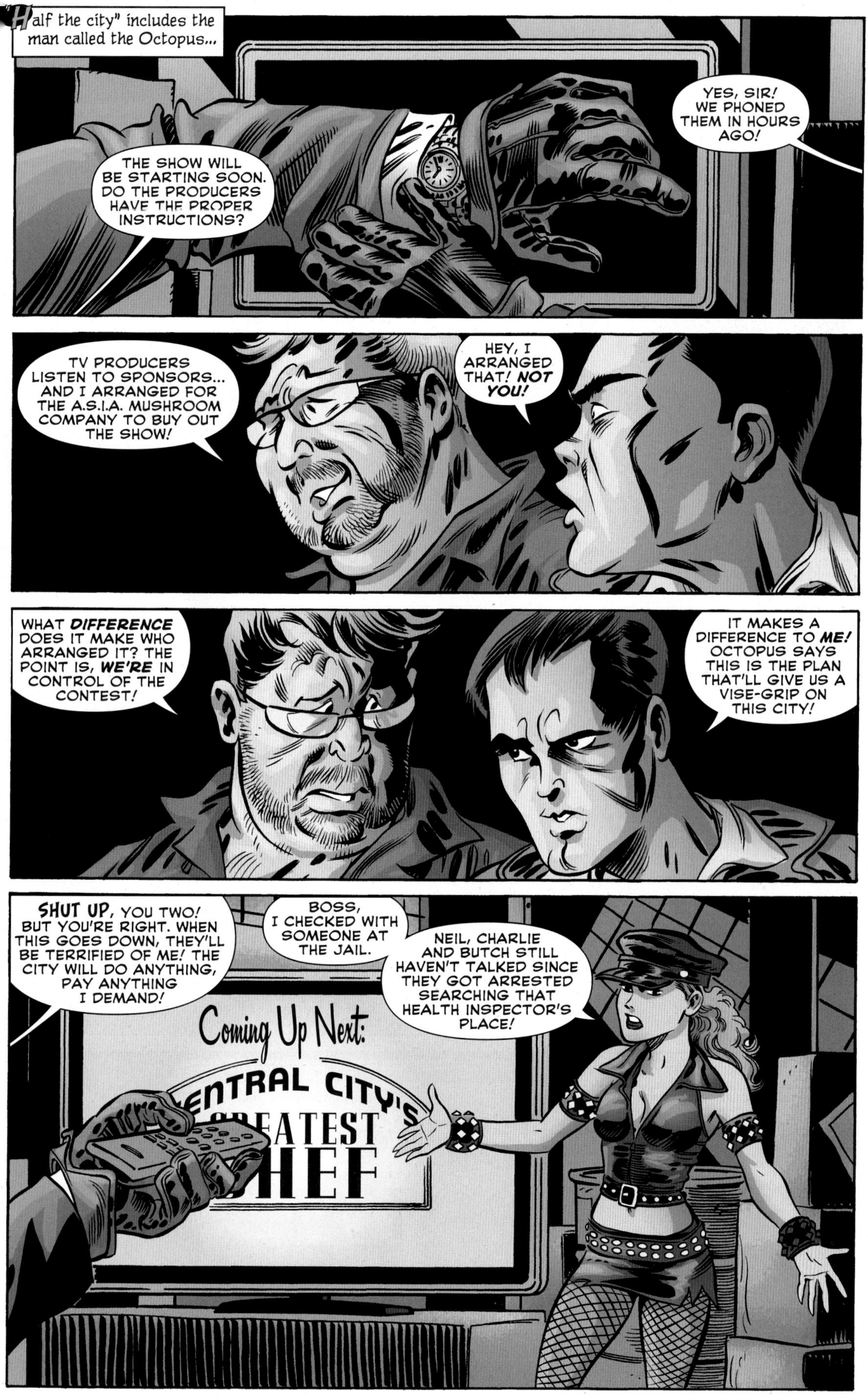
"Half the city" includes the man called the Octopus...
THE SHOW WILL BE STARTING SOON. DO THE PRODUCERS HAVE THE PROPER INSTRUCTIONS?
YES, SIR! WE PHONED THEM IN HOURS AGO!
TV PRODUCERS LISTEN TO SPONSORS... AND I ARRANGED FOR THE A.S.I.A. MUSHROOM COMPANY TO BUY OUT THE SHOW!
HEY, I ARRANGED THAT! NOT YOU!
WHAT DIFFERENCE DOES IT MAKE WHO ARRANGED IT? THE POINT IS, WE'RE IN CONTROL OF THE CONTEST!
IT MAKES A DIFFERENCE TO ME! OCTOPUS SAYS THIS IS THE PLAN THAT'LL GIVE US A VISE-GRIP ON THIS CITY!
SHUT UP, YOU TWO! BUT YOU'RE RIGHT. WHEN THIS GOES DOWN, THEY'LL BE TERRIFIED OF ME! THE CITY WILL DO ANYTHING, PAY ANYTHING I DEMAND!
BOSS, I CHECKED WITH SOMEONE AT THE JAIL.
NEIL, CHARLIE AND BUTCH STILL HAVEN'T TALKED SINCE THEY GOT ARRESTED SEARCHING THAT HEALTH INSPECTOR'S PLACE!
Coming Up Next:
ENTRAL CITY'S
GREATEST
HEF

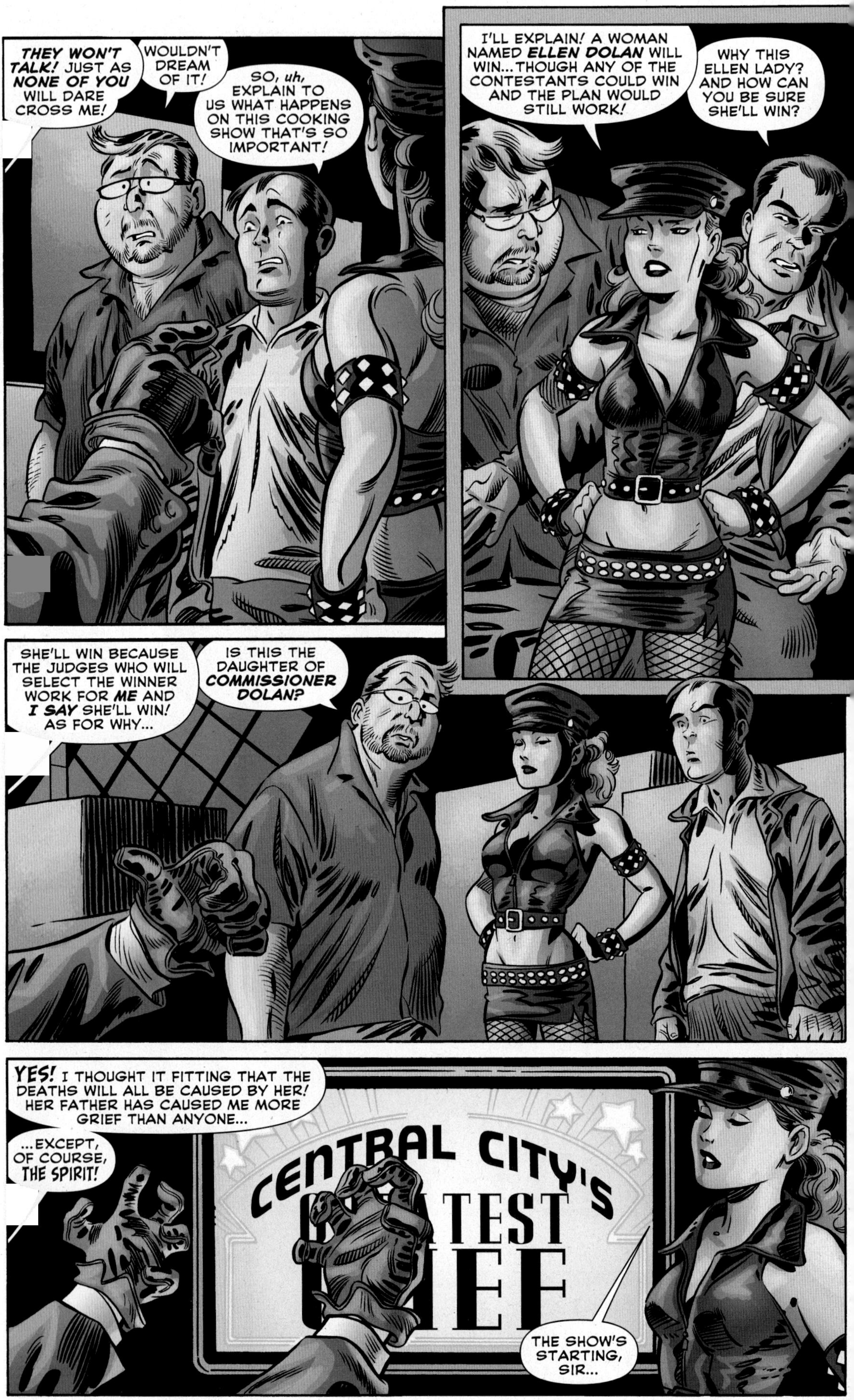
THEY WON'T TALK! JUST AS NONE OF YOU WILL DARE CROSS ME!
WOULDN'T DREAM OF IT!
SO, uh, EXPLAIN TO US WHAT HAPPENS ON THIS COOKING SHOW THAT'S SO IMPORTANT!
I'LL EXPLAIN! A WOMAN NAMED ELLEN DOLAN WILL WIN... THOUGH ANY OF THE CONTESTANTS COULD WIN AND THE PLAN WOULD STILL WORK!
WHY THIS ELLEN LADY? AND HOW CAN YOU BE SURE SHE'LL WIN?
SHE'LL WIN BECAUSE THE JUDGES WHO WILL SELECT THE WINNER WORK FOR ME AND I SAY SHE'LL WIN! AS FOR WHY...
IS THIS THE DAUGHTER OF COMMISSIONER DOLAN?
YES! I THOUGHT IT FITTING THAT THE DEATHS WILL ALL BE CAUSED BY HER! HER FATHER HAS CAUSED ME MORE GRIEF THAN ANYONE...
...EXCEPT, OF COURSE, THE SPIRIT!
CENTRAL CITY'S
THE SHOW'S STARTING, SIR...

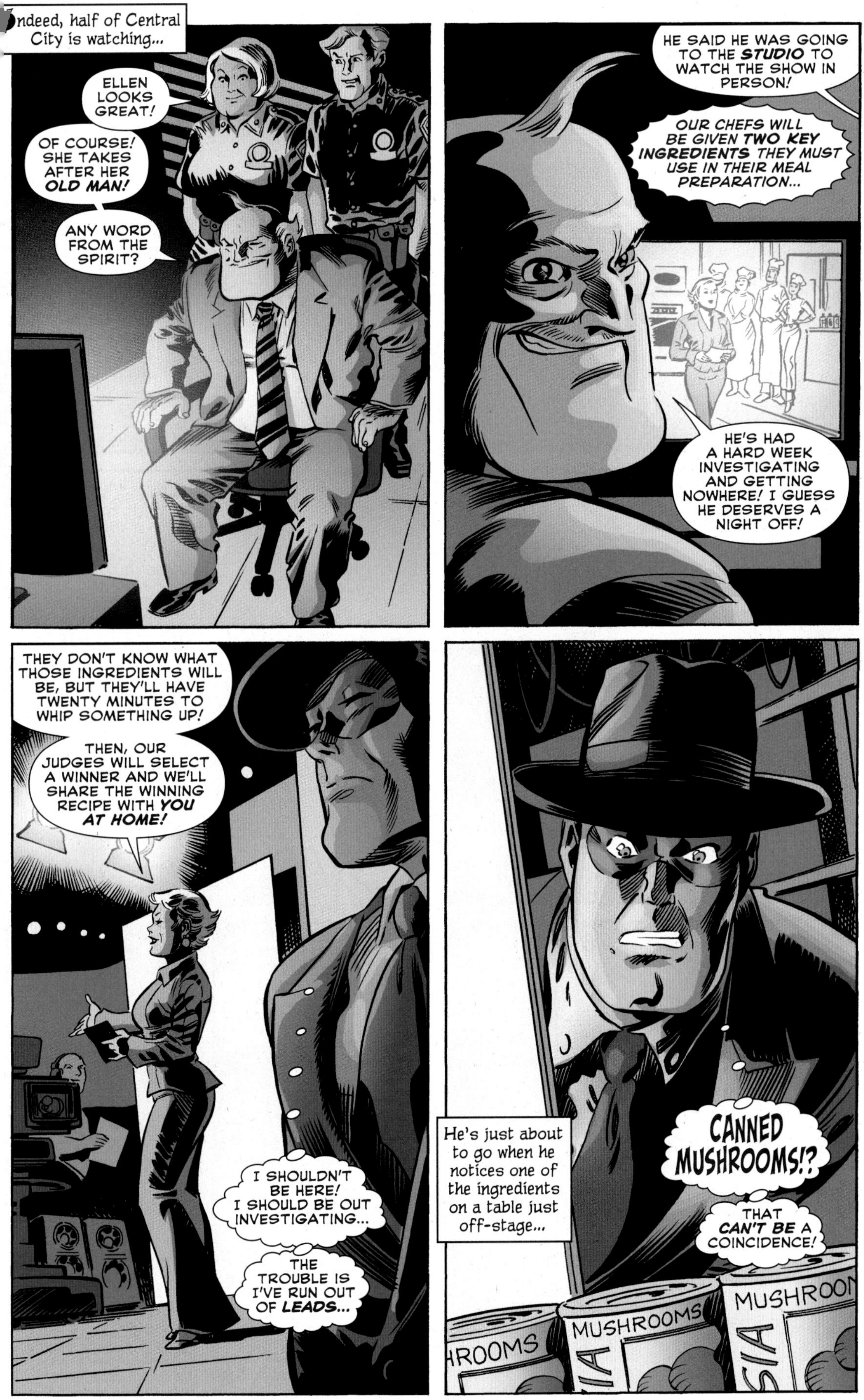

Indeed, half of Central City is watching...
ELLEN LOOKS GREAT!
OF COURSE! SHE TAKES AFTER HER OLD MAN!
ANY WORD FROM THE SPIRIT?
HE SAID HE WAS GOING TO THE STUDIO TO WATCH THE SHOW IN PERSON!
OUR CHEFS WILL BE GIVEN TWO KEY INGREDIENTS THEY MUST USE IN THEIR MEAL PREPARATION...
HE'S HAD A HARD WEEK INVESTIGATING AND GETTING NOWHERE! I GUESS HE DESERVES A NIGHT OFF!
THEY DON'T KNOW WHAT THOSE INGREDIENTS WILL BE, BUT THEY'LL HAVE TWENTY MINUTES TO WHIP SOMETHING UP!
THEN, OUR JUDGES WILL SELECT A WINNER AND WE'LL SHARE THE WINNING RECIPE WITH YOU AT HOME!
I SHOULDN'T BE HERE! I SHOULD BE OUT INVESTIGATING...
THE TROUBLE IS I'VE RUN OUT OF LEADS...
He's just about to go when he notices one of the ingredients on a table just off-stage...
CANNED MUSHROOMS!?
THAT CAN'T BE A COINCIDENCE!
MUSHROOMS
MUSHROOMS

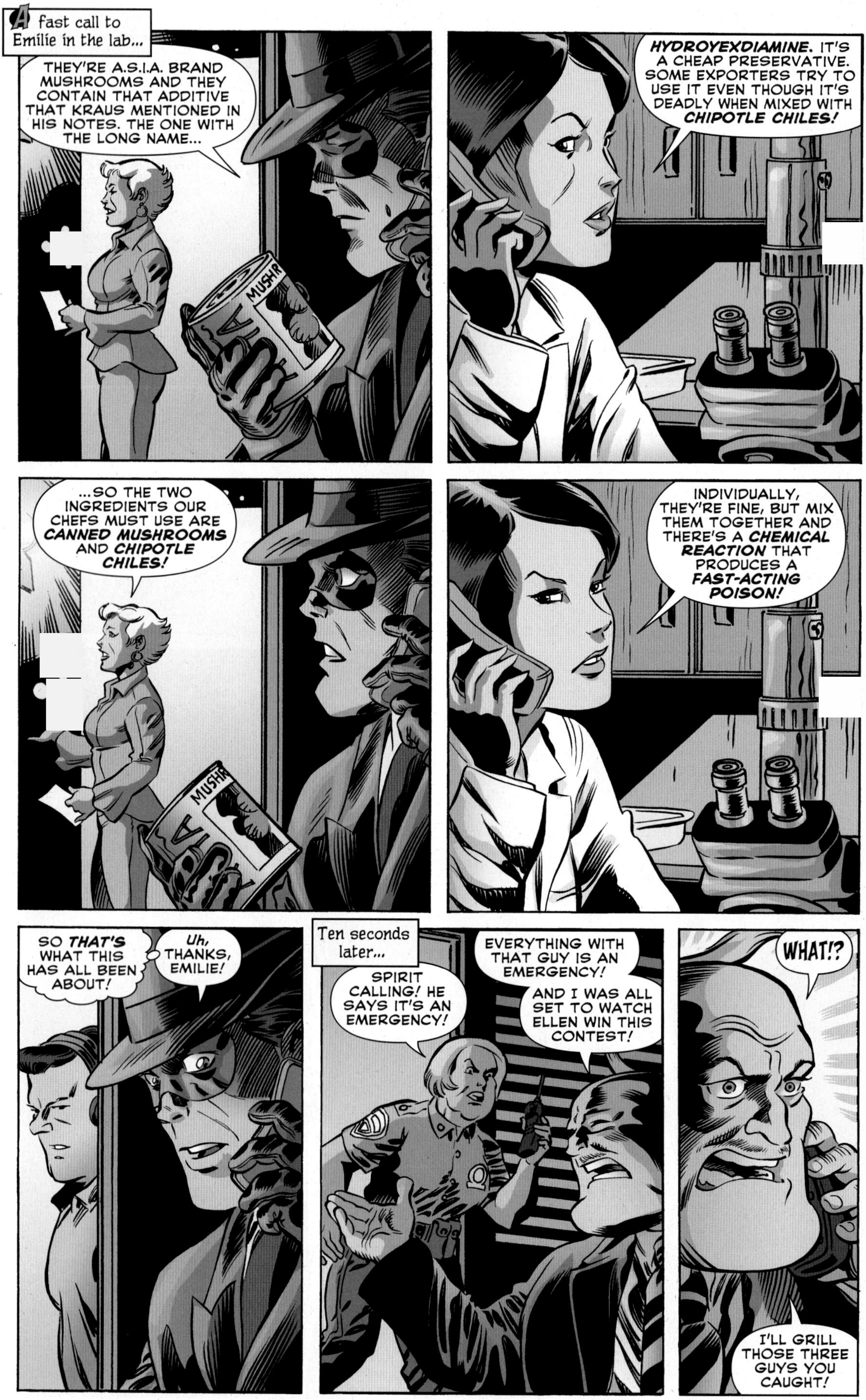
A fast call to Emilie in the lab...
THEY'RE A.S.I.A. BRAND MUSHROOMS AND THEY CONTAIN THAT ADDITIVE THAT KRAUS MENTIONED IN HIS NOTES. THE ONE WITH THE LONG NAME...
MUSHR
HYDROYEXDIAMINE. IT'S A CHEAP PRESERVATIVE. SOME EXPORTERS TRY TO USE IT EVEN THOUGH IT'S DEADLY WHEN MIXED WITH CHIPOTLE CHILES!
...SO THE TWO INGREDIENTS OUR CHEFS MUST USE ARE CANNED MUSHROOMS AND CHIPOTLE CHILES!
MUSHR
INDIVIDUALLY, THEY'RE FINE, BUT MIX THEM TOGETHER AND THERE'S A CHEMICAL REACTION THAT PRODUCES A FAST-ACTING POISON!
SO THAT'S WHAT THIS HAS ALL BEEN ABOUT!
Uh, THANKS, EMILIE!
Ten seconds later...
SPIRIT CALLING! HE SAYS IT'S AN EMERGENCY!
EVERYTHING WITH THAT GUY IS AN EMERGENCY!
AND I WAS ALL SET TO WATCH ELLEN WIN THIS CONTEST!
WHAT!?
I'LL GRILL THOSE THREE GUYS YOU CAUGHT!

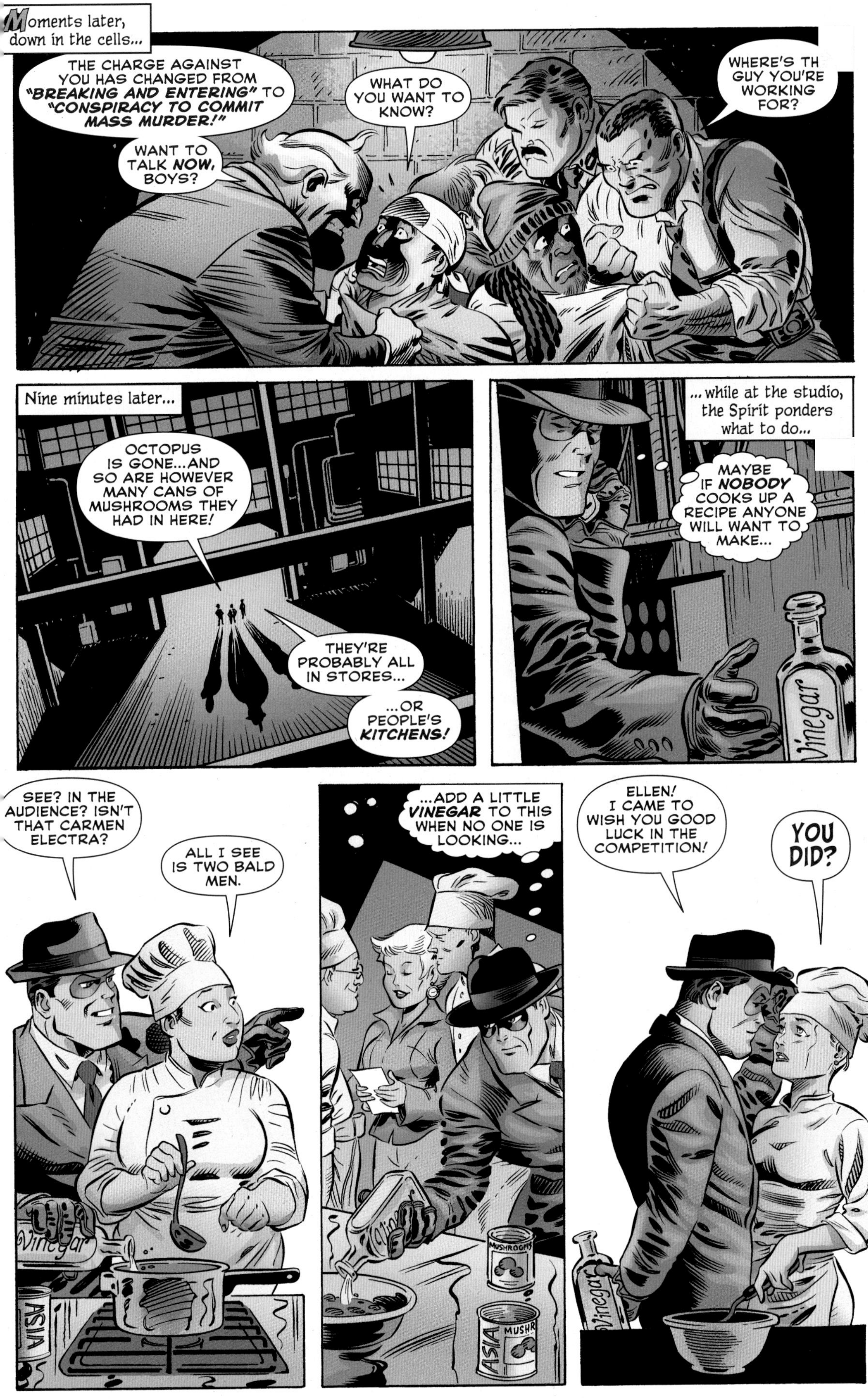
Moments later, down in the cells...
THE CHARGE AGAINST YOU HAS CHANGED FROM "BREAKING AND ENTERING" TO "CONSPIRACY TO COMMIT MASS MURDER!"
WANT TO TALK NOW, BOYS?
WHAT DO YOU WANT TO KNOW?
WHERE'S TH GUY YOU'RE WORKING FOR?
Nine minutes later...
OCTOPUS IS GONE...AND SO ARE HOWEVER MANY CANS OF MUSHROOMS THEY HAD IN HERE!
THEY'RE PROBABLY ALL IN STORES...
...OR PEOPLE'S KITCHENS!
...while at the studio, the Spirit ponders what to do...
MAYBE IF NOBODY COOKS UP A RECIPE ANYONE WILL WANT TO MAKE...
Vinegar
SEE? IN THE AUDIENCE? ISN'T THAT CARMEN ELECTRA?
ALL I SEE IS TWO BALD MEN.
Vinegar
ASIA
...ADD A LITTLE VINEGAR TO THIS WHEN NO ONE IS LOOKING...
MUSHROOMS
ASIA MUSHR
ELLEN! I CAME TO WISH YOU GOOD LUCK IN THE COMPETITION!
YOU DID?
Vinegar

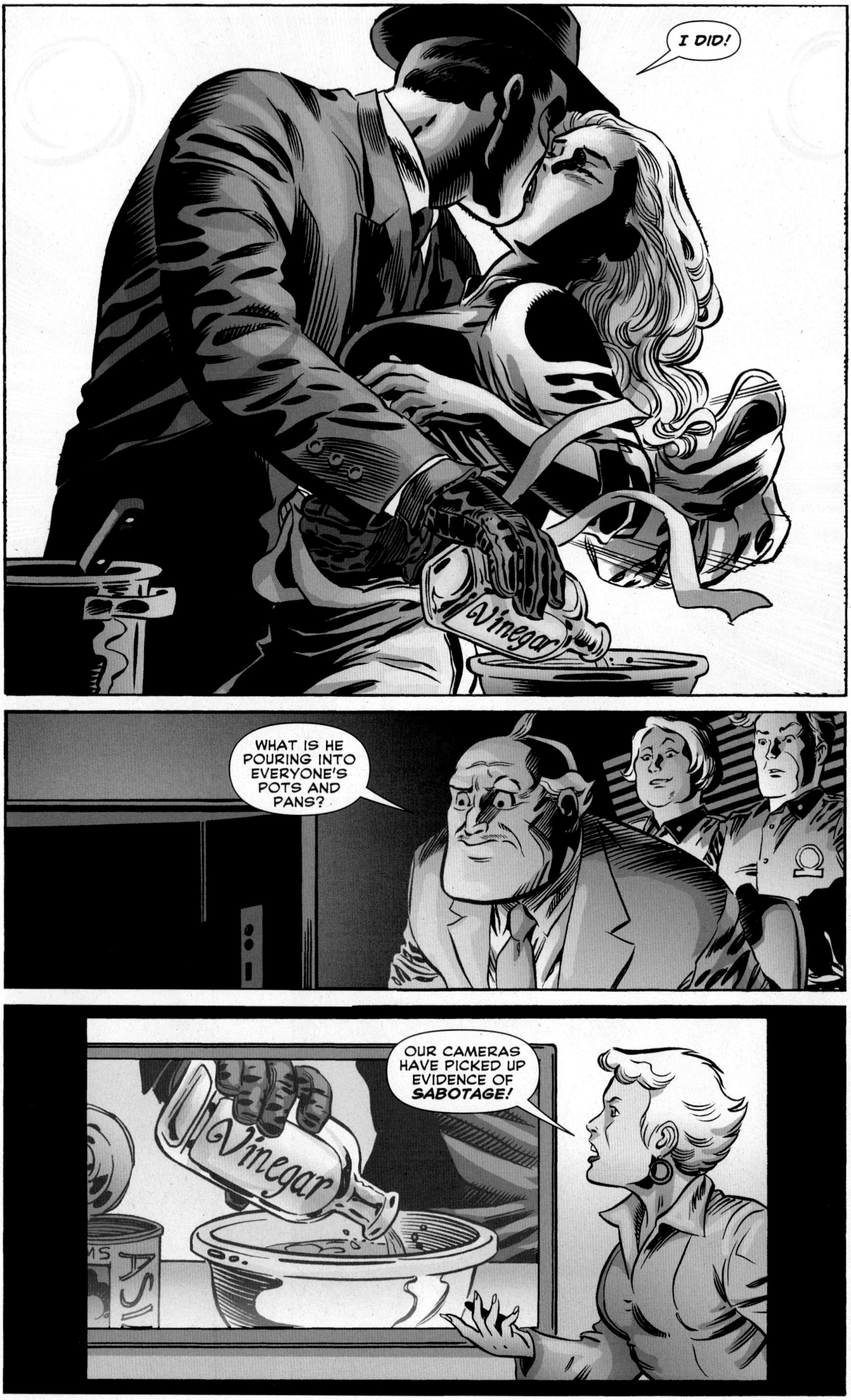
I DID!
Vinegar
WHAT IS HE POURING INTO EVERYONE'S POTS AND PANS?
OUR CAMERAS HAVE PICKED UP EVIDENCE OF SABOTAGE!
Vinegar

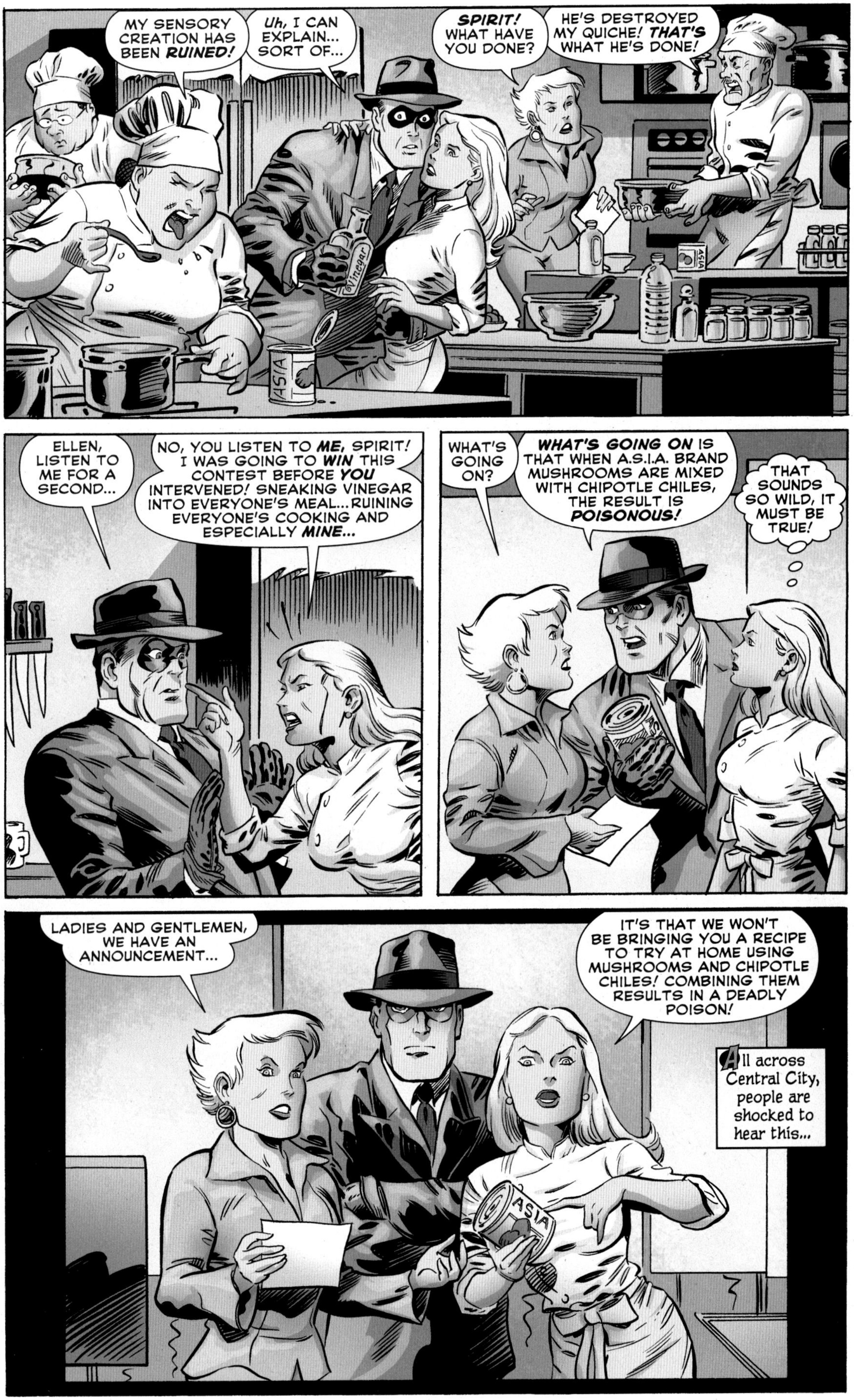
MY SENSORY CREATION HAS BEEN RUINED!
Uh, I CAN EXPLAIN... SORT OF...
SPIRIT! WHAT HAVE YOU DONE?
HE'S DESTROYED MY QUICHE! THAT'S WHAT HE'S DONE!
Vinegar
ASIA
ELLEN, LISTEN TO ME FOR A SECOND...
NO, YOU LISTEN TO ME, SPIRIT! I WAS GOING TO WIN THIS CONTEST BEFORE YOU INTERVENED! SNEAKING VINEGAR INTO EVERYONE'S MEAL...RUINING EVERYONE'S COOKING AND ESPECIALLY MINE...
WHAT'S GOING ON?
WHAT'S GOING ON IS THAT WHEN A.S.I.A. BRAND MUSHROOMS ARE MIXED WITH CHIPOTLE CHILES, THE RESULT IS POISONOUS!
THAT SOUNDS SO WILD, IT MUST BE TRUE!
LADIES AND GENTLEMEN, WE HAVE AN ANNOUNCEMENT...
IT'S THAT WE WON'T BE BRINGING YOU A RECIPE TO TRY AT HOME USING MUSHROOMS AND CHIPOTLE CHILES! COMBINING THEM RESULTS IN A DEADLY POISON!
All across Central City, people are shocked to hear this...
ASIA

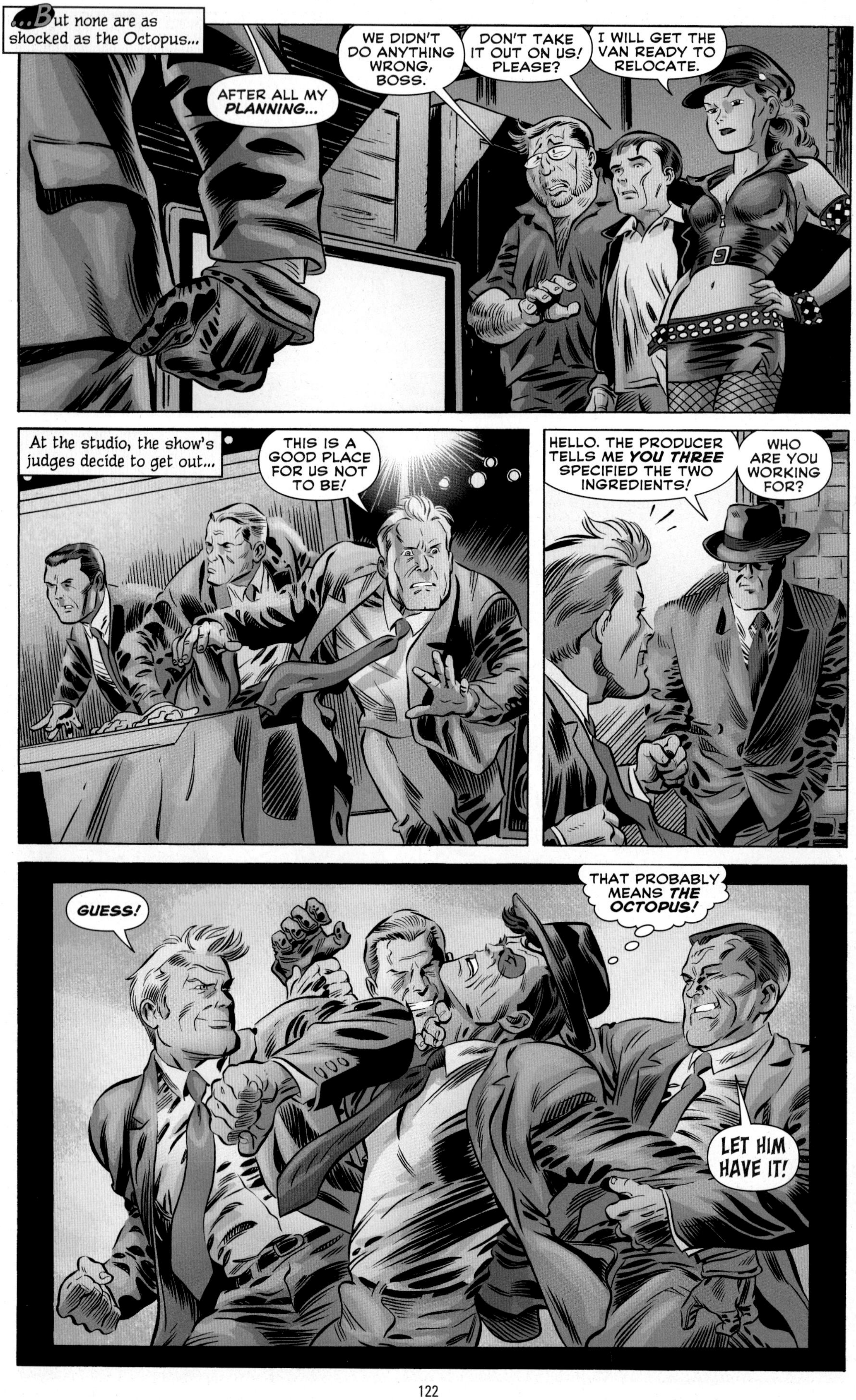
...But none are as shocked as the Octopus...
AFTER ALL MY PLANNING...
WE DIDN'T DO ANYTHING WRONG, BOSS.
DON'T TAKE IT OUT ON US! PLEASE?
I WILL GET THE VAN READY TO RELOCATE.
At the studio, the show's judges decide to get out...
THIS IS A GOOD PLACE FOR US NOT TO BE!
HELLO. THE PRODUCER TELLS ME YOU THREE SPECIFIED THE TWO INGREDIENTS!
WHO ARE YOU WORKING FOR?
GUESS!
THAT PROBABLY MEANS THE OCTOPUS!
LET HIM HAVE IT!

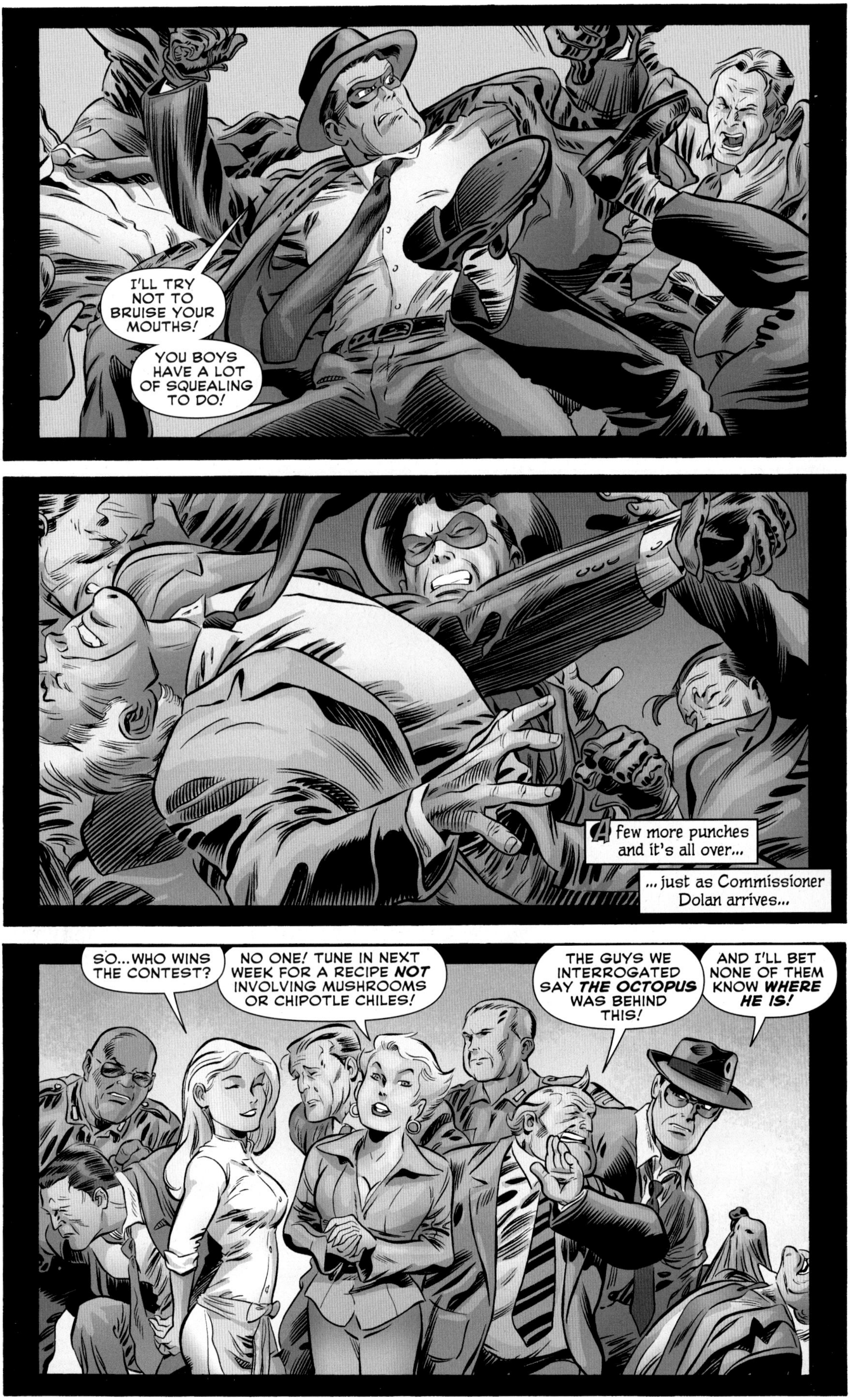
I'LL TRY NOT TO BRUISE YOUR MOUTHS!
YOU BOYS HAVE A LOT OF SQUEALING TO DO!
A few more punches and it's all over...
...just as Commissioner Dolan arrives...
SO...WHO WINS THE CONTEST?
NO ONE! TUNE IN NEXT WEEK FOR A RECIPE NOT INVOLVING MUSHROOMS OR CHIPOTLE CHILES!
THE GUYS WE INTERROGATED SAY THE OCTOPUS WAS BEHIND THIS!
AND I'LL BET NONE OF THEM KNOW WHERE HE IS!

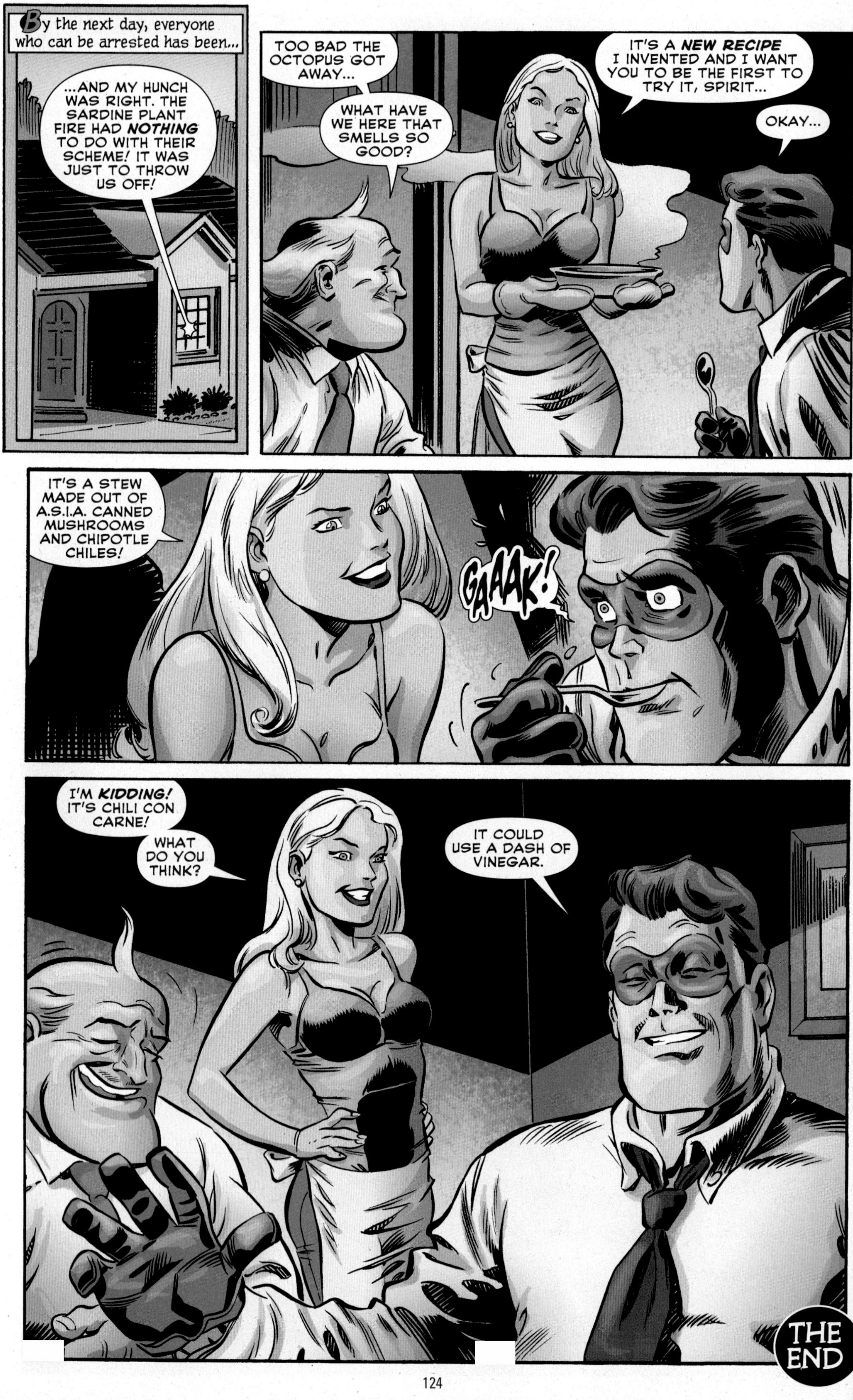
By the next day, everyone who can be arrested has been...
...AND MY HUNCH WAS RIGHT. THE SARDINE PLANT FIRE HAD NOTHING TO DO WITH THEIR SCHEME! IT WAS JUST TO THROW US OFF!
TOO BAD THE OCTOPUS GOT AWAY...
WHAT HAVE WE HERE THAT SMELLS SO GOOD?
IT'S A NEW RECIPE I INVENTED AND I WANT YOU TO BE THE FIRST TO TRY IT, SPIRIT...
OKAY...
IT'S A STEW MADE OUT OF A.S.I.A. CANNED MUSHROOMS AND CHIPOTLE CHILES!
GAAAK!
I'M KIDDING! IT'S CHILI CON CARNE!
WHAT DO YOU THINK?
IT COULD USE A DASH OF VINEGAR.
THE END

MORE CLASSIC TALES OF THE DARK KNIGHT

BATMAN: HUSH
VOLUME ONE

**JEPH LOEB
JIM LEE**

BATMAN: HUSH
VOLUME TWO

**JEPH LOEB
JIM LEE**

BATMAN:
THE LONG HALLOWEEN

**JEPH LOEB
TIM SALE**

BATMAN:
DARK VICTORY

**JEPH LOEB
TIM SALE**

BATMAN:
HAUNTED KNIGHT

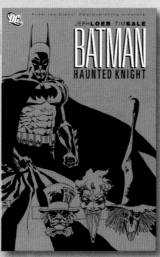

**JEPH LOEB
TIM SALE**

BATMAN:
YEAR 100

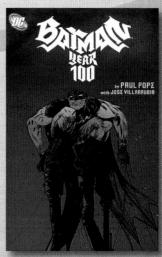

PAUL POPE

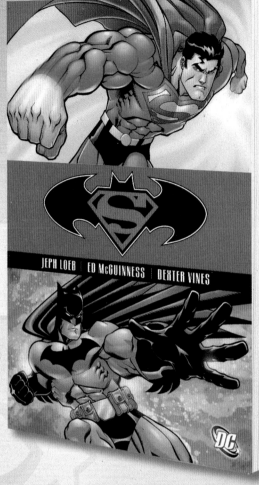